CONSTRUCTING THE HIGHER EDUCATION STUDENT

Perspectives from across Europe

Rachel Brooks, Achala Gupta, Sazana Jayadeva,
Anu Lainio and Predrag Lažetić

D1609864

First published in Great Britain in 2022 by

Policy Press, an imprint of
Bristol University Press
University of Bristol
1–9 Old Park Hill
Bristol
BS2 8BB
UK
t: +44 (0)117 374 6645
e: bup-info@bristol.ac.uk

Details of international sales and distribution partners are available at
policy.bristoluniversitypress.co.uk

© Rachel Brooks, Achala Gupta, Sazana Jayadeva, Anu Lainio and Predrag Lažetić 2022

The digital PDF version of this title is available Open Access and distributed under the terms of the
Creative Commons Attribution-NonCommercial-NoDerivatives 4.0 International licence (https://
creativecommons.org/licenses/by-nc-nd/4.0/) which permits reproduction and distribution for non-
commercial use without further permission provided the original work is attributed.

British Library Cataloguing in Publication Data
A catalogue record for this book is available from the British Library

ISBN 978-1-4473-5962-3 paperback
ISBN 978-1-4473-5963-0 OA PDF

The right of Rachel Brooks, Achala Gupta, Sazana Jayadeva, Anu Lainio and Predrag Lažetić to
be identified as authors of this work has been asserted by them in accordance with the Copyright,
Designs and Patents Act 1988.

All rights reserved: no part of this publication may be reproduced, stored in a retrieval system, or
transmitted in any form or by any means, electronic, mechanical, photocopying, recording, or
otherwise without the prior permission of Bristol University Press.

Every reasonable effort has been made to obtain permission to reproduce copyrighted material. If,
however, anyone knows of an oversight, please contact the publisher.

The statements and opinions contained within this publication are solely those of the authors and
not of the University of Bristol or Bristol University Press. The University of Bristol and Bristol
University Press disclaim responsibility for any injury to persons or property resulting from any
material published in this publication.

Bristol University Press and Policy Press work to counter discrimination on grounds of gender, race,
disability, age and sexuality.

Cover design: Clifford Hayes
Front cover image: Group of people talking and interacting with each other
© Vectorarte/Freepik.com
Bristol University Press and Policy Press use environmentally responsible print partners.
Printed and bound in Great Britain by CMP, Poole

Contents

List of figures and tables

Figures

Tables

Acknowledgements

We are very grateful to all the students, staff and policy actors who gave up their time to be interviewed for the project or join a focus group. We would also like to thank the European Research Council for awarding a Consolidator Grant to Rachel Brooks (grant reference EUROSTUDENTS_ 681018), which funded the empirical research upon which this book draws.

Many people have contributed to the project in various ways since we began our research in 2016. We would like to thank our advisory group – Barbara Kehm, Marek Kwiek, Lea Meister, Maria Slowey, Aina Tarabini, Carlos Vargas-Tamez and Susan Wright. We are also grateful to Dominik Antonowicz, Vikki Boliver, Sarah Bulloch, Daniel Faas, Maria Fernandez Mellizo-Soto, Alicia García Fernández, Sara Gil, Jakub Krzeski, Emanuel Kulczycki, Ralf Lottman, Heather Mendick, Gritt Nielsen, Katia Nielsen, Martin Portos, Maite Santiago-Garabieta, Laura Louise Sarauw, Christina Silver, Isabel Steinhardt, Krystian Szadkowski and Lars Ulriksen, all of whom have made important contributions to the project. We are particularly indebted to Jessie Abrahams, for her sterling work as part of the research team between 2016 and 2018.

We are also grateful to those who read drafts of chapters and gave extremely useful feedback: Anna Bull, Kay Calver, Karen Gravett, Paul Hodkinson, Anesa Hossein, Avril Keating, Hugh Lauder, Rob Meadows, Beth Michael-Fox, Rille Raaper, Steve Roberts, Michael Tomlinson and Lars Ulriksen, and to Christine Hine, for co-supervising Anu's PhD project with Rachel, which has fed into this book. Rachel would also like to thank colleagues at the University of Surrey and elsewhere for support when putting the original research proposal together and at many points subsequently – particularly Sarah Neal, Christine Hine, Paul Hodkinson, Andy King, Jon Garland, Johanna Waters, Michael Kearney, Maria Sega-Buhalis and Sarah O'Shea.

Parts of this book draw on articles we have published previously. We are grateful to the editors and publishers of these journals for permission to use material from the following papers:

Brooks, R. (2021) 'The construction of students within higher education policy: a cross-national comparison', *Compare: A Journal of Comparative and International Education*, 51(2): 161–180. (Used in Chapter 7.)

Brooks, R. and Abrahams, J. (2021) 'European higher education students: contested constructions', *Sociological Research Online*, 26(4): 810–832. (Used in Chapters 1, 4 and 8.)

Brooks, R., Gupta, A. and Jayadeva, S. (2021) 'Higher education students' aspirations for their post-university lives: evidence from six European nations', *Children's Geographies* (advance online access). (Used in Chapter 4.)

Brooks, R., Gupta, A., Jayadeva, S., Abrahams, J. and Lažetić, P. (2020) 'Students as political actors? Similarities and differences across six European countries', *British Educational Research Journal*, 46(6): 1193–1209. (Used in Chapter 3.)

Jayadeva, S., Brooks, R. and Lažetić, P. (2021) 'Paradise lost or created? How higher-education staff perceive the impact of policy on students', *Journal of Education Policy* (advance online access). (Used in Chapters 1 and 4.)

Jayadeva, S., Brooks, R. and Abrahams, J. (2022) The (stereo)typical student: how European higher education students feel they are viewed by relevant others, *British Journal of Sociology of Education*, 43(1): 1–21. (Used in Chapters 4 and 7.)

1

Introduction

There are currently over 35 million students within Europe and yet, to date, we have little knowledge of the extent to which understandings of 'the student' are shared. A central aim of *Constructing the Higher Education Student: Perspectives from across Europe* is thus to investigate how the contemporary higher education (HE) student is conceptualised and the extent to which this differs both within nation-states and across them. This is significant in terms of implicit (and sometimes explicit) assumptions that are made about common understandings of 'the student' across Europe – underpinning, for example, initiatives to increase cross-border educational mobility and the wider development of a European Higher Education Area. It is also significant in relation to exploring the extent to which understandings are shared within a single nation and, particularly, the degree to which there is congruence between how students are conceptualised within policy texts and by policymakers, and the understandings of other key social actors such as the media, HE staff and students themselves. Should nations be understood as 'coherent educational entities' (Philips and Schweisfurth, 2014) – or is there, instead, a high degree of contestation within nation-states about what it means to be a contemporary HE student?

To help contextualise the arguments that follow in this book, in this introductory chapter we discuss previous scholarship that has explored, first, the extent to which students have become increasingly similar as a result of processes of globalisation and, with respect to students in Europe in particular, Europeanisation. We then consider some of the dominant ways in which students have been constructed and analysed in the academic literature. Following this, we provide detail about the empirical research upon which *Constructing the Higher Education Student: Perspectives from across Europe* is based, before giving a brief overview of the countries in which we collected data and the structure of the book.

Increasingly similar students?

The arguments we make in *Constructing the Higher Education Student: Perspectives from across Europe* articulate with extant debates – conducted across the disciplines of education, sociology, geography and social policy – about the extent to which educational processes have been globalised and the experience of being a student has become increasingly similar worldwide.

Some scholars have argued that, in contemporary society, education policy and practice have both been profoundly changed by globalising pressures. Usher and Edwards (1994), writing almost three decades ago, asserted that globalisation had undermined the modernist goals of national education as a unified project and, as result, education could no longer control or be controlled. Some scholars have contended that the state's capacity to control education has been significantly limited by the growth of both international organisations and transnational companies (Ball, 2007). Ozga and Lingard (2007) suggest that one consequence of this questioning of the nation-state as the 'natural' scale of politics and policy has been the emergence of alternative interpretive frames – some of which draw on more localised traditions and values. With respect to HE in particular, Sam and van der Sijde (2014) have contended that the three traditional models of university education in Europe (Humboldtian, Napoleonic and Anglo-Saxon) have been replaced by a single Anglo-American model, characterised by, inter alia, competition, marketisation, decentralisation and a focus on entrepreneurial activity. Moreover, policy convergence in such areas has been explicitly encouraged by the European Union (EU), through its desire to create a European Higher Education Area and the Bologna Process, which has aimed to achieve 'harmonisation of the overarching architecture of European higher education' (Dobbins and Leišyté, 2014: 989). Indeed, Slaughter and Cantwell (2012) have argued that the European Commission is committed to 'reverse engineering' Anglo-American HE models. While much of the literature in this area has focused on national policies, institutional structures, governance and management, a small number of studies have suggested that students, themselves, have been directly impacted. Moutsios (2013), for example, has argued that, as a result of reforms introduced through the Bologna Process, students across Europe have increasingly been positioned as consumers – and as part of a 'knowledge industry' rather than a traditional university. Similar arguments about the rise of consumerism have been made by other scholars, reflecting on how funding reforms, and particularly the introduction of tuition fees, in many European nations have changed what it means to be a student (for example, Kwiek, 2018). (We return to these points below.)

Nevertheless, this analysis – of increasing convergence of HE across Europe around an Anglo-American model – is not shared by all. Many writers contend that the demise of the nation-state has been overstated and that national governments retain considerable influence – in shaping education policy within their own borders, as well as upon the nature of globalisation itself (Green, 2006). For example, not all European nations have sought to establish elite universities or maximise revenue through attracting international students, and significant differences remain in how HE is funded (for example, Hüther and Krücken, 2014). Moreover, there is variation in the extent to which European nations have embraced marketisation (see

Dobbins and Leišyté, 2014), and the nature of the Anglo-American model of HE that has been implemented in different national contexts (Sam and van der Sijde, 2014). In explaining such variations, scholars have pointed to differences in political dynamics, politico-administrative structures and intellectual traditions, as well as the flexibility and mutability of neo-liberal ideas themselves (for example, Bleikie and Michelsen, 2013). However, much research to date has focused primarily on the extent of convergence (or divergence) with respect to top-level policies; as a result, little work has explored the perspectives of social actors – and particularly students themselves. Our knowledge of the 'lived experience' of HE across Europe is thus partial.

Dominant constructions of the student

When we turn to the literature on conceptualisations of the HE student, in Europe and elsewhere, the majority of discussion has tended to focus on a relatively small number of constructions. In this section, we introduce four of the most prominent of these – students as consumers (rather than learners), political actors, future workers and socialites.

Consumer not learner?

In much of the scholarship, within education and other cognate disciplines, it is often assumed that students are, first and foremost, learners. There is clearly a substantial amount of research devoted to enhancing the teaching and learning that takes place within higher education institutions (HEIs), typically underpinned by the belief that this is the primary function of the sector. However, over recent years, various scholars – as well as a range of social commentators – have asserted that students are understood less as learners and more as consumers (for example, Morley, 2003; Cardoso et al, 2011; Woodall et al, 2014). Typically such arguments are advanced as part of a critique of the neo-liberalisation of the HE sector. In countries such as Australia, the US and the UK, high fees are often seen to have inculcated more consumerist behaviours on the part of students, and led to their clear positioning as consumers by both HE institutions and policymakers (Tight, 2013). This has been brought into sharp relief in the UK by the government's encouragement of students unhappy with their degree programme to seek redress through the Competition and Markets Authority – a governmental body that ensures that 'consumers get a good deal when buying goods and services, and businesses operate within the law' (CMA, 2020: np). In countries in which fees are either not payable by HE students or have been kept at a low level (such as across much of mainland Europe), similar arguments about the emergence of new forms of student identity are also advanced, suggesting that the widespread introduction of principles of new public management (even if payment has not shifted to the individual) has had a similar effect of encouraging a broad range of HE stakeholders to view students as consumers of an educational product (Moutsios, 2013; Kwiek, 2018). Some researchers have suggested that a shift to more highly marketised systems, particularly those in which students pay fees, has had a direct impact on how the process of learning is understood by both students and staff. Molesworth et al (2009), examining developments in the UK, have argued that students have come to conceptualise learning in highly transactional terms – as a product to be bought, rather than a process that requires a considerable amount of effort on their part and that might, in places, be difficult and challenging. In such analyses, the previously dominant construction of student as learner is seen to have come under significant pressure through the reconfiguration of the HE sector along market lines.

There is now, however, an emerging body of work that questions some of these assumptions and provides more nuanced accounts of the impact of market mechanisms within HE (for example, Budd, 2017). Research conducted in the UK by Tomlinson (2017), for example, has shown that while some students have embraced a consumer identity that informs their approach to their studies, a considerable number of their peers actively reject this construction on the grounds that it fails to recognise the effort they themselves put into their learning, and has the potential to undermine their relationships with lecturers (see also O'Shea and Delahunty (2018) who have made similar arguments with respect to Australian students). Research has suggested that constructions may differ at the institutional level, too, with higher-status and more financially secure universities better able to insulate themselves from the pressures of marketisation and thus protect their students from being positioned as consumers (Naidoo et al, 2011). Comparative research by Muddiman (2020) has evidenced differences – across nations – by discipline, as well: in her study in Singapore and the UK, students studying business were more likely to assume consumer-like orientations to their degree than their counterparts in sociology departments. Nevertheless, intra-European comparisons are rarely conducted, while research on the impact of market mechanisms on student identities is uncommon outside nations with neo-liberal welfare regimes and that charge high tuition fees. Our study sought to fill both these gaps.

Political actor

The construction of 'student as consumer' is often held in tension with that of the student as a political actor. Indeed, in many societies, there is now an assumption that students *should* be politically active, driving social change and challenging enduring inequalities, and students are often criticised – by journalists, HE staff and other interested parties – when they are perceived not to be acting in this way (Brooks et al, 2020b). Nevertheless, as Williams (2013) has argued, this conceptualisation of students as political actors became common only in the 1960s, and is frequently based on a misreading of that particular period – a misreading that incorrectly assumed a majority of students were involved in the US and European campus protests of the 1960s and early 1970s (Sukarieh and Tannock, 2015). Such contemporary constructions also tend to operate with a relatively narrow understanding of political engagement. While involvement in on-campus activities associated with *formal* politics tends to be limited, and students' unions in a number of countries of the world have become less 'activist' in their orientation (for example, Rochford, 2014; Nissen and Hayward, 2017), students nevertheless have a relatively high level of political interest (Abrahams and Brooks, 2019; Brooks et al, 2020b) and graduates are more likely than others to be politically engaged in later life (Olcese et al, 2014). Moreover, comparative work in Australia, the US and UK has shown that small student societies can play an important role in encouraging students to develop their political identity and emerge as 'student citizens' (Loader et al, 2015).

Future worker

Studies across the Anglophone Global North have indicated that, within national policy, students are frequently constructed as 'future workers' – typically as part of a broader 'human capital' discourse in which the primary purpose of HE is increasingly presented as labour market preparation – and are assumed to be motivated primarily by employment-related concerns (for example, Waters, 2009; Allen et al, 2013; Moore and Morton, 2017). In the wider European context, increasing the 'employability' of students has also constituted a key focus of the Bologna Process and informed various national-level policies (Stiwne and Alves, 2010). Within Denmark, for example, Nielsen and Sarauw (2017) have argued that there has been a growing demand on the part of policymakers that students 'focus on and work towards their future employability from the day they enrol at the university' (p 162) and move through their studies quickly to enable prompt labour market entry.

There are, however, some subtle differences in how this 'future worker' focus is played out, which are related to national models of HE funding and broader education policy traditions (about the role of public funding and the position of universities in national development). Antonucci (2016) notes that in what she calls the 'social investment' model of HE, which typifies Anglo-Saxon countries such as England (and also Australia, New Zealand and the US, although they were not covered by her research), students are constructed by policymakers explicitly as individual investors in their future careers and, as such, are expected to make significant private contributions to their HE fees and living costs. In contrast, in the 'public responsibility' model of HE funding that characterises the Nordic countries, this language of individual investment (in becoming a future worker) is largely absent. Instead, and as noted above, students are expected to develop skills relevant to the labour market and move quickly through their studies into a job, to repay the public investment in their education.

Socialite

Finally, students have often been viewed – by others, if not often by themselves – as socialites, 'party animals' or even hedonists, interested primarily in the social opportunities afforded by HE. This particular construction tends to be stronger in nations with a dominant 'residential' model of HE, in which it is common for students to leave their parental home in order to pursue their studies and live in dedicated student accommodation or shared private houses. Williams (2013) has argued that this specific construction has a long history within the UK particularly, dating back at least to the first half of the 20th century. However, some scholars have suggested it has taken on new significance in contemporary society, as a number of HE institutions have chosen to stress their 'party credentials' as a means of differentiating themselves from their competitors and thus attracting students who prioritise social life over study. This is articulated well in Armstrong and Hamilton's (2013) ethnography of a large state university in the US, entitled *Paying for the Party*. They identify various 'pathways' that students can take through the university, but argue that it is the 'party pathway' which is dominant. It is, they suggest 'the main artery through the university', and the primary means of attracting 'those whose dollars fuel the university' (p 21). By stressing the highly developed social life of the campus and the correspondingly modest academic demands, the university targets extremely affluent students with middling academic records. As a result, Armstrong and Hamilton contend, it fails to support those from less privileged backgrounds who are more focused on their academic studies. Writing with respect to the UK, Sykes (2021) has shown how students often feel that they have to live up to the stereotype of the partying student in how they present themselves to others, even when their day-to-day lives are focused almost exclusively on studying and work.

This literature provides an important point of departure for the chapters that follow. Indeed, in a number of chapters, our arguments articulate with some of the points made above. We also, however, introduce some new constructions that are captured less well in the extant literature. Moreover, we demonstrate the complexity of such conceptualisations, by showing how some understandings differed *within* as well as across nations.

Researching understandings of the student

The subsequent chapters of this book draw on data that were collected as part of a European Research Council-funded project – 'Eurostudents' – that explored how HE students are understood across Europe. The research was designed to enable us to make comparisons between the ways in which students were constructed by different social actors within individual nation-states, as well as across nations. To facilitate cross-national comparisons, data were collected from six countries – Denmark, England, Germany, Ireland, Poland and Spain – chosen to provide diversity in terms of relationship to the EU, welfare regime, mechanisms of funding HE, and the type of financial support offered to students (see Table 1.1). We provide more detail about the specific policy contexts in each of these countries at the time we were collecting data later in the chapter. To compare the perspectives of different social actors within the same nation, we analysed how students were understood in policy and the media, and by HE institutions and students themselves. Fieldwork was conducted during 2017–20, and a full list of all the data collected can be found in Table 1.4.

We are cognisant of some of the critiques of comparative research that uses the nation-state as the unit of analysis. These tend to argue that such an approach reinforces methodological nationalism – that is, the assumption that the nation is the natural social and political form of the modern world (Wimmer and Glick Schiller, 2002). However, while employing a cross-national design, as discussed above, our research aimed to assess the perspectives of students and other stakeholders in a Europe where policy over the past two decades has been intended to bring about convergence of HE systems and, it is argued, has led to the conceptualisation of students in increasingly similar ways (for example, Moutsios, 2013). Moreover, our research design was intended to question explicitly whether nations, themselves, should be considered as 'coherent educational entities' (Philips and Schweisfurth, 2014), through exploring the perspectives of different social actors in each nation and being aware of likely inter-dependencies between the global, national and local levels (Kosmützky, 2015). No a priori assumptions were thus made about the relative importance of national borders. We now discuss each of the four strands of our research in turn.

Policy perspectives

The first strand of the research focused on the understandings of the HE student held by policy actors and disseminated through relevant policy documents. In each of the six countries, between 12 and 16 policy documents were selected, produced by government (including key strategy documents and speeches given by HE ministers); national unions representing HE staff and students;

Table 1.1: Characteristics of the countries involved in the research

Country	Welfare regime	Accession to the EU	Tuition fees for full-time undergraduates (2017/18)	Student support for full-time undergraduates (2017/18) – with amounts per annum[1]
Denmark	Social democratic	1973	No tuition fees	c.85 per cent receive needs-based grants (of up to €9703); loans available to those entitled to state grant
England	Liberal	1973 (left in 2020)	High fees, typically £9250 per year	No grants; loans available to all
Germany	Corporatist	1952	No tuition fees; administrative fee of up to €300 per semester	c.25 per cent of students receive need-based grants (up to €8820 – includes integrated loan)
Ireland	Catholic corporatist	1973	No tuition fees; 'student contribution' of €3000 per year	c.44 per cent of students receive need-based grants (up to €5915); no loans available
Poland	Post-Communist	2004	No tuition fees; one-off administrative fee of c.€47 per year	c.16 per cent of students receive need-based grants (€1244) and eight per cent merit-based grants (average €113); loans available to those on lower incomes
Spain	Mediterranean/ sub-protective	1986	c.71 per cent of students pay fees; average amount of €1213 per year	c.30 per cent of students receive need-based grants (up to €6682); no loans available

and bodies representing graduate employers. Documents were chosen based on the extent to which they focused on students, specifically; their national significance; and their date of publication (the most recent documents that met the first two criteria were chosen). In total, 92 documents were analysed.[2] Where they were not available in English, they were translated prior to analysis.

Interviews were conducted in each of the countries with a similar range of stakeholders, representing government (a civil servant working on HE policy and/or a government minister); unions (in most countries a leader of the national students' union, although in Spain we interviewed a leader of a union representing staff); and graduate employers/business organisations. In addition, we interviewed a member of staff from the national body representing universities (often called 'rectors' conferences' in mainland Europe). In total, we interviewed 26 such policy actors across the six countries. All interviewees were asked a similar range of questions about how they understood students in their own country and the extent to which their understandings had changed over time. They were also asked about specific ways in which students have been understood by others (for example, as consumers, political actors, future workers) and the degree to which they shared such views. Additionally, they were asked to respond to an extract from a key policy document from their own country. All interviews were conducted in English and lasted, on average, an hour.

In the subsequent chapters of the book, policy documents are referred to in terms of their country of origin and type (for example, German government document, Polish union document). Full references can be found in the Appendix, along with a list of all 92 documents analysed. The interviews are referred to by giving the country and type of organisation the interviewee represented.

Media perspectives

The second strand of the research concentrated on how HE students were represented in the media, with respect to newsprint and popular culture. Our decision to focus on newspapers was informed by the belief that the views of print journalists, and how they construct HE students within newspapers, are significant. As Williams (2011) notes, journalists 'are subject to the same influences as other people and in order to sell articles, pieces must chime with the opinions of at least a section of the population' (p 170). They thus reflect dominant understandings of what it means to be a student, but can also 'help reconstruct ways of being a student for new generations' (Williams, 2011: 170). In each of the six countries, two national newspapers were selected for analysis (see Table 1.2). When sampling the newspapers, we chose to include only national – not regional or local – publications, and restricted ourselves to those that were available through an online database or

Table 1.2: Sampled newspapers

Country	Name of newspaper	Tabloid/ broadsheet	Political orientation	Other information[3]
Denmark	*Politiken*	Broadsheet	Centre left	Largest circulation of broadsheets
	BT	Tabloid	Centre right	Largest circulation of tabloids
England	*The Guardian*	Broadsheet	Centre left	Third largest circulation of broadsheets
	Daily Mail	Mid-market/ tabloid	Right	Second largest circulation of all newspapers
Germany	*Süddeutsche Zeitung*	Broadsheet	Centre left	Largest circulation of broadsheets
	Die Welt	Broadsheet	Centre right	Third largest circulation of broadsheets
Ireland	*Irish Independent*	Mid-market/ tabloid	Centre right	Largest circulation of all newspapers
	The Irish Times	Broadsheet	Centre left	Second largest circulation of all newspapers
Poland	*Gazeta Wyborcza*	Broadsheet	Centre left	Largest circulation of broadsheets
	Rzeczpospolita	Broadsheet	Centre right	Second largest circulation of broadsheets
Spain	*El País*	Broadsheet	Centre left	Largest circulation of broadsheets
	ABC	Broadsheet	Right	Fourth largest circulation of broadsheets

archive. Two different newspapers from each country were sampled: either 'a tabloid' and 'a broadsheet'[4] newspaper, or two broadsheets that differed in terms of political alignment.

We then searched for articles that were published between 2014 and 2016 using search terms (for example, students, higher education, university) relevant to each national context. In total, we gathered 1159 articles from the six countries, which were analysed using (largely qualitative) content analysis. On the basis of this content analysis, a sub-sample of the articles was chosen for more detailed discursive analysis. When material was not available in English, it was translated using Google Translate or professional translators.

In the second part of this strand, up to two popular films or drama-based television programmes that feature students prominently were selected from each country, where available (see Table 1.3). We included only those that had been made in the last ten years, and which had been widely distributed and/or

Table 1.3: Sampled TV series and films

Country	Name	Format	Date of production	Other information, including genre
England (or UK)	*Clique*	TV series	2017–2018	Psychological thriller; two seasons
	Fresh Meat	TV series	2011–2016	Comedy; four seasons
Germany	*13 Semester*	Film	2009	Romantic comedy
	Wir Sind Die Neuen (We Are the New Ones)	Film	2014	Comedy
Ireland	*Normal People*	TV series	2020	Drama and romance; one season
Spain	*Fuga de Cerebros (Brain Drain)*	Film	2009	Romantic comedy
	Merlí: Sapere Aude (Merlí: Dare to Know)	TV series	2019	Drama; one season

had high viewer numbers. Popular culture texts are created and consumed mainly for the purposes of entertainment but may, nonetheless, help to inform dominant societal constructions of the student (Farber and Holm, 2005) and can be analysed as a source of 'public narratives' (Thornham and Purvis, 2005). In Denmark and Poland, no such films or TV shows were available and only one was found in Ireland. Moreover, both series that comprised the English sample were produced in the UK (rather than England specifically). With respect to language, all the material was either in English or had English-language subtitles. The analysis of these texts employed a discursive approach, paying attention to the visual and aural landscape, as well as the words that were spoken. Summaries of the plots of the films and TV series are provided in the Appendix. When we refer to the media data in the chapters that follow, we focus on the ways in which students are represented or constructed – and do not assume that these are necessarily accurate portrayals.

Institutional perspectives

The third strand of the research focused on institutional perspectives, that is, how HE students are constructed through official university texts and staff understandings. Semi-structured interviews were conducted with staff members from three HEIs per country.[5] In general, the institutions were chosen to represent key elements of the diversity of the relevant national HE sector. However, in some cases, our choice was limited by logistical factors, such as where we were able to secure access and the practicalities of travel. In Denmark, we chose two universities of different ages (one established after the Second World War, the other earlier) and a university college with a vocational focus. In England, which has the most vertically differentiated system in our sample, we included three institutions of different ages, which mapped onto different league table positions. One belonged to the 'Russell Group' of 'research intensive' universities, a second conducted both research and teaching but was not a member of the Russell Group, and the third was a relatively recently established institution, with a strong teaching focus. The German sample comprised one large, old and prestigious institution, one younger (post-war) mid-sized university, and one university of applied sciences. In Ireland, we chose one institute of technology, as well as two universities of different statuses – one that was considered prestigious, and another that was less so. In Poland, we included one large technical university and two more general universities located in cities of different sizes in different parts of the country, and of different ages (one established post-war, the other older). The Spanish sample comprised two public universities (in different parts of the country – one established post-war, the other older) and one private university. (We say more about the structure of the HE sectors in each country below; see also the Appendix, which shows the label we gave to each HEI.) In each institution, four members of staff were selected – giving a total of 72 staff across the project as a whole. We aimed to include two members of staff who had teaching-related roles and two employed in professional services and/or leadership roles. However, in some HEIs this was not possible for logistical reasons. While we tried to ensure that a wide range of disciplines was represented among staff, this was sometimes limited by the nature of the HEI: in both Germany and Denmark, for example, as noted above, we included one institution that offered primarily vocationally oriented programmes.

Respondents were asked about their own conceptualisations of HE students in their countries, the extent to which these had changed over their career, and the factors they believed had informed these understandings. As with the policy actors mentioned above, staff were also asked for their views about some of the common ways in which students were understood by others. These interviews lasted, on average, an hour, and were all conducted in English. In the subsequent chapters, when we refer to members of staff we provide an identifier that relates to the institution for which they worked (see Appendix for details). Further information about staff members' roles, discipline, years of experience, and gender are provided in the Appendix.

Student perspectives

The fourth strand examined the constructions of HE students held by students themselves. Three focus groups were conducted in each of the 18 HE institutions where we also conducted staff interviews (see above). Thus, in total we conducted 54 focus groups, involving 295 undergraduate students.

Although numbers varied, on average there were five or six participants in each focus group. All were undergraduate students who held citizenship of the country in which they were studying.[6] We aimed to select participants so that the focus groups were broadly representative of the undergraduate population at each HEI. However, for logistical reasons this was not always possible. Across the sample as a whole, mature students and those from ethnic minority backgrounds tended to be under-represented, while women and those on arts and social science courses were over-represented (see Appendix for further details of the sample composition).

The focus groups lasted, on average, 90 minutes. Participants were asked a wide range of questions about their understandings of what it means to be a student today. An open, semi-structured approach was used to ensure that the conversation was led by students themselves. We also made use of plasticine modelling. This creative method, as discussed by Ingram (2011) and Abrahams and Ingram (2013), is a useful tool for eliciting rich data on a subject such as social constructions, as it enables participants to make tangible relatively abstract ideas, and allows greater time for reflection. At the start of each group, we asked all participants to make two plasticine models: the first focusing on how they understood themselves as HE students, and the second on how they thought others viewed them. Students were subsequently asked to talk us through what they had made and why. In addition, towards the end of the focus group, participants were asked for their views about specific constructions discussed in the academic literature (such as student as consumer, political actor, future worker and learner), and examples of representations (of students) drawn from the sampled policy and newspaper texts (see above) were introduced as prompts to encourage discussion. The focus groups were conducted in English in England, Ireland and Denmark. In Germany, Poland and Spain, they were conducted in the national language, with the transcriptions translated into English prior to analysis. We also conducted one individual interview with a student in Denmark, as she was the only participant to turn up to one of the planned focus groups. Although we rescheduled this group, she could not make the new time but was nevertheless keen to take part in the project. When we report the focus group data, we note the relevant country and have given each of the three HEI focus groups a number.

A note about language

Throughout our data collection (see Table 1.4 for a summary of all data collected), we were aware that various terms, including some of those central to our research, such as student and worker, have different connotations in particular languages. To increase our awareness of these, sometimes key terms were discussed explicitly as part of the interviews and focus groups. This was particularly the case for the

Table 1.4: Summary of all data collected

	Data collected in each of the six countries	Data collected across the project as a whole
Policy constructions	12–16 policy texts 4–6 in-depth interviews with policy actors	92 policy texts 26 in-depth interviews with policy actors
Media representations	Relevant articles from two newspapers over three-year period Up to two popular films or TV series	Content of 12 newspapers over three-year period (total of 1159 articles) Seven popular films or TV series
Institutional perspectives	12 in-depth interviews with HEI staff	72 in-depth interviews with HEI staff
Student understandings	Nine focus groups (each with 4–6 students)	54 focus groups (total of 295 students)

German word *Bildung* and the Danish word *Dannelse* – neither of which have a direct equivalent in English but refer to the idea of personal development or self-formation through education. In the chapters that follow, we refer to these two concepts (and a small number of additional terms) in the original language. Elsewhere, we use English translations. The extracts we present from focus groups in Germany, Poland and Spain have been translated into English, as have the quotations we use from newspaper articles from the four countries where English is not the national language and some of the policy extracts (others had English-language official versions).

National policy contexts

In the chapters that follow, we show how some understandings of students were common across the six countries in our study. We also, however, demonstrate that in some cases, particular conceptualisations were informed by the specific national policy context. To help situate these arguments, as well as provide more detail about the contexts in which our data collection took place, in this section we outline various key features of the HE sectors in the six nations. We also discuss some of the particular reforms which, our analyses suggest, had exerted influence on how students were understood. This overview is not intended to be exhaustive, but rather to highlight salient points to inform the reading of later chapters.

Denmark

The Danish HE sector is relatively small compared to the other five countries in the sample, comprising just over 310 000 students in 2018. Nevertheless, it

Table 1.5: Salient higher-education-related data, by country

	Denmark	England (figures given for UK as whole)	Germany	Ireland	Poland	Spain
Total number of students enrolled in tertiary education, 2018 (thousands)*	310.9	2467.1	3127.9	231.2	1492.9	2051.8
25–34-year-olds with tertiary education (bachelor's level or above) (%), 2019**	43	44	33	63	43	33
New entrants to bachelor's programmes below age of 25 (%)**	76	87	83	89	87	91
Unemployment rates of 25–34-year-olds with tertiary education (%), 2019**	7	2	3	4	3	12
Public expenditure on tertiary education (as % of GDP), 2017*	2.45	1.44	1.25	0.97	1.08	0.93

Sources: *Eurostat (2019a); **OECD (2020)

is characterised by a high level of spending (2.45 per cent of Gross Domestic Product (GDP) in 2017) and a generous funding system, whereby the cost of tuition is covered by the state and students typically receive a non-means-tested grant for the duration of their studies (see Tables 1.1 and 1.5). Around 43 per cent of the 25–34-year-old population in Denmark has at least a bachelor's degree, and the age profile of students is rather higher than the other countries in the sample, with just under a quarter of those enrolling on bachelor's programmes aged 25 or over (see Table 1.5). HE programmes are offered by universities, university colleges and academies of professional education. Denmark, in common with many other countries in central, north and eastern Europe, has been influenced by the Humboldtian model of the university – which emphasises the unity of teaching and research, academic freedom, institutional autonomy (despite funding from the state), freedom of study for students (*Lernfreiheit*), and the ideal of self-cultivation or *Bildung* (Anderson, 2004). We discuss these ideas in greater depth in Chapter 2 (with respect to students' transitions), Chapter 4 (in relation to learning) and Chapter 5 (in our examination of work).

Over recent years, some in Denmark have argued that these principles have been undermined by various government reforms – particularly those known as the 'Sizing Model' and the 'Study Progress Reform'. The 'Sizing Model' was introduced across the Danish HE sector in 2014 and aimed to link the annual student intake in specific subjects to the number of graduates from that subject area who successfully secured work on graduation. Caps on admissions were introduced for programmes which, according to the model's calculations, had 'systematic and striking excess unemployment' (Madsen, 2019: 73). 'Excess' unemployment was defined as two per cent or more above the average unemployment for all Danish graduates in the fourth to seventh quarters after leaving university, while unemployment was categorised as 'systemic' if it was evident in seven of the last ten years (Madsen, 2021). Degree programmes in the arts and humanities were the main casualties of this initiative (Madsen, 2019). The Study Progress Reform, also implemented in 2014, aimed to increase the pace at which students progressed through their degree programmes. It made use of a key feature of the Bologna Process reforms, namely the European Credit Transfer System (ECTS) – an ostensibly neutral means of measuring a course's workload – to accomplish the country's own objectives, namely reducing the cost of education (incurred by the state) and ensuring that students enter the labour market quickly (Nielsen and Sarauw, 2017; Sarauw and Madsen, 2020). These objectives are in part achieved through regulating duration of study. Since 2014, students have been incentivised to complete their courses within the prescribed time limit: they must sit exams after completing a certain number of ECTS points and are allowed to fall only a specific number of ECTS points behind schedule before they lose access to financial support. HEIs have, in turn, made courses more standardised, with fewer optional elements, in order to ensure efficiency and quick completion. Alongside this, a modularised and competence-based curriculum has been introduced to promote the future employability of students, and students have been encouraged not to assume that they will automatically progress to a master's degree (as has been the case in the past). Empirical examinations of the impact of these reforms have suggested that students feel they are sometimes restricted to a superficial and instrumental engagement with their studies, choosing 'safe routes' through their studies, to maximise their chances of passing their exams and completing their studies in the required time (Nielsen and Sarauw, 2017; Sarauw and Madsen, 2020). Moreover, there is often a poor match between how 'study time' is understood within policy and by students themselves (Ulriksen and Nejrup, 2021).

England

England was chosen as a case study country rather than the whole of the UK because HE is governed separately in the four 'home nations' that make up the UK, and because of the differences in funding structures in England,

Wales, Scotland and Northern Ireland. For example, at the time of our data collection, English undergraduates studying at English HEIs had to pay very high fees (£9250) while Scottish undergraduates studying in Scottish HEIs paid no fees at all. Nevertheless, HE data are often collected at the UK level (see Table 1.1), and so in this section we discuss both the UK in general as well as England, specifically.

As Table 1.5 indicates, the UK has a relatively large number of students as a whole, when compared to other European countries (although fewer than Germany), and most are quite young (87 per cent of those starting a first degree were under the age of 25). In 2019, 44 per cent of the UK population between the ages of 25 and 34 had attained at least a bachelor's degree and, in 2019, very few graduates were unemployed (only two per cent). Despite the high fees charged to students (see Table 1.1), public expenditure on tertiary education as a proportion of GDP is the second highest in our sample, at 1.44 per cent (Table 1.5). As noted above, the English HE sector (as well as that of the UK as a whole) is more vertically differentiated than in many countries (Hazelkorn, 2015), with divisions typically drawn between larger, older, 'research intensive' universities (commonly members of the 'Russell Group' mission group); smaller, research-focused universities, which held university status prior to 1992; and more modern, often teaching-focused institutions, which gained university status in 1992 or later.

The English HE sector differs from many of its European counterparts with respect to its early embrace of marketisation and its associated decision to charge individual students a high level of fee (albeit with the option of taking out a loan, the repayment of which is tied to future earnings) (see Table 1.1). Indeed, a number of studies have illustrated how HE policies in England – through the introduction of a range of market mechanisms including student charters (contracts between students and their HEIs), student satisfaction surveys, and institutionalised complaint mechanisms, as well as high tuition fees – construct students as consumers, and HE as a commodity in which they will be willing to invest for personal gain (Naidoo and Williams, 2015; Brooks and Abrahams, 2018; Raaper, 2018). As discussed earlier in this chapter, it has also been argued that these policies have had a significant impact on classroom practices and the learner identities taken up by students themselves (for example, Nixon et al, 2010; Naidoo and Williams, 2015). These analyses of the contemporary English university often stand in stark contrast to the 'idea of a university' proffered by the theologian John Henry Newman in his classic text of the 19th century, and which has exerted a significant influence, historically, on how HE has been understood in England. In this, he argued that university scholars should be engaged in intellectual pursuit as an end in itself, not for any external purpose. Moreover, he advocated a broad, liberal education, focused on teaching students to think, reason, compare, discriminate and analyse, and was critical of narrow vocational education (Newman, 1996 [1858]). Such ideas have not vanished entirely from the English HE system, and were referred to by some of our research participants (see Chapter 4). Over recent years, the English HE system has also been caught up in the so-called 'culture wars'. Influenced by ideas from the US (Bloom, 1987; Lukianoff and Haidt, 2018), various politicians and journalists have expressed concern that free speech is being compromised on campus and students' learning is being adversely affected by an emphasis on 'safetyism' (for example, protecting students from potentially challenging ideas). Nevertheless, these accusations are strongly contested by many within the HE sector, and studies have suggested that students themselves are broadly supportive of how their HEI promotes freedom of expression (Grant et al, 2019). We engage with this debate in Chapter 7, in particular.

Germany

The German HE sector is the largest of the six in the research, with over three million students (Table 1.5). Nevertheless, the proportion of young people with at least a bachelor's degree in Germany is joint lowest – at 33 per cent. This is largely due to the enduring strength of the vocational sector in Germany, with many young people choosing to take up an apprenticeship or other form of vocational education or training rather than enrol in HE. Those who do progress to HE are typically quite young – with 83 per cent of new entrants on bachelor's programmes below the age of 25 – and are very likely to move into employment on graduation (the unemployment rate for graduates under 35 was only three per cent in 2019) (Table 1.5). HE is not predominantly regulated at the national level in Germany, but by the 16 individual states (*Länder*). There are, however, some important commonalities across the country: tuition fees are not payable and means-tested grants are available to those whose family income is below a certain level (around a quarter of students are eligible for such funding) (see Table 1.1).

Three main types of institution make up the German HE system: universities (including some that specialise in particular areas, such as technical universities); universities of applied sciences (that are practically oriented, and include a period of paid practical training); and colleges of art, film and music. There is a strong vocational system in Germany and, as noted above, many young people opt to pursue an apprenticeship rather than an HE qualification. Although, historically, the German HE system has been a relatively 'flat' one, with few status differences between institutions, since 2005, steps have been taken by the German government to introduce more vertical differentiation into the system. This has been done through the 'Excellence Initiative', which has concentrated funding in a small group of

HEIs, with the aim of enabling them to compete more successfully with comparable 'top performers' from other countries (Kehm, 2013).

Currently, a bachelor's degree takes three years or six semesters to complete and a master's degree usually two years or four semesters. However, it is only since the early 21st century that bachelor's and master's qualifications have been available in Germany, as a result of the Bologna Process. Previously, students studied for a *Diplom* or *Magister* and, because these allowed students to study very flexibly, they often took a long time to complete (Ertl, 2013). Indeed, since the turn of the century, there has been a concerted effort in Germany to encourage students to move faster through their degree programme – bearing some similarities to the Danish reforms discussed above. German politicians have been concerned at the cost to the taxpayer of slow completion (Ertl, 2013). Student support is now available only for the number of semesters it is expected to take a student to complete a degree (six for most bachelor's programmes). After this time, students are still able to continue with their degrees, but have to fund their studies themselves. As in Denmark, there has been considerable opposition to these reforms, with students believing they are being rushed through their studies, and denied the freedom to decide on their own pace of learning. This opposition is often framed in terms of the Humboldtian principles upon which German HE was built and particularly the idea of *Lernfreiheit* (the freedom to learn) (see Brooks et al (2021a) for further discussion).

Ireland

The Irish HE sector is the smallest of the six covered by the research, with just over 230 000 students (Table 1.5), and government spending in this area is fairly low (0.97 per cent of GDP). However, Ireland has the highest participation rate in the study, with 63 per cent of 25–34-year-olds having gained at least a bachelor's level qualification (Table 1.5). Irish students tend to be young, with 89 per cent of those starting bachelor's programmes under 25, while unemployment among graduates has been relatively low (four per cent in 2019). Although Irish students do not officially pay tuition fees, they do have to pay a reasonably high 'student contribution', which, at the time of our research, stood at €3000 a year. Means-tested grants are available for students from low-income families; when we collected data in Ireland, around 44 per cent of students were entitled to such grants, up to a maximum of €5915 (see Table 1.1).

The Irish HE sector is comprised of universities, institutes of technology, colleges of education and some specialist institutions. However, it is generally considered a binary system, with distinctions made between universities on the one hand and institutes of technology on the other. Institutes of technology are largely teaching-focused, and the majority of their students tend to be undergraduates. Although there are only nine universities in Ireland, these are differentiated to some extent, with Trinity College Dublin and University College Dublin – founded in 1592 and 1854, respectively – considered the most prestigious. Ireland is sometimes seen as similar to England in relation to the marketisation of its HE system, having introduced various aspects of new managerialism (Lynch et al, 2012; Fleming et al, 2017). Market reforms have, however, been less thorough-going. For example, the student contribution has remained relatively low when compared to the fees charged in England and other Anglophone nations of the Global North (Clancy, 2015). Moreover, Hazelkorn (2015) has argued that the underpinning model of HE in Ireland adheres to social democratic, rather than neo-liberal, norms. She notes that unlike the emphasis within neo-liberal models on vertical differentiation between HEIs with the aim of creating elite institutions able to compete internationally, social democratic models seek to balance excellence with support for good quality institutions across the country. Thus, while as we noted above, there are some status differences between HEIs, these are largely related to the different institutional histories and profiles, rather than specific steps taken by the government to increase vertical differentiation. Ireland has also, historically, been influenced by Newman's view of university education (see above). Indeed, his *The Idea of the University* is a collection of lectures he delivered on becoming the first rector of the newly founded Catholic University in Ireland in 1851.

Poland

Polish HE has a long history, with the first university established in the 14th century. It has been influenced by both Humboldtian principles (see above), and the country's Communist past (Antonowicz et al, 2020). It has, however, undergone significant change over the past three decades since the end of Communist rule in 1989. Although the HE participation rate is now similar to that seen in many other European countries (43 per cent of 25–34-year-olds held at least a bachelor's degree in 2019 – see Table 1.5), the rate of expansion has been much higher. During the Communist period, HE was centrally planned, with places strictly linked to labour market need and, by 1989, despite massification in many other parts of Europe, only about ten per cent of each cohort went on to HE (Kwiek, 2016). Within 15 years, however, the participation rate had risen to over 50 per cent – a process that Kwiek (2016) describes as both abrupt and uncoordinated. The main drivers of this expansion were changes within the labour market, which required a more highly educated workforce, and greater demand for HE from the population (and an increased ability to pay fees, as salaries increased post-Communism) (Kwiek, 2016).

Much of this increase in demand was absorbed by less prestigious public sector universities and a large number of new private institutions – facilitated by a laissez-faire state policy, and the willingness of academic staff to work across both public and private HEIs (Kwiek, 2016). Higher-status institutions also developed new part-time, fee-based courses to cater for the increase in demand – although such courses were often of lower quality than those available to full-time, state-funded students, and tended to be taken up by students from lower socio-economic backgrounds (Kwiek, 2016). Since 2006, however, a sharp demographic decline in the number of young people in Poland has led to a contraction of the private sector (Kwiek, 2016). Alongside the decline in the number of private institutions, Poland's public HEIs are becoming increasingly stratified – driven by the concentration of research funds in a relatively small number of universities through Poland's own 'Excellence Initiative' (Kwiek, 2016). The sector currently comprises private and public HEIs. The latter includes comprehensive universities, specialist universities (focusing, for example, on technical subjects, medicine and economics), specialist academies and small higher vocational schools.

Polish students are typically young, with 87 per cent of those entering bachelor's programmes below the age of 25 (see Table 1.5), and most go on to find jobs at the end of their studies (the unemployment rate for 25–34-year-olds with tertiary education was three per cent in 2019 – see Table 1.5). Students attending public HEIs do not have to pay tuition fees, only an annual administration fee which, at the time of our data collection, was around €47. A small number of needs- and merit-based grants are available to students; in addition, loans are offered to those from low-income families (see Table 1.1 for further details). Those attending private HEIs pay for their tuition; they typically study on a part-time basis and engage in paid work at the same time. Fees are also payable for those studying on a part-time basis in public HEIs.

Spain

Despite the Spanish HE sector being relatively large (in terms of the size of its student population), only a third of those in the 25–34 age group have a bachelor's degree or above, and public expenditure on the sector is the lowest of all our six countries (see Table 1.5). Those who do go on to HE are typically young, with 91 per cent of new entrants to bachelor's programmes under the age of 25 – the highest proportion across the sample. One of the factors that distinguishes Spain from the other five countries in the research is the relatively high level of unemployment (see Table 1.5). At the time of our data collection in Spain (2017–2018), the youth unemployment rate was 34.3 per cent – more than double the EU average of 15.2 per cent and the highest of all the countries in our study (Eurostat, 2019a). Moreover, Spain was also one of the four EU Member States with the highest rate of *graduate* unemployment (running at 22.1 per cent), while all the other countries in our study had a graduate unemployment rate below the EU average (of 14.5 per cent) (Eurostat, 2019b). This was largely a result of the 2008 global recession, which hit Spain, along with other countries in southern Europe, particularly hard (Martínez-Campillo and Fernández-Santos, 2020).

The majority of Spanish students (around 70 per cent) pay fees – at the time of our data collection the average annual amount was €1213 (see Table 1.1) – and a relatively small proportion (about 30 per cent) are eligible for needs-based grants. No loans are available to cover either tuition fees or living costs, and student support was cut back quite substantially following the 2008 recession (de la Torre and Perez-Esparrells, 2019). As in Denmark and Germany, there have been some substantial reforms to the Spanish HE system as a result of the Bologna Process (Elias, 2010; de la Torre and Perez-Esparrells, 2019). For example, the time required to complete an undergraduate degree was shortened from five to four years in 2007, and then to three years in 2015 – although universities still have the right to offer a four-year degree if they wish. While these changes were controversial at the time of introduction (Phillips, 2008; Elias, 2010), they were commented on by only a very small minority of our interviewees, and appeared to have been largely accepted by the time of our data collection (see Brooks et al (2021a) for further discussion). In general, European policies have been viewed favourably by politicians and policymakers in Spain. Bonal and Tarabini (2013) have contended that Spanish official discourse (in education policy as well as elsewhere) consistently underlines the advantages of Europeanisation as a means of advancing both social and economic progress: 'in order to become "real Europeans" it is crucial to follow the reforms already implemented by other European countries' (p 337).

Structure of the book

In the subsequent chapters of the book, we draw on the data collected in the Eurostudents project to explore six of the most dominant constructions of HE students that emerged from our data. Not all of these were equally strong in all of the countries in which we conducted fieldwork – and, where relevant, we explore the reasons for this variation. Moreover, we also examine differences in the extent to which the particular conceptualisations were evident among the various social actors in the research; indeed, a key part of our overall argument is that there is often a significant disconnect between the understandings of students themselves and those of others in society.

The first construction we discuss, in Chapter 2, is that of students as 'in transition' – understood in terms of transition to the labour market, but also a period of self-development. While, in general, being 'in transition' was viewed positively, we suggest that it sometimes has the effect of marginalising students, through their positioning as 'not yet fully adult'. Chapter 3 picks up some of these themes in its exploration of students as citizens. This was a key way in which students constructed themselves – emphasising what they believed was their responsibility to think and act critically for the benefit of society. We also show, however, that their views were not always shared by other social actors, with staff and policy actors more likely to reject the construction of students as active and engaged citizens. In Chapter 4, we focus on students as 'enthusiastic learners and hard workers', again contrasting students' own accounts, which emphasised their high degree of engagement with their learning, with those of other stakeholders who were more likely to stress passivity and instrumentality. Chapter 5 focuses on students as 'future workers', contending that while this is a common construction across the dataset, it is played out in different ways. While policy discourses tend to foreground ideas associated with human capital, students themselves understand the 'future worker' in more divergent terms – stressing, for example, the importance of vocation and self-development. In Chapter 6, we demonstrate how in almost all the countries in our research students were couched as stressed. This was typically understood in negative terms, and explained in terms of HE-specific factors as well as broader societal trends. Chapter 7 shows how students were often seen by other social actors as threats and/or objects of criticism, and then examines the impact these negative constructions had on the students to whom we spoke. Finally, in Chapter 8, the conclusion, we draw together various themes from the preceding discussion, considering their significance for both academic debate and HE as it is lived on the ground.

Different authors have taken a lead on particular chapters, so some variation in authorial voice may be evident across the book. However, we have all shared the analysis across both country and data strand, and discussed the content of each chapter together in considerable depth. *Constructing the Higher Education Student: Perspectives from across Europe* should thus be considered very much a common endeavour.

2

In transition

Introduction

With the growing massification of HE in Europe – as well as across OECD countries more generally – and the majority of students entering HE fairly soon after completing their compulsory schooling, HE students are often seen as 'in transition'. In our study, this was common, too. Moreover, students were also conceptualised, by themselves and other research participants, as people undergoing a series of potentially transformative changes. In this chapter, we explore this conceptualisation of HE students, examining how they are understood as 'in transition' and how this construction varies within and across our six countries.

We first draw on the extant literature to help contextualise the subsequent discussion of students as 'in transition'. We then outline how many students in our study considered attending university to be a rite of passage and examine two common ways in which the idea of being 'in transition' is understood in our data: as preparation for the labour market and as a personally transformative experience. Here, we explore both commonalities and variations within and across countries, suggesting that the HE funding regime, national traditions of HE, cultural norms, and other socio-historical factors may all affect how the construction of students as 'in transition' is understood. We then discuss the implications of this construction, maintaining that by positioning students as in a transitional period of their lives and thus 'not fully adult', their roles as political actors and citizens may be marginalised.

Understanding higher education students in transition

While most of the literature on HE and transition focuses on students' transition *to* university, there has been relatively little discussion of the construction of students within HE as *in transition*. The limited research on this topic unveils a variety of aspects pertaining to students' transitional experiences – both personal (for example, as students entering adulthood) and professional (for example, as HE students preparing for future jobs) within university settings. We will now discuss both of these aspects in turn.

Transitioning to adulthood is one of the main ways in which HE students are discussed in this literature. For example, based on their research in the UK, Bristow and colleagues (2020) show that students are often seen by academic staff as dependent and fragile children who need to be socialised into adulthood roles (noted, too, in Gravett et al, 2020). Various other studies have also suggested that HE is a critical turning point in students' lives as it offers them space to inculcate new habits and practices (Blichfeldt and Gram, 2013) and, as a result, they come to craft their understanding of their role and purpose in society (O'Shea, 2014). These experiences of transitioning are, however, often patterned by students' social characteristics such as gender, race and social class. Christie (2009) notes that the formation of a student identity commonly intersects with one's class position and related sense of belonging – or exclusion – within the university space. For many young students who entered university from non-traditional routes (and who had participated in an access to HE course before pursuing a university degree) in Christie's study, for example, the transition was not necessarily about 'leaving home and developing a new identity as an (independent) adult' (p 131) – in contrast to what appeared to be the case for many of their peers who studied full-time, lived on the university campus and were middle class. Instead, these students spoke about how, as 'day students' who would commute to university and had a full-time job, being a student was only one of their many identities (see also Reay et al, 2010).

Another common way in which students are considered to be in transition is with respect to graduate employment. Although this topic has been explored well from policy perspectives (see, for example, Tomlinson, 2013; Brown et al, 2020 – we discuss these further in Chapter 5), recent research has begun to engage more closely with the views of students themselves. For example, in a study conducted with marine sports science students in a relatively new HEI in the UK, Gedye and Beaumont (2018) documented several changes to how students understood their employability – their views shifted over their degree programme 'from those that centred on what employers want (extrinsic) to what the student had to offer the employer (intrinsic)' (p 406). In another study, Donald and colleagues found that while students considered themselves to be employable, they felt less confident about getting jobs when they factored in the competition in the labour market (Donald et al, 2018). Both of these studies (and others, such as Berg et al, 2017; McManus and Rook, 2021) allude to the transition within the university as crucial and life-changing 'identity work' – a broader process in which students form ideas about who they are and what they want to become. Developing a career identity is held to be a critical part of this work. Such processes are, however, again often affected by students' social characteristics – with social class, in particular, often exerting a significant influence on how students envisage their future career path and identity (Roberts and Li, 2017; Bathmaker, 2021).

The nature of transition within HE is conceptualised in different ways within the literature. Gale and Parker (2014), for example, delineate three key approaches, evident in both education policy and HE research: transition as induction (a period of students adjusting to HE settings); transition as development (a trajectory or a life stage at which students mature and form their career identity); and transition as 'becoming' (something that is not specific to HE students and instead is a part of a lifelong process of change). The authors suggest that the first two ways of understanding transition – more common in policy and in research – tend to view students as relatively passive actors, assuming that they need to be moulded in a specific way throughout their degree programme to ensure successful outcomes. In contrast, viewing transition as 'becoming' may provide a more nuanced understanding of the transitional experiences of individual students. We use this framework in this chapter to understand differences in conceptualisations of the changes students experience during their time in HE.

While the research in this area offers valuable insight into the complexity of being a student in transition, to date, we have had no clear understanding of how this complexity plays out across countries. Therefore, in the subsequent discussion, we focus on how students are thought of – in relation to ideas associated with transition – by the social actors in our study, identifying similarities and differences within and across our sample countries.

University as a 'rite of passage' – normalising students as 'in transition'?

The various groups who participated in our study tended to normalise the idea of students in transition – through viewing HE as a transitional period and a rite of passage in people's lives. For example, several policy actors, media and staff across the six countries viewed progression to HE as an increasingly typical transition in one's life course. Moreover, many students themselves spoke about pursuing tertiary education after secondary schooling as an 'obvious next step' rather than a deliberate choice (as also discussed in Chapter 5). Indeed, many of our participants attributed these views to what they held to be the widespread societal norm regarding entering HE, which they considered to be a direct result of the massification of HE over recent decades. Although students from non-traditional backgrounds remain under-represented in most national HE systems (Weedon and Riddell, 2015), students across the six countries – including those from non-traditional backgrounds themselves – spoke about what they held to be a general societal view that it was necessary to pursue a university degree in order to improve one's life chances. The following quotations are illustrative:

'Well, I think that I began studying because that's just what you're expected to do, because everyone else starts studying, eventually someone has a gap year, but he/she is still planning on studying. Nowadays virtually everyone goes to the university and after graduating from high school […].' (Focus group, Polish HEI2_1)

'[I decided to go to college] To be able to get a job, to improve our lives, and as well, I think it's kind of just what everyone does, like you're kind of expected to finish school and then either go join a trade or go to college.' (Focus group, Irish HEI1_1)

Alongside comments about social expectations about entering HE, there was also a high degree of consensus across the focus groups that gaining a university education is 'a lot more accessible' for contemporary students than used to be the case for previous generations. For example: "[B]efore you … like you were very … lucky if you got to university, whereas now it's a lot more accessible, so a lot more people have degrees. … So I think it's, it's almost like a rite of passage to a lot of people" (Focus group, English HEI1_3).

Many students across the six countries (and from a variety of different social backgrounds) suggested that, while in the past HE had been considered a transitional space for only those from privileged backgrounds, more recent developments – such as the increasing number of students from lower income families and minority ethnic groups, and an increasing belief that a degree was necessary to access even quite low-level jobs – had made the idea of university education as a normative transitional phase more widespread in society (see also Chapter 5). In our sample, we found little evidence to suggest that progression to HE was considered 'normal' only by those with family experience of HE – indeed, well over a third of our student participants were first in their family to enter HE (see Appendix). This tends to support Harrison's (2019) argument that the massification of HE and the perceived need for a university degree in order to secure even relatively low-level work has reconfigured the perceived social and financial risks associated with attending HE among lower socio-economic groups. We acknowledge, however, that these are the views of the students who were already enrolled in HE and that there remain many young people from more disadvantaged backgrounds, across Europe, who do not progress to HE (Powell et al, 2012; Haj et al, 2018; Irwin, 2020) and may thus have very different views.

There were, nevertheless, some differences by institution in the extent to which students' entry to university was normalised. For example, many students from the most nationally prestigious universities in our sample, most notably in Ireland (HEI3), discussed how attending such institutions was deemed a 'tradition' in their families. For example:

'I wanted to go to university because my father had gone to university, that's why I think … [HEI3], my dad came here, my brothers and sisters, all my family came here, so it's kind of a bit of a joke like through the years, like oh … you'll have to go to [HEI3], but I actually wanted to come here because I had seen the experiences that they'd had.' (Focus group, Irish HEI3_1)

Moreover, our data indicate that the students with more privileged schooling experiences and family backgrounds may have had more resources to draw upon to transition successfully – to and from – HE (in alignment with studies by Ball et al, 2002a and Bathmaker et al, 2013, for example). Nevertheless, the perception that it is commonly expected by society for young people to gain a university degree – alongside the massification of HE – appears to have led to a general view among students (in our research at least) that their transition within university is a critical phase in their lives. Indeed, for many of our participants, HE was deemed a crucial period for facilitating preparation for future work and life more broadly – although, as we discuss below, these understandings of students in transition varied within and across countries.

Students in transition to the labour market

As noted above, constructing students as in transition was a common theme across our dataset. This was articulated most prominently in terms of preparation for professional work in the future. Research participants discussed how HE provides avenues for students to make a transition from education to gainful employment. This section will discuss how students and other social actors conceptualised students as people entering the labour market, as well as how this conceptualisation varied cross-nationally.

Students' perspectives

Across the focus groups, most students positioned themselves as in transition to future employment, and most of them foregrounded this when discussing their reasons for pursuing HE (as discussed in detail in Chapter 5). They spoke, for example, about university as the place where they would acquire the knowledge and skills for graduate jobs in a variety of fields. For many of our student participants, a university degree was a pathway to secure 'high-skilled' 'office' jobs – and the experiences students had while at university were believed to be essential to achieving this goal. This view is illustrated in the following excerpts from our English and Irish focus groups.

'[T]hey [at university] are trying to prepare us for more like office jobs now, it's like less jobs that are kind of like hands-on, like in labour and things like that. Coming here gives you the experience and like

they set [you] up more for an office job or something similar to that.'
(Focus group, English HEI1_2)

'Well I think it [HE] trains you how to work in a workplace as well, like you know you learn a lot of skills that are obviously helpful, obviously we couldn't just walk into a lab if we didn't go to college.' (Focus group, Irish HEI1_1)

Comments such as these show how students perceive university as a facilitator of their transition from HE into the labour market (Berg et al, 2017; Donald et al, 2018). Implicit in many of the focus group discussions was the idea of transition as 'development', suggesting that students believe they go through 'qualitatively distinct *stages* of maturation' during their HE (Gale and Parker, 2014: 738, italics in original). Here, maturation relates to the formation – and growth – of students' career and professional identities as they progress through their degree programme, and engage in various other activities such as mentoring and field placements.

While this view of constructing students as immersed in a period of planning, preparing and training for future jobs was prevalent in most of our focus groups, there were some notable country-level differences. Students in England, Ireland and Spain were more likely than their peers in the other three countries to understand their transition to the labour market as a matter of personal investment and benefit (also see Donald et al, 2018). This emphasis on individual gain is likely because, in these countries, many students make a significant contribution to the cost of their education through paying tuition fees (see Chapter 1), and therefore it is understandably important for students to realise returns on their investment through securing a graduate job. In contrast, while students in Denmark, Poland and Germany – where students do not pay fees – also viewed themselves as in training for future high-skilled jobs, they were more likely to understand this as a way to contribute to society rather than solely a path to realise their personal goals. This variation by country regarding whether this period of transition was considered a subject of private investment or a public good also emerged in the policy documents and the narratives of the policy actors, which we now discuss.

Views of other social actors

Policy documents from all six countries often constructed students as in transition to the world of work. Many of these documents, for example, were *premised* on the discourse of viewing students as 'workers-in-the-making' – and, therefore, they positioned HE students first and foremost as individuals preparing for the labour market (this stance has been problematised in the literature on student identity formation – see, for example, Daniels and Brooker (2014) – and we will return to this specific construction of students as future workers in Chapter 5). In alignment with this discourse, constructing students as in transition to the workforce emerged strongly in the narratives of many policy actors we interviewed and is exemplified in the following excerpts from interviews with English and Irish policy actors.

> '[W]e see students as a very important contributor to the skills, needs and productivity of the country, so … higher education and the products from higher education, i.e. trained and educated students are sort of a critical part of the UK's skills … supply.' (Representative of English government)

> '[W]e want the cultivated, well-rounded citizen because it just so happens they're the ones that bring the biggest contribution to the workplace.' (Representative of Irish employers' organisation)

While this theme was common across all six nations in our sample, there were specific country-level differences in whether the policy actors discussed its importance in terms of public good or private commodity. These differences mirror the variations in students' stances mentioned previously. In Denmark, Germany, and Poland, policy actors often spoke about students as people who have a responsibility to contribute to societal progress through realising their role as citizens and integral members of the future national workforce. The stress on responsibilising students in this way is likely because, in these nations, students' pay no or low fees. As such, students are understood as beneficiaries of societal investment and thus have particular obligations to the taxpayer. This dynamic is articulated in the following excerpts from interviews with policy actors in Poland, Germany and Denmark:

> 'I think if students, particularly students with their intellectual potential, they should be expected to contribute far more to society than just being a student and just reading books and passing exams and then clutching to an employer.' (Representative of Polish government)

> '[The role of higher education students is] to get a job. But of course it's also to be a good democratic person that can enlighten … it's also to be a part of the workforce and be part of how we're going to have a society afterwards.' (Representative of Danish government)

> '[O]f course we want also all this knowledge these people get and all their competencies they achieve, they should also bring into society,

I mean that's the idea of education, it's not just for them and not just for their … income.' (Representative of German government)

The theme of HE students as preparing to contribute to society more broadly, as a future worker and citizen, was particularly prominent in Denmark – the country that spends a higher proportion of GDP on tertiary education than any other in our sample (see Table 1.5). The role of the state in managing students' transitions through university was evident in interviews with the Danish policy actors and in the Danish media. For example, the Danish newspapers, *Politiken* and *BT*, covered a wide range of topics on this theme, noting for example: government initiatives to shape students' choice of disciplines (in line with projected future earnings), changes to the HE system to make it more closely aligned with labour market demand, and the state's view that students lacked skills at securing jobs.

> The jungle of nearly 1,500 higher education programmes currently offered in Denmark must definitely be cleared up as they do not always provide the best prospects for finding a job … the government is prepared to push universities to educate fewer on those programmes where there are no jobs waiting after the final exam. (*Politiken*, 28 April 2014)

> It is 'very pleasing that the young people have chosen education with good future prospects,' says Ulla Tørnæs, Minister for Higher Education and Science. … 'We have long had a particular focus on education targeted at engineers, teachers and IT at the universities, thus it goes to show that our work to ensure a better match between education and jobs is working,' she says. (*Politiken*, 7 July 2016)

The above excerpts show how, within media discourse, students are commended when they are perceived to be making 'rational choices' about HE – by taking into account their future employability. They reflect not only the ways in which the alignment between the HE sector and the demand for skilled labour is articulated in Denmark, but also the extent to which the state intervenes to ensure a strong link between education and work (see also Wright and Shore, 2017).

Students in the process of personal transformation?

Many social actors across our six countries spoke about students as individuals in transition, not just in relation to the production of workers for the labour market or the training of people for particular professions, but also in terms of the development of the self – a journey of self-discovery, advancement of critical thinking and broadening of horizons. However, again, there was notable geographical variation. While in England, Ireland and Poland, the construction of students in transition was viewed by many of our participants through a predominantly 'developmental' lens – deeming that students are in transition to the life stage of adulthood – it was spoken about primarily as a form of 'becoming' in Denmark, Spain and Germany; that is, as a process of growth and development more broadly, and without mapping this on to any particular life stage (Gale and Parker, 2014).

Students in transition to adulthood: England, Ireland and Poland

Many students and other social actors in England, Ireland and Poland spoke at length about how they believed HE represented a period of transitioning to adulthood. Many students in these countries discussed the HE transition as a process of finding their own identity as individuals (Ecclestone et al, 2009) and growing socially and emotionally as independent adults (Bristow et al, 2020). There were notable similarities, as well as some differences, between the three countries – both of which will be explored here.

Many staff members in these three countries viewed students as people undergoing a deeply personal transformation while at university. They said that students were preparing for their future lives, not merely learning about the subjects they were studying and training for future jobs. Several staff members articulated this preparation in terms of becoming an independent adult and growing as a person. For example, one English staff member characterised the university experience as comprised of 'magical' years, a period of tremendous growth, transformation and transition:

> 'I think it shouldn't … just be about study, no, not at all, it's a really magical … three years in your life, you're an adult, you're learning to be an adult, you're learning about yourself, what you want to do and who you want to be. You're making friends, who might potentially be your friends for the rest of your life. You're learning skills, finding hobbies that will be almost your salve at some times … I don't think university should ever just be about dedicating yourself to study.' (Staff member, English HEI1_1)

This interview excerpt captures the views of many other English staff members that suggested that the experiences one gains while *in transition* during HE impact not only future employment opportunities but also one's life more broadly. Similarly, Irish and Polish staff members also spoke about the importance of HE, beyond curricular learning, for development and transition to adult life.

Such staff views were in close alignment with the perspectives of students themselves. Many of our participants in England, Ireland and Poland viewed themselves as in the process of becoming independent adults. They spoke about their HE experiences as transformational and discussed this in terms of learning to care for themselves (such as 'how to cook') and gaining social and emotional maturity (such as 'how to be sociable' and 'how to survive'). Many of these accounts were used by students to illustrate what they believed were their more 'adult-like' ways of living, being and doing things. In this way, the transition was understood as a combination of various elements of student life. The following focus group excerpts are illustrative.

'I made a frying pan [see Figure 2.1] … It [represents] independence and being on your own, having to look after yourself, whilst carrying out like the things that you need to do for everyday life and stuff like that.' (Focus group, English HEI1_2)

'[F]irst year was for purpose of letting off steam, it was fun to experience this, I was partying but okay now it is time to change your life and it can be like that for all the time. I moved to [name of the city] and it is time to gain some independence. If I spend all 5 years of studies on parties it will be really hard for me to start a regular job, get up at 6 am, go to the office, provide for myself, cook for myself, do laundry, etc. Of course, this change wasn't fast and easy but it was very needed.' (Focus group, Polish HEI1_2)

'I think it's about like becoming more independent, you know like OK, obviously you're not totally independent, because like most of us, our parents are paying for things. But certainly like I've always had jobs throughout college, sometimes more than one at a time! And like it's about kind of learning to manage everything. But then it's also kind of like being able to get a job at the end of it, hopefully.' (Focus group, Irish HEI3_3)

Notably, though, the conceptualisation of students as in transition – associated primarily with independent living and moving out of the parental home – featured most prominently in England. Many of our English student participants made plasticine models of food, kitchen equipment and beds to show that they had been moving from being reliant on their parents or other family members for basic everyday needs to being independent. Many students in the English focus groups commented on what they deemed to be their own and their peers' 'baby-ish' behaviour – such as not knowing how to take a bin out, boil water, or not to put foil in a microwave – as 'normal'. This normalisation was also evident in the depictions of students

Figure 2.1: Frying pan

in the TV series *Fresh Meat*, set in England. Various scenes in *Fresh Meat* illustrate the social, emotional and behavioural changes that students may go through. Many characters leave their parental home (and hometown) to go to university in a new location and start to live together in a shared student house, where they socialise, cook and 'hang out' together. In the early episodes of the series, we see students negotiating house rules and beginning to take responsibility for particular chores. Although studies show that many English students may not actually move out of the parental home for HE (see, for example, Abrahams and Ingram, 2013; Donnelly and Gamsu, 2018; Holton and Finn, 2018), this emphasis on 'moving away' in both the TV series and the focus groups is likely informed by the historically dominant cultural norm of a 'residential model' of university education in England that remains pervasive (Whyte, 2019).

Similar cultural norms do not operate in Ireland and Poland. Moreover, not many Irish and Polish students opt for living independently. In both of these countries, a significant proportion of students (39 per cent in Ireland and 41 per cent in Poland) live with their parents, and only a minority of students move into student accommodation (19 per cent in Ireland and 11 per cent in Poland) (Eurostudent, 2018). Nevertheless, in our study, those Polish and Irish students who had chosen to move out of their parents' home considered this decision as instrumental to their personal growth and crucial for their transition to adulthood.

Overall, this conceptualisation of students as becoming adults in our study resonates strongly with the work by Bristow and colleagues (2020), who show that students are cognisant of the changes to their lifestyle during university and often see them as integral to what they perceive to be part of their HE transition. They contend that students consider learning practical life skills as important opportunities offered by their university education. These narratives in our English, Irish and Polish datasets also reflect Gale and Parker's (2014) categorisation of transition as 'development': maturation and moving from one stage of life to another, defined by 'linear, cumulative, non-reversible movement' (p 738). Transition in this sense involves the personal transformation of students as they mature into adults and form their own social, personal and professional identities.

Contested views: Spain, Denmark and Germany

Within the extant literature, transition in HE is often understood primarily as transition to adulthood – a construction that was also prevalent in England, Poland and Ireland (as shown in the preceding discussion). This way of conceptualising transition was, however, notably absent in the other three countries in our sample. The reasons for this varied across Spain, Denmark and Germany, as we will now explain.

Spain: students as dependent children?

In our Spanish dataset, views of students as in transition related primarily to their perceived dependence on their family and assumptions about the relatively high degree of parental involvement in students' everyday lives (also discussed in Chapter 7). Spanish policy actors often framed students as part of a family unit rather than individuals with rights of their own; similarly, many Spanish newspaper articles in both *El País* and *ABC* alluded to the reliance of HE students on their parents – evident in reports about parents' involvement in degree programme choices, and their provision of financial support (see Lainio and Brooks (2021) for further discussion). In addition, many Spanish staff members reflected on parents' concern about students' academic performance and their tendency to "protect their children". They spoke about how this often had the effect of infantilising students and dissuading them from taking on the responsibility that university students should, in their view, assume as adults. One interviewee, for example, suggested:

'Every year I gave the speech to the new students, many of them came with mum or dad, and I always said, mum and dad remember,

I may not tell you the grades of your son, because they're adults ... the administration will never give you any information about them. Sorry for that but it's how it works. Ah, my kid! My little kid! No, your ... your kid is eighteen years old. ... [I]t's not that they are more infantile and more childish, maybe it's just society as a whole treats them that way, we are more protective, more, more infantilising.' (Staff member, Spanish HEI1_1)

Hence, in the narratives of staff members in Spain, we find a general assumption that students *should* be becoming independent and a belief that HE *should* act as this space of transition, alongside a belief that this may not be the reality for a majority of Spanish students. Assumptions about the dependence of students – and general views about them being child-like – were also linked to staff reflections on students' typical living arrangements. Furthermore, many Spanish students in our study spoke themselves about living with their parents or relatives, with very few renting accommodation of their own. This is broadly in line with trends documented nationally: within Europe, Spain has one of the highest proportions of students living with their parents or relatives, with very few individuals in university halls of residence (Eurostudent, 2005).

Some Spanish participants in our study made explicit contrasts between what they saw as the familial dependence of Spanish students and what they believed were the more independent attitudes of students elsewhere in Europe. For example, some staff compared Spanish students with their counterparts in England and Germany, arguing that many Spanish students lack 'typical' university experiences, such as learning to take responsibility for themselves, living independently, and making decisions autonomously. Moreover, the majority of Spanish students we spoke to suggested that while they were growing as individuals and creating their own personal and professional identities, their lifestyle was not drastically different from how it had been when they were in school. These and other observations presented in this section align with Chevalier's (2016, 2018) contention that social citizenship – with respect to young people in particular – is played out differently across Europe. He suggests that the welfare regime dominant in Spain, alongside cultural and historical factors linked to the influential role of the Catholic Church, has led to the rise of what he calls 'familialised' (rather than 'individualised') citizenship. In this conceptualisation of citizenship, parents, rather than the state, are held legally responsible for financially supporting their children (see also Lainio and Brooks, 2021). These various factors perhaps explain why many Spanish students in our study did not perceive themselves as undergoing a 'transformational change' in the ways described by others – and particularly those from England.

Denmark: students as already grown up?

Many Danish participants in our study viewed Danish students as more mature than their counterparts in other European countries. This is likely to be related to the average age of Danish students and prevalent cultural norms. As shown in Table 1.5, Danish students tend to be older than their peers elsewhere in Europe on entry to HE. Relatedly, our data suggest that views about Danish students as 'already adults' were linked to a perception that the majority of them are more likely to have already achieved some of the traditional markers of adulthood, such as living with a partner in independent accommodation, and being less financially reliant on their parents. Indeed, many Danish students compared their lives with those of their counterparts in other European countries and concluded that they were 'more mature' than many of their European peers.

> '[M]aybe we Danes are like more adult than [students in other European countries] ... because we have to like get an apartment maybe really sooner than other student[s] ... even though we get payment we still have to have work to get it like going on. So yeah, I think we're like really mature and ... But again, I have some co-students who is like really helpless ... it's shocked me because how can you do this study ... if you don't know how to research for yourself and do some proactive things by yourself?' (Focus group, Danish HEI3_3)

Moreover, some Danish staff members and policy actors went further, suggesting that 'being a student' is only one of many identities of HE students in Denmark. This is illustrated in the interview extract below.

> '[I]n Denmark, being a student is [only] part of your identity. So I studied to be a nurse, but I'm also living in my own flat with my girlfriend that does something completely different. We have people over for dinner, I have a job ... You know it's, it's sort of like being a student in Denmark is not ... our identity.' (Representative of Danish employers' organisation)

This view, common across the Danish dataset, can be explained in terms of the wider social, political and cultural norms we discussed above in relation to Spain. Indeed, Chevalier (2016) asserts that Nordic countries follow the logic of 'individualised citizenship' (as opposed to 'familialised citizenship' in the case of Spain), linked to Protestant traditions and values. As a result, young people are typically viewed as independent social citizens, the state provides support to facilitate early independence, and parents tend not to have legal obligations to support their children after compulsory schooling (see Lainio and Brooks (2021) for more details). Furthermore, across the Danish focus groups, students' narratives about transition were often linked to the concept of *Dannelse* – which understands the value of education in a broader sense, beyond inculcation of academic skills and knowledge, and which involves various ethical, cultural and philosophical dimensions of personal growth and enrichment (see Chapter 1). From this perspective, the HE transition is thus conceptualised as part of a lifelong experience, in some ways similar to Gale and Parker's notion of 'becoming', rather than a 'developmental' stage with an end goal of moving into adulthood. We found somewhat similar narratives in Germany, as we discuss below.

Germany: a more expansive understanding of student transition?

Within our German dataset there were also relatively few discussions about students' transitions to adulthood. This may have been because of the particular age profile of our focus group participants and the influence of Humboldtian concepts such as *Bildung* and *Lernfreiheit* (see Chapter 1). While many students in Germany enter university soon after compulsory schooling (see Chapter 1), the age profile of the students in our sample was more diverse (see Appendix). Moreover, some of our participants also reflected on the increasing enrolment of students with substantial professional experience. For example, an employer interviewee noted that "25 per cent of all our students already have a qualification in the vocational training sector" – for many of these students, the interviewee continued, HE offers a route to explore a new career path or enhance their skills and knowledge to excel in their chosen field of work rather than merely facilitate transition to the labour market (for the first time) or adulthood. Students also acknowledged how the nature of transition may differ for particular student groups. For example: "[S]ome people are already adults but some have only just left home and are in the process of turning into independent adults and it's all part and parcel of that, the fact that you have to deal with things yourself and learn as you go along" (Focus group, German HEI2_3). Many German students acknowledged that while, for many younger students, transitioning in HE means progressing towards adulthood (similar to their counterparts in England, Ireland and Poland, as discussed above), for older peers who have already reached this life stage, this will not be the case. Furthermore, irrespective of age, we found that many of our German student participants viewed themselves as undergoing a more profound personal transition than just maturing or growing up, as the following excerpt illustrates:

> '[A]t university you have the opportunity to dip your toe into other things, perhaps to think about things more deeply, things people

wouldn't normally think about and perhaps that's a little bit of what university has to offer, the opportunity to delve into other topics … how a person defines him or herself and what their attitude is to the world.' (Focus group, German HEI3_2)

This perspective is informed by the Humboldtian concept of *Bildung* – a process of self-cultivation (see Chapters 1, 4 and 5). Reflecting on the application of *Bildung* in contemporary society, Biesta (2002) defines this as a 'lifelong challenge and a lifelong opportunity' (p 343). The core principle of this German tradition of education, Biesta argues, transcends the simplistic ideas of education as a process of gaining skills and acquiring knowledge and instead brings to the fore the *nurturing* experience of education that produces an individual subjectivity in terms of 'becoming and being somebody' (Biesta, 2002: 343). Furthermore, linked closely to the Humboldtian concept of *Lernfreiheit* (the freedom to learn), there has been a tradition in Germany of students taking a long time over their studies while combining it with other pursuits, including paid work (Ertl, 2013) (see Chapter 1). As a result, HE has traditionally not been conceived of as a short and self-contained period between school and work but, rather, a longer period that is not so tightly bounded (see Brooks et al (2021a) for further discussion). Thus, broadly, we find that the ways in which transition is made sense of in Germany is, as in Denmark, rarely linked to ideas of 'development' (in terms of reaching a particular life stage) and more closely aligned to Gale and Parker's (2014) understanding of transition as becoming, a lifelong process of self-formation.

Students in transition: entering adulthood or prolonging youth?

A large number of our research participants discussed the construction of students as in transition in relation to students' particular life stage. Notably, such discussions were least prominent in Germany and Denmark for reasons discussed above. Nevertheless, many students in our study felt that they were neither children nor 'fully adults' – and that they were in a distinctive transitional phase 'in-between' the two life stages. Being in this phase has been discussed in the HE literature using the concept of 'liminality' (Gravett, 2019). Indeed, some students in our study characterised this phase as 'a pause' between being a child and an adult. At the same time, the majority of students saw this period as a time of growth, learning and possibilities. The following extracts capture this in-betweenness in students' narratives, as we see participants emphasising the flexibility that being an HE student brings with regards to time management, career and life planning, and (partial) dependency on one's family despite starting to live independently and away from home.

'I think like being a college student, you do have a bit of leeway to like oh but I'm only a student … you're not fully an adult yet, you still have that small bit of excuse to act a small bit more like a child or not knowing where you're going with life or what you're doing.' (Focus group, Irish HEI1_3)

'For me it's also just to enjoy … being young and being flexible with like my time schedule, as opposed to when I grow up and get like a job that requires more time.' (Focus group, Danish HEI1_1)

'It's a good way of launching yourself, quite gradually actually, because it is something, even though it's a big deal leaving home, we're still back like half the year, so it's a bit, it's quite a good like halfway rather than friends of mine who have stayed at home, to then move out is kind of a bigger deal.' (Focus group, English HEI2_1)

Notwithstanding the points made earlier about some research participants being very aware that not all students are of a 'young' chronological age, many of our focus group members saw themselves in a phase in-between a dependent child and independent adult. At the same time though, they usually articulated the idea of transitioning within university spaces as a stage in and of itself. This idea aligns with the concepts of 'youthhood' ('an additional step [after adolescence and] toward adulthood') (Côté, 2000: 4) and 'emerging adulthood' (Arnett, 2004). Côté argues that youthhood as a life stage emerged as an outcome of larger socio-economic shifts – such as the extension of compulsory education, the massification of HE and later labour market entry – that have changed understandings of maturity and identity. The transition to adulthood, therefore, Côté suggests, is often now effectively delayed and, as a result, can be more challenging for many young people. This aspect of transition as delaying adulthood was spoken about by many of the staff members in our study. Again, however, this was articulated differently across countries. For example, Spanish staff members were the most likely to view HE students as 'young' and 'immature'. Many of them felt that while indeed HE offers students an opportunity to 'cross the bridge' between school (where they are 'obligated' to study) and university (where this decision is left to students), in reality, HE appears to be merely an 'extension of childhood' for Spanish students. This may be because of students' living arrangements and wider cultural assumptions in Spain, as discussed in the previous section. In other countries, staff members were more likely to talk about postponing adulthood as synonymous with prolonging youth – as evidenced below.

'It's a phase of many, many questions, where do I head for and did I do the right … did I choose the right subject, etc., etc., a lot of self-questioning, etc. It's basically I think a prolonged phase of youth, which is typical for our society, and that phase which we call crossed adolescence might well last until the mid-thirties for many of them … unless they found their families, yeah, or start to job very soon.' (Staff member, German HEI1_1)

'I think for many of them, it's almost prolonging their adolescence or holding off or suspension of their adulthood by coming here.' (Staff member, Irish HEI1_3)

Views such as these, along with other aspects, such as extensive exploration of one's identity, a focus on oneself, feelings of being in-between, and individualism, which staff members alluded to when discussing HE students, are described by Arnett (2004) as central features of emerging adulthood. HE was often seen by students themselves as an opportunity to try out new things, grow as a person, and shape their identity. Students felt that while at university, they are gradually being prepared to think for themselves by delving deeper into subject knowledge, on the one hand, and exploring who they are and how they will position themselves in the world, on the other. Hence, instead of framing HE as a way to delay the inevitable future, students considered that this 'extended period' of exploration offered them the opportunity to gain a greater understanding of the 'real world'. The following quotations are illustrative:

'I think of it as a fun transition period. It's like being thrown from a plane with a parachute. Fall is not so quick then, you don't come crashing down on the ground, but you are simply gliding through the air for some time. There is time to think things through, organise them.' (Focus group, Polish HEI3_2)

'It [university], it does shape you a lot as a person, you learn an awful lot. It's like a kind of buffer time between entire … independence and being a child! And having independence, yeah, you do a lot of growing in that time. And it's a definite like safe space to be trying out new things and seeing what works and what doesn't.' (Focus group, English HEI3_2)

'And I was thinking that I kind of view myself … like a flower [see Figure 2.2] that blossomed throughout my education. And the reason why I used different colours for the different petals, because I think that … not only have I learned some nursing knowledge, but also I learnt a lot about myself [and] my social skills.' (Focus group, Danish HEI2_1)

Figure 2.2: Flower

This idea of transition as self-discovery in preparation for the next phase of one's life was common – although in some countries this was discussed as a part of students' transition to adulthood more often and more explicitly than in others (as outlined in the previous section). Furthermore, we notice parallel narratives of transition in relation to students' life stage. While for many staff members and some students, the HE period was understood as a way for students to delay growing up, becoming mature, and entering adulthood, many of the students, in contrast, identified being 'in transition' as a stage in itself, associated with a variety of positive experiences, not merely a phase between childhood and adulthood.

Students in transition as a marginalising construction?

So far, we have looked at the various ways in which HE students are constructed as in transition. This section explores how the assumptions often underlying this construction – that students are 'young people' and not yet fully formed adults – may marginalise students' voices. Although, of course, there is no one single way in which students can be defined and understood – and, indeed, many students in our study offered a nuanced understanding of how experiences of being a student can be differentiated by social factors such as class, gender and age (see Brooks et al (2020a) for further discussion), this section focuses on how many narratives regarding the construction of students as 'in transition' may, in fact, have negative implications for students. We show how these narratives often tended to construct a deficit discourse around youthhood.

Students across the focus groups mentioned how they are often seen by others as not 'fully adult' – this was evident in countries where the majority of students are relatively young (such as England) as well as in nations where, on average, students tend to be slightly older (for example, Denmark), albeit articulated rather differently. In England, students said that society, in general, perceives them as 'naive', 'sheltered', 'mollycoddled', and as 'avoiding dealing with life', whereas we found that many Danish students mentioned that (despite the previous discussion) staff members usually saw them as a 'step behind being adult'. The following quotations from an English and a Danish focus group reflect this.

'I think there's an image of the student as kind of avoiding the real world ... I think like some people do see us as quite naive because it's like, well they haven't had a job, they're avoiding going into the world of work, you know, they're in like a safe institute with a big pastoral like network that's looking after them and ... I think it's easy to see us as kind of, kind of like mollycoddled, like you know, like wrapped up in cotton wool, like we're kind of being protected from what we eventually will have to deal with.' (Focus group, English HEI2_1)

'I think they, at least what I've experienced, is that they [HEI staff] sort of see us as unfinished projects, their projects, which are exciting, you want to work on ... And also that we're just the step behind being responsible, the step behind being adults. I've heard several ... of the staff telling us, you are adults and *you don't say to an adult, you are an adult!* ... that they sort of remind us what we are, that ... but we aren't quite there yet.' (Focus group, Danish HEI3_3)

Focus group participants felt that considering them as merely in transition also meant that while they are valued for what they would become and how they would contribute to the labour market and society in the future, their current role and contribution to society as students is significantly undervalued. As a result, they believed their opinions and views as members of society were frequently overlooked (see also Chapter 3). Many Spanish students mentioned that they are often labelled as a 'poor little thing', and their political stances 'ridiculed' by the media (discussed in Chapter 7). Similarly, English students claimed that everyday infantilising practices often undermined their voices and authority as political actors.

'I think they see you as a child because you have to study, they don't think of any other possibilities so it's like, "He's a poor lad who's growing up and doesn't yet know anything about life", when in reality you know many other things because the university give you the tools to enrich yourself, which you won't find anywhere else and you probably consider yourself as someone who is growing strongly at a personal level.' (Focus group, Spanish HEI1_2)

'I feel like when people protest, like we want like fees to be lowered or whatever, we're, like in the media we're talked about like it's students that are doing this, it's not like adults, we're not classed as that. And we're supposed to be like the next generation that's going to you know have a say in politics and stuff, but I don't think at all that's what we're recognised as.' (Focus group, English HEI1_2)

Students' views also contrasted with those of other social actors who often perceived them as only 'people with a promising future', a key means of securing the economic and social prosperity of the nation-state (see Chapter 5 on the theme of students as future workers), rather than significant political stakeholders in the present as well. These tensions, associated with defining students in transition as being in a liminal position – and valuing them primarily in terms of what they would become after graduation – fail to acknowledge what 'being' a student in the here and now might mean. Indeed, Lesko (2012) has argued that young people have been defined as 'always "becoming", waiting for the future to arrive' (p 131). (Here, the use of the word 'becoming' is not the same as Gale and Parker's definition of this term, which recognises transition as becoming and occurring throughout one's life.) This definition has provoked, she maintains, 'endless watching, monitoring and evaluating' (p 111) on the part of adults, and passivity on the part of young people as they are told that only the future matters, and that it is the end of the adolescent story that is key. It is important to note that, as mentioned in the previous section, some students themselves reinforced this deficit view (of students as 'not yet adults') in their own narratives. Such ways of viewing students may take away the legitimacy of students' voices and, in doing so, undermine the formative processes involved in this transitional phase in students' lives, which we have discussed above.

Conclusion

This chapter began by showing how it has become normal to see students as 'in transition' across our six countries. We then discussed three main themes in relation to this construction of HE students – transition to the labour market, personal transformation, and the understanding of students as entering adulthood or prolonging youth. This discussion has illustrated some important differences in how students are viewed. While students are commonly seen as people transitioning to the world of work, we demonstrated that, in countries where students pay high fees, they were more likely to view this transition in terms of the desired return on their personal investment. In contrast, in nations where no fees were payable, students typically saw their transition to the workforce as a more collective endeavour, and a way to contribute to wider society. Moreover, we have shown that transition within HE is not just about the readiness to secure future jobs; it is valued highly for the personal transformation students undergo in this period. This also, however, is played out differently by nation-state – with variation according to social, cultural and historical factors as well as prevalent citizenship regimes. Finally, we have discussed how the 'transitional' status of students can be seen in more negative ways – including as 'not yet adults'. Such an understanding of transition often marginalises students' voices, fails to appreciate their current societal contributions, and potentially delegitimises their political activity.

3

Citizens

Introduction

Over the past few decades, there has been increasing interest on the part of many policymakers around the world in measures to inculcate 'citizen behaviours' among school pupils and HE students. Such initiatives have often been developed in response to: the demise of the welfare state in many developed nations and an associated emphasis on the importance of citizens taking care of their own wellbeing; an increase in the diversity of many countries and an attendant perceived need to strengthen social cohesion; a concern about young people's political knowledge and skills; and unease at the rise of individualism (Brooks and Holford, 2009). Within Europe, these have been played out at the regional level, through the actions of the European Commission and the Council of Europe, as well at the level of nation-states (Hoskins, 2006; Keating, 2014). In this chapter, we show that many of the participants in our research engaged with ideas related to citizenship in some capacity, although there was not always consensus between social actors in the extent to which students should be seen as citizens or the nature of this citizenship.

The chapter begins by briefly outlining some of the ways in which the 'student as citizen' has been understood in the extant literature. We then go on to examine the perspectives of students themselves, arguing that they often positioned themselves clearly as citizens – with a responsibility to think and act critically. While acting as a citizen was not necessarily viewed as synonymous with being politically engaged, many students did also consider themselves to be – potentially at least – significant political actors, but believed that their capacity to effect change in this way was often constrained by others. We then compare these student perspectives with the views of other actors, contending that while a certain degree of ambivalence is evident in media portrayals of students, staff and policy actors were much more likely to reject the construction of students as active and engaged citizens.

Conceptualising the student as citizen

There is now a large literature on education and citizenship. Much of it is informed, to some extent at least, by debates about *active* citizenship. The shift to talking about students as active citizens can be seen as part of a broader movement, evident within both scholarship and policy development, away from legalistic and narrow definitions of citizenship (focusing primarily on rights and legal status) towards broader conceptualisations that emphasise the importance of active involvement within a civic community and, equally, of being recognised as a full member of that community (Evans, 1995; Harris et al, 2021). Thus, for some scholars and policymakers, active citizenship is a progressive concept, which signals a turn away from understanding citizens solely as passive rights-bearers. It has also informed various policy initiatives, not least European-level programmes to develop 'active citizenship' within HE, and enhance the 'civic competence' of students (Hoskins, 2006).

The focus on active citizenship has not, however, been uncontentious. Taken at face value, there may seem substantial merit in encouraging citizen-like behaviours on the part of students across the world. However, such policy measures and educational initiatives have frequently been critiqued – for obscuring the importance of individual rights through an over-emphasis on responsibilities, and tending to privilege non-contentious forms of 'active citizenship', such as volunteering, over more overtly political forms, such as protesting and taking direct action (Ahier et al, 2003; Coffey, 2004; Cunningham and Lavalette, 2004). Scholars who have charted the rise of more 'activated' forms of citizenship across social policy in general have argued that while they have often drawn on social democratic and communitarian conceptions of the citizen, they have tended to be dominated by the neo-liberal concern to 'liberate' the individual from the state (Clarke, 2005). Similarly, university programmes aimed at inculcating a global active citizenship often have a strong neo-liberal orientation, linked closely to promoting an institutional brand in a competitive HE marketplace and/or enhancing the production of 'globally competent workers' (Hammond and Keating, 2018: 927). Such programmes are also more likely to be taken up by those from more privileged backgrounds.

Writing with respect to European HE specifically, Biesta (2009) has argued that its emphasis on promoting active citizenship is problematic because it is functionalist (that is, it approaches citizenship from the putative 'needs' of the socio-political order); it assumes that individual action (rather than collective action, or action on the part of the state) is the main solution for collective problems; and it tends to see democracy in consensual terms – active citizens are those who subscribe to the existing political order and actively work to ensure its reproduction. On the basis of this analysis, Biesta argues that the EU has tended to promote a 'socialisation' model of civic learning, which aims at 'inserting' individuals into a pre-existing socio-political order. He advocates instead what he calls a 'subjectification' model, whereby greater recognition is given to collective and political concerns, and alternative conceptions of democracy, liberty and equality are explicitly recognised. This critique of citizenship learning informs our discussion below.

In the rest of the chapter, we make reference to these debates, and explore some of the various ways in which our participants talked about students as citizens – providing a more nuanced picture than is sometimes evident in the extant literature. Given some of the ambiguity and contestation associated with the term 'active citizen', we refer primarily to the broader term of 'citizen'.

Responsible citizens: the perspectives of students

Strong self-identification

A common theme within much of the literature that has charted the increasing marketisation of national HE systems is the passivity of students. Scholars have argued, for example, that as students have increasingly had to make significant financial contributions to their own HE, their interest in wider social issues has declined (for example, Morley, 2003; Pusey and Sealey-Huggins, 2013; Della Porta et al, 2020). Indeed, writing with respect to the UK, Williams (2013: 110) has contended that:

> Today's active campaigning students, who are heralded as agents of change within their institutions, are quick to learn the bureaucratic language of agenda items, assessment patterns, learning outcomes and programme monitoring, and are more likely to be found sitting on Staff-Student Liaison Committees than on picket lines. This domestication of the student voice and limiting of campaigning confirms the consumer identity of students rather than challenging it.

Such arguments have been rehearsed outside Europe, too. Shin et al (2014) have argued, for example, that in South Korea, student activism has narrowed in its focus – to be primarily concerned with education-related issues – after the introduction of tuition fees. Moreover, Nissen (2019) has shown how, in New Zealand, increasing levels of HE-related debt have had considerable impact on students' political activity. She outlines how the students in her research, who had taken on debts to fund their studies, felt shame at their financial position, which discouraged them from being open about their situation and concerns. This, in turn, made collective action harder. Moreover, their need to earn money during their degree programme reduced the time they had available for other activities, including political participation. And, for those who did find time for such activities, their overriding concern to do nothing to jeopardise their employment prospects on graduation led them to pursue cautious and non-controversial forms of politics, measured by what they believed actors external to the university (such as employers) would consider acceptable. Focusing more on pedagogical change, Grant (2017) has contended that market-informed pedagogies introduced across the Global North in the past few decades – including the disaggregation of learning into semesters and modules, and the introduction of regular student evaluations of teaching – have shifted students' concerns. In her analysis, a commitment to the communal good has come to be replaced with 'a sense of personal entitlement' (p 139).

Nevertheless, the students in our research – across all six nations – presented a rather different picture. On the whole, they tended to view themselves as active and engaged citizens, who were making an important contribution to their societies at present, and/or were developing the skills, knowledge and dispositions to enable them to make such a contribution in the future. Such identities were clearly important to them and, in some cases, fundamental to their understanding of what it meant to be a student. In Denmark, for example, focus group participants often made explicit reference to their status as citizens when asked a general question about how students in their country should be understood. The following two excerpts, both from focus groups at Danish HEI3, illustrate this point well:

Interviewer:	How should students be understood?
Focus group participant:	As citizens, as we are the new generation, we are going to be the, the leaders; whatever we're going to do, we're going to lead the future in some way.
Focus group participant:	What we learn today is actually going to form the future that we're going to have. (Focus group, Danish HEI3_2)

'What an education does is also to educate you kind of to be a citizen in society, and in the society that you grow up in or that you live in. So I think it's, it doesn't only educate you to become a worker or to do some kind of job, but it also educates you in, yeah, societ[al] aspects, in how to be a citizen, how to be, for example democratic ... and what it means.' (Focus group, Danish HEI3_3)

Explicit reference to students as citizens was also made in Spain, with one focus group participant commenting that, alongside knowledge acquisition, the role of the university is "to develop you as a citizen" (Focus group, Spanish HEI3_ 2). In other cases, students did not make explicit reference to being a citizen, but drew on ideas commonly associated with this term, through emphasising their own agency (rather than the passivity often alluded to in the literature mentioned above) and ability to effect societal change. An English participant, for example, described how she believed HE played an important role in fostering beliefs, first, that change is possible and, second, that individuals need to play their role in bringing such change about. She explained:

'[I say to myself] well if I do it and no one else does it, nothing's going to happen, but if we all think that way, then obviously nothing's going to happen, so [university helps] develop this mindset that you, you are yourself and you have an opinion and you have a choice and you have the chance to effect, effect change. ... if this mindset is developed in university ... then it's more likely change or anything will be brought about, rather than you know if we all passively sit and wait for things to happen.' (Focus group, English HEI3_3)

Democratic participation was also discussed by some students in terms of their understanding of what it meant to be a student:

'[T]he idea of making, of not just creating workers and bringing students in and teaching them about whatever subject they're studying and then send them out into the workplace, but making people politically aware that when they're living in their house and it comes to the general elections, so you know like how to vote, what [your elected representatives] are going to kind of give to you.' (Focus group, Irish HEI1_3)

In this quotation, the participant acknowledges the construction of students as learners and future workers (see Chapters 4 and 5, respectively), but suggests that – alongside this – they are also citizens who are increasing their political knowledge and ability to participate in democratic society.

The responsibility to be critical?

As we noted above, a key debate within the literature on citizenship, as it has been played out in education, and also with respect to youth generally, is whether young people's responsibilities have tended to be emphasised at the expense of their rights. Numerous scholars have argued that educational programmes, in schools as well as universities, have typically focused on responsibilities – and 'active citizenship' proffered as a means of ameliorating what are deemed to be students' 'deficient' citizenship values and practices (for example, Landrum, 2002; Ahier et al, 2003; Pole et al, 2005). This sits in tension, however, with moves within HE policy to encourage students to be more aware of their rights and entitlements (in England couched in terms of their 'consumer rights') as a means of improving the quality of teaching and learning (Naidoo et al, 2011; Bunce et al, 2017; Nyland and Tran, 2020). Within our data, there was, however, relatively little discussion by students of their rights. Indeed, when citizenship was discussed explicitly, or referred to implicitly, it was articulated much more commonly in terms of participants' responsibilities – to their local communities, nation-states and, in some cases, the world in general (see discussion below). To some extent, this emphasis on responsibilities, rather than rights, can be seen as largely in line with what Biesta (2009) has termed the 'socialisation' model of civic learning. In the extracts below, for example, we see students emphasising the importance of volunteering, supporting social norms and contributing to society as it exists around them.

> '[Students] should be viewed as someone who want to learn and want to … find the best way possible for us to contribute.' (Focus group, Danish HEI1_3)

> 'I think there's an expectation from your parents and those around you to be a contributing member of society. And I think that university is kind of where they want you to start, if that makes sense. I think you're kind of, it's not so much about what you can get from it but what you can then give to others.' (Focus group, Irish HEI2_2)

Such sentiments were also echoed by the focus group participant who made a model of a book and a quill (see Figure 3.1), explaining that it

Figure 3.1: Book and quill

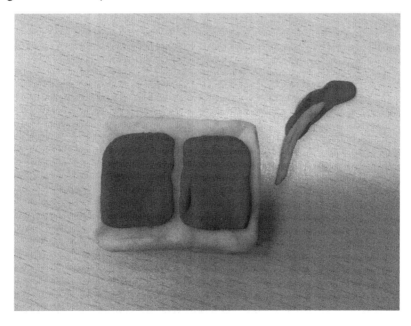

represented her belief that 'everything that I am learning is something that I'll be able to give back to other people and help them progress' (Focus group, Irish HEI2_2).

For some participants, while they talked about the importance of making a social contribution, this was seen as inextricably linked to the job they hoped to take up on graduation. Such accounts were relatively common in England and Ireland, although not in the other four countries.

'I think we are preparing ourselves to contribute to the society. [Agreement from other members of focus group.] Like it's just how we've chosen to go about it, like because one of the reasons why we do come to university is so that we can have a better future, so that we, well my job, well I feel like I will be definitely contributing to society because I'll be teaching the young generation, so … but I can't contribute, I can't make that contribution without coming to university and getting a degree and being trained in doing so.' (Focus group, English HEI3_3)

'So yeah, I think we are preparing ourselves to be workers, you know, we are being scrutinised by employers, hence why we're being scrutinised by employers and politicians and whatever, because we are being conditioned to become a worker, to gain our role in society and be an active citizen and all that.' (Focus group, English HEI3_3)

In these narratives, citizenship appears to be elided with labour market participation, and the citizen reconfigured, to some extent at least, as a worker-citizen (Isopahkala-Bouret et al, 2014). (See Chapter 5 for a more extended discussion of students as future workers.)

Nevertheless, it would be wrong to assume that the foregrounding of responsibilities was always associated with this 'socialisation' perspective. Indeed, it was striking that across many of the focus groups and various different nation-states, participants emphasised the responsibility they felt – as students, who were benefiting from a higher education – to be critical and to play an active role in changing society, rather than just accepting the state of affairs they saw around them.

'[The] university [experience] must be to produce citizens having a critical faculty, with critical thought.' (Focus group, Spanish HEI3_2)

'We also learn to be critical, we learn to be critical of the state, we learn to be critical of society in general. '(Focus group, Danish HEI3_2)

'[Students should be seen as] young people that are trying to learn something, like learn a lot and get a lot of knowledge, so they can come out there at the other side and maybe make the society even better than it is right now.' (Interview, Danish HEI2)

'[We are not here] like to see, like not just engage in society but kind of here to improve it and where we're going ... [To] think outside the box as well.' (Focus group, Irish HEI1_1)

In some cases, participants contrasted this view of students – as critical and activist citizens – with the construction of them as future workers, which they felt often dominated debates within their nation (see Chapter 5). This is articulated in the extract below – along with an explanation of how the participant thought the experience of HE encouraged students to develop more critical perspectives on the world around them:

'Yeah, and I think it's not just become a worker, but like be an activist and like an active citizen and just having our own voice because we kind of develop our own mindset here [agreement from others in focus group], as opposed to like people that are not at university. We have all these experiences, different cultures all thrown at us, and then we come out like with our own mindset and things, and we have a, like a voice and are kind of leaders in our own right, which makes us different to those that maybe didn't go to university, not all but ... yeah, some.' (Focus group, English HEI3_3)

In comments such as these, the students appeared to affirm the contentions of those who have argued that HE campuses can act as important spaces for social mixing (Altbach, 1997; Bennett et al, 2017), akin to what Massey (2005) has referred to as the 'thrown-togetherness' of public space.

Taken together, the data presented above suggest that while the students tended to focus primarily on their responsibilities rather than their rights, these responsibilities were often – although not always – framed in a critical manner. Although, as we discussed previously, various scholars have argued that a conception of citizenship that places primary importance on individuals' responsibilities rather than their rights is commonly associated with a conservative political stance, and frequently invoked by governments as a means of rolling back the welfare state (Coffey, 2004; Pickard, 2019), our data demonstrate that students often understand their responsibilities differently, constructing active citizens as those who subject social norms and current practices to critical scrutiny, with the aim of effecting change. In such cases, students appear to understand the role of HE and their place within it as much closer to Biesta's (2009) progressive 'subjectification' model of civic learning, than its conservative 'socialisation' alternative.

National citizens?

In the data derived from our focus groups, particular spatialities are evident. In most cases, it appeared that when participants were referring to the particular communities or societies to which they hoped to 'give back' or 'change for the better', they had in mind either their nation-state or a more local community. The former was evident, for example, when they spoke about the important part HE played in furthering their knowledge of democracy and the role played by their elected officials. The latter was often implicit and sometimes explicit in narratives about engaging in voluntary activity near where they lived. There were, however, a small minority of cases where focus group participants made reference to larger-scale communities, which crossed national borders. In the following examples, students talk about making change that helps the world, and the importance of paying attention to the inter-dependencies between nation-states:

'[I want] to be enlightened about ideas that can move the world to a better place, and not just a job. It's something deeper.' (Focus group, Danish HEI3_1)

'And I don't think we have a perfect society, far from it, [and] there are lots of problems in the world that are not [related to] the labour market. And I think that's more important [that education prepares us to solve these other problems, not just for entering the labour market]. … An earthquake in … in Thailand doesn't, maybe doesn't really affect our labour market here in Denmark or in some part of Copenhagen, but it's still important to the world.' (Focus group, Danish HEI3_1)

'Well, I chose my degree because I feel like I could really, like it's in my interest and I want to help people with what I'm studying, so […] I wanted to go on and do nutrition after my course and I want to help the world, you know, the whole [world] make a change!' (Focus group, Irish HEI2_3)

Interestingly, and linking back to the earlier discussion about 'worker-citizens', the first two extracts above contrast an interest in or commitment to global change with what the participants saw as the narrower perspective associated with viewing students only as future workers. The third extract, however, positions the two as more interlinked: it is through securing a particular job that change can be effected. In general, however, despite the emphasis on promoting 'global citizenship' in many HE institutions across the world (Hammond and Keating, 2018) and a recognition that younger generations are more likely to be interested in global social and political issues (Devinney et al, 2012; Sloam and Henn, 2019), relatively few participants had such geographically expansive horizons, irrespective of how they understood the relationship between citizenship and paid work.

Merely future citizens?

Notable in much of the data presented above is an emphasis on the future. As has been evident from the preceding discussion, when our participants talked about themselves as active citizens, this was often in relation to developing the knowledge, skills and critical capacities to prepare them for life after graduation. Some, however, argued that this future orientation, particularly when deployed by policymakers and other social actors, obscured the important ways in which they were engaging as active citizens in the present (see also discussion in Chapter 2). Participants from Danish HEI2, for example, drew attention to the action they were taking *now*, maintaining that, if this was recognised more fully, students may be understood differently:

'[Students should be seen as] an asset, like ... right now there's all this ... refugee problems and there's one place [name] that they are trying to make like these places to live, where students can live cheaply and then they can live with the refugees and they can like help refugees integrate more in the society and stuff like that. And I think stuff like that is ... like ... well a different way of seeing students.' (Interview, Danish HEI2)

Indeed, a commonly articulated theme was that students were often not treated as full citizens, with views of equal worth to other adults. The following excerpts from Ireland and Poland are illustrative:

'I think I'd like to see students taken more seriously above all [...] because I feel like a lot of people either dismiss students' views or opinions or things like that [...] I don't think anyone's views should be ... or opinions should be discounted because they're just students, it would be nice to I think see, yeah, to be viewing students as members of society, already participating.' (Focus group, Irish HEI3_3)

'I would say that the society, in general, has this feeling that young people don't know anything and they shouldn't speak their minds. Even if some protests occur or some marches and a young person speak his mind, then on the internet or in another place they show different speech of someone who is saying "Oh, he is young, he doesn't know anything, why he is speaking at all. If he lives for as long as I have lived …".' (Focus group, Polish HEI2_2)

Here, we can see strong echoes of previous research on citizenship and education that has emphasised the ways in which students and pupils are often addressed as 'proto-citizens' or 'citizens-in-the-making' rather than individuals (or indeed groups) able to make substantial contributions to their society in the present (Pickard, 2019). This is often reinforced by social policies that have tended to reduce the welfare rights available to young people (because they are not viewed as fully formed adults) and so increase their dependence on their families (Furlong and Cartmel, 2007).

Political participation

A further way in which students articulated ideas associated with citizenship was in relation to political participation. As we explained in Chapter 1, we asked our participants specifically about whether they considered students to be significant political actors, and this was also a theme that came up spontaneously in other parts of the focus groups. Some talked about the political activity they were currently engaged in – relating to both formal and informal modes of engagement. As an example of the latter, a focus group participant at Irish HEI2_3 made a model of a fist (see Figure 3.2) to represent her political activism.

The vast majority of the students we spoke to believed that they had the potential, at least, to be significant political actors – a view that was echoed, to some extent, in the staff interviews. Students from all six countries described themselves as the political future of their country. In part, this was linked to the particular knowledge and skills they had gained through their degree programmes, as the quotations below illustrate.

'[S]tudents have an influence on politics because they represent a large number of young people who bring new ideas into the world but who are old enough to stand up for these ideas and to consider them logically and to bring forward logical arguments.' (Focus group, German HEI3_2)

'[W]e're informed … like the older people would just have a view from when they were younger and what they were told, but they didn't know all the facts, whereas we would be more knowledgeable.' (Focus group, Irish HEI1_1)

Moreover, some focus group participants typically saw the space of the university as an important site, in itself, for political activity, while others

Figure 3.2: Fist

emphasised the unique opportunity HE presented, in terms of both time and space, for such engagement.

> 'I think university students, as well as being adults and therefore having a little wider conception of things than students in secondary education … as a student you … have a little more time and you can organise [more easily] because of your proximity [to your fellow students].' (Focus group, Spanish HEI1_2)

Nevertheless, across most of the focus groups, our participants also spoke of the factors that limited their political activity or prevented them from being as engaged as they wished to be. They described feeling ignored and infantilised by politicians and others with power. In Spain, however, although it was more common for students to believe they were taken seriously as a political force by politicians, they also asserted that the state sometimes took steps to limit their political impact. They commented:

> 'It's in the psyche of society that students are seen as a bomb that can explode at any time, but if they [the students] are skilfully manoeuvred and modified they can become another tool for the system and fall into the hands of the politicians so that the country can function.' (Focus group, Spanish HEI1_1)

Thus, despite the importance they placed on acting as critical and active citizens (discussed above), participants in all countries believed that specific constraints tempered their ability to exert political influence as students. Here, there is significant continuity with previous research (albeit in youth studies rather than education) conducted over the past few decades that has suggested that young people in general are acutely aware of the limitations of the political systems around them. Indeed, Pilkington and Pollack (2015) have argued, with respect to the young people in their cross-national European research, that a paradox exists whereby youth 'are not so much "anti" politics but profoundly disillusioned with the current democratic system while continuing to be, in principle, supportive of democratic reforms of government and seeking to "be heard" through it' (p 8).

Variation between and within nation-states

In many ways, the students we spoke to across Europe held quite similar views to one another: they frequently drew on the construction of the citizen in explaining how they understood the role and identity of HE students and, while they typically associated this with the carrying out of responsibilities, these were often framed in terms of criticality and bringing about substantial change, rather than the affirmation of societal norms. While a minority discussed this citizenship in terms of global society, most appeared to relate it to their nation-state or local community and, despite critiquing politicians for viewing them as merely citizens-in-the-making, often held a strong future orientation themselves (here, there are links to the understanding of students as in transition, discussed in the previous chapter). Students also commonly saw themselves as political actors, with the potential to make a significant contribution to their communities through various types of political engagement, including both formal and informal means.

Nevertheless, despite these commonalities across the sample, there were also differences between nations and within them. It was notable that, as mentioned above, it was only in England and Ireland that participants made implicit reference to the figure of the 'worker-citizen'. Moreover, it was striking that Danish students tended to place more emphasis on their contributions to wider society and the importance of collective action than their counterparts in the other nations. These differences map on the different welfare regimes evident in the six nations (see Chapter 1), with neo-liberal norms more entrenched in Anglophone nations than elsewhere and social democratic influences remaining relatively strong in Denmark (despite the introduction of some market-based HE reforms). Such differences have been observed in other studies, too. Indeed, Della Porta et al (2020) have contrasted student political activity in England which, they argue is influenced by the construction of students as consumers, with that evident in continental Europe, which has more in common with wider social movements. It is also possible that the funding of HE in Denmark – with the state covering both fees and living costs (see Chapter 1) – encourages students to conceive of HE as a public good and emphasise their future societal contribution.

With respect to political engagement, specifically, differences were also evident. For example, while Danish students typically considered involvement in politics to be an important element of what it means to be a student, this view was not shared in all nations, and was particularly rare in Poland. Such variations relate not just to the welfare regimes discussed above but also to the particular histories of student politics in the various nations. In Denmark, for example, students' unions have a strong and long-standing tradition of influence, with access to significant material resources, and formal and informal links to government actors (Klemenčič, 2014; Della Porta et al, 2020). In contrast, Polish unions have, since the 1990s, become increasingly corporatist in nature, moving from being seen as a social movement-type organisation to a professional association (Antonowicz et al, 2014). As a consequence, the Student Parliament (the national body representing students) has been criticised for not defending well students' interests, and has also found it hard to mobilise students in general (Antonowicz et al, 2014).

Some within-nation differences were also played out in our data. For example, with respect to political engagement specifically, although not broader discussions of citizenship, students at some of the more prestigious institutions in the sample (particularly in England and Germany) tended to be more optimistic about their future political influence than students at the less prestigious institutions – possibly linked to the social characteristics of the students who attend such institutions, and differences in institutional habitus. As Della Porta et al (2020) have argued, elite universities often convey different messages about the importance of citizenship-related activities than less prestigious institutions which, by virtue of their different market position, have to be more commercially oriented. Moreover, because of structural inequalities in access to both HE and the labour market, graduates from elite institutions are more likely to take up positions of political influence after graduation. In Spain, political activity appeared to be higher at the two public universities in our sample than the private institution. As the majority of the activity the students talked about was related to protests against higher fees, it is likely that those attending a private institution would be less concerned about this, as they have already made a positive choice to attend an institution charging higher fees, than their peers within the public sector (see Brooks et al (2020b) for a fuller discussion). Finally, some differences were also observed at the disciplinary level, with students studying social sciences often apparently more politically engaged and interested than those from other disciplines. Differences in political interest and engagement by discipline may, of course, be because students who are already more interested in politics and political issues tend to choose to study such subjects. However, there is also some evidence that social science subjects can inculcate greater political interest, awareness and engagement – not necessarily by making more time available to explore political issues, but by bringing about more profound changes in how students think about the world and their own place within it (for example, Abbas et al, 2016; Muddiman, 2020).

Contestation within media

When we turn to other social actors, we see a rather different view of students emerge. With respect to the media – TV series and films as well as newspaper articles – students were often discussed as citizens, either implicitly or explicitly, but there was considerable ambivalence about both the nature of this citizenship and its impact.

In four of the seven TV series and films we analysed (see Chapter 1 for details of the sample), students' political activity was referenced quite frequently – including student protests, elections for students' unions, and debates and discussion about political matters between key characters. These suggest that the trope of 'student as political actor' is reasonably strong across various European nations. Students' political activity was also referenced, at least to some extent, in the newspapers in our sample. Here, however, there were quite significant differences by country. In both Spanish newspapers, for example, over a third of the articles referred in some way to students as political actors, whereas under ten per cent of the articles in the German newspapers discussed students in this way. This articulates, to some extent, with previous research that has shown that in southern Europe (and also France) protest actions by young people are more likely to be covered by newspapers than elsewhere in the continent (Loukakis and Portos, 2020). Moreover, in Spain students had assumed an important political role in the years preceding our period of data collection, by initiating anti-austerity protests and helping to mobilise other social actors to this cause (Zamponi and González, 2017). Such protests were more significant in Spain than in the other countries in the sample because the impact of the crisis was worse, and this legacy may have informed ongoing newspaper perspectives.

In some cases, media representations of students as political actors and/ or citizens more broadly were positive. For example, in the Spanish TV series, *Merlí: Sapere Aude* (referred to as '*Merlí*' hereafter), students' political activity is depicted as stemming from their genuine care for the society in which they live. Some of the main characters participate in various sustained discussions about political issues, including the impact of colonialism in contemporary society. They also take part in student protests and strike action (by not attending class). Moreover, in the newspaper articles, students' political activity and other forms of social action are often framed in a positive manner, and as a justified response to inequalities in society. This is discussed, for example, in the Polish paper *Gazeta Wyborcza* with respect to student action in response to the sexual harassment experienced by female students; in the Spanish papers *El País* and *ABC*, in relation to student protests against the inequities brought about by the changes to the structure of degrees; and in *The Irish Times* with respect to students' concerns about environmental degradation.

Such perspectives were not, however, shared in a consistent manner across the media. Indeed, there is also a clear critique of student political activity that pervades some of the TV series and newspaper articles (see also Chapter 7). Apathy and/or general disinterest in wider societal issues is mentioned in a small minority of articles, echoing some widely documented policy discourses on this theme (Marsh et al, 2007). This is evident in the German newspaper, *Süddeutsche Zeitung*, for example, where several articles focus on alleged apathy, with headlines such as, 'Only one in three students has a keen interest in politics' (29 October 2014). The paper's editorial on the same day notes, disapprovingly, that '[t]he politically active and belligerent have shrunk to a splinter group' in universities across the country. More common, however, is criticism of the *nature* of students' political engagement. The English TV series, *Fresh Meat*, for example, devotes a considerable amount of time to covering students' politically related activities, including protests at what are perceived to be the damaging environmental policies of the oil company BP, and students' union elections. Nevertheless, such activities are presented as often being immature, driven by self-interest and largely ineffective. For example, during the elections for the students' union president, one of the main characters stands as a candidate for the 'Cheap Chips' party and, despite her absurd policy ideas, receives many more votes than candidates with more serious manifestos. Another candidate stands primarily to please his father and has no interest in students' concerns or political issues more broadly. Moreover, while student politics is a central theme of the second series of the UK thriller *Clique*, it is again depicted in somewhat negative terms – with two groups of students presented as pursuing oppositional and antagonistic political agendas, leaving no space for dialogue or resolution of the issues that are important to them. Similarly, within the newspaper articles, students' political activity is sometimes criticised for being violent. This is evident in a number of articles in the Spanish newspaper *ABC*, for example, with headlines such as, 'They entered with their faces covered and one of them attacked a security guard with a bat; Incidents in Zaragoza and Valencia during a student strike which had little support' (9 May 2014). Another relatively common criticism is that students' political activity – particularly that related to 'no-platforming'[1] and the insistence on 'trigger warnings'[2] – is serving to limit freedom of speech on campus, evidenced by headlines such as the following:

'Professor says free speech is stifled'. (*Daily Mail*, 30 November 2015)

'The mollycoddled students who fuel campus zealotry'. (*Daily Mail*, 20 February 2016)

'Life can be rough. Our students must learn that'. (*Irish Independent*, 5 April 2016)

'The boycott of the debate at the Autónoma [Autonomous University of Madrid] has been widely condemned'. (*El País*, 21 October 2016)

This particular problematisation of student political activity is a prominent theme in England, Ireland and Spain, which we discuss further in Chapter 7.

Students are framed as citizens not only in relation to their political activity, however. A relatively common point of discussion in some of the newspapers was whether students should have particular rights to education. This is pursued, for example, with respect to whether education should be a public good in *The Guardian* (as part of a broader discussion about the high level of fees in England), and whether students should have the right to choose their discipline of study and progress to postgraduate study in *BT* and *Politiken* (in relation to Danish reforms that have introduced change in both areas – see Chapter 1) and to pursue a second subject free of charge, in *Rzeczpospolita*. In addition to constructing students as rights-bearers, many newspapers also framed them as citizens by virtue of their future labour market contribution. This construction of students as 'economic citizens' was evident in many countries including Denmark, Ireland and Poland – with *Rzeczpospolita*, for example, focusing on this in its article 'Young people offer a lot to companies' (26 March 2016). Often, however, this construction was held alongside others that foregrounded the civic learning undertaken by students within HE, and which emphasised a more expansive view of citizenship. A clear example of this is an article in *Politiken* (19 January 2014) where considerable space is given to critics of government policy, who emphasise the importance of 'ideals of enlightenment, including free thinking, democracy and moral development' for HE students and outline concerns that these will be damaged as a result of the Study Progress Reform (see Chapter 1). Thus, across the sample, media perspectives were complex. Although students were quite frequently constructed as citizens in the newspaper articles, TV series and films, the nature of this citizenship often differed considerably, as did the way in which it was evaluated.

Staff and policy perspectives

A more straightforward rejection of understanding students as active and engaged citizens was evident among HE staff and many of the policy actors we interviewed. Our staff interviewees, across all six countries, tended to articulate this in three main ways. First, many claimed that students had become more demanding about their education – questioning, for example, why they have not received higher grades, and expecting immediate responses from teaching staff – and yet more passive in their broader civic and social orientations. Although they noted that some students were now more aware of their rights (as students), they tended to view this not as a manifestation of citizenship, but more as evidence of what they viewed as an 'entitled' consumer mindset (see also Chapter 4). Second, and relatedly, staff members claimed that students' interests were narrow, and that it was only those that related directly to their education that animated them:

'[I]t's almost always something [like], please don't touch our grant from the government and please don't put too much pressure on us, on completing our studies on time, and sometimes it's very hard to be a student nowadays [...] They are focused mainly on taking care of their own position in society, that they don't have to pay for study programmes, that they don't have to complete their studies too quickly ... that the society should procure better dormitories, etc.' (Staff member, Danish HEI1_1)

'Students [are] not engaged with politics, they [are] engaged with their own local politics, so our students are concerned about, you know, they pushed for a fifteen day turnaround for assessment, they want the library open 24/7, they want, you know that sort of thing, and that's what they talk to us and that's what [students' union leaders] get elected on, so they're not being elected on a Communist or a Tory or a ... so we don't have a lot of political debate at a national level.' (Staff member, English HEI3_1)

These accounts mirror the arguments of some extant research that has suggested that, in various nations, the scope of students' political engagement has reduced significantly, often coalescing around issues that impact directly on them as students (see, for example, Shin et al, 2014).

The third theme, outlined by staff, was that there had been a marked decline in collective political activity by students, when compared to the past – and that this was a negative development. This was a strong discourse in all six countries, and is illustrated in the following quotations:

'So formerly, the, well in the sixties of course obviously, but also, I think also still later they were kind of a force, so the ... extra parliamentary opposition that was mainly student driven, but now I think there is no such thing as students as a political voice.' (Staff member, German HEI2_4)

'I think that students played an essential role, for example 30 years ago, or even 40 years ago, and in Europe since the revolution of the sixties, seventies [...] I think that the students played a central role in politics. And I think that that's not the case anymore. I think that not only in Spain but also in the rest of Europe.' (Staff member, Spanish HEI3_3)

In such references to a putative 'golden age' of political participation, there is little recognition that those who took part in the campus protests of the late 1960s comprised only a small minority of students (Sukarieh and Tannock, 2015). Moreover, there is an implicit assumption that students (perhaps more so than other social actors) *should* engage in political activity, typically understood as that stretching beyond educational issues.

The policy actors tended to frame students in less pejorative ways but, like the staff members, also raised questions about the extent to which they could be viewed as active citizens – making particular reference to what they perceived to be their reluctance to become involved in political activity. Moreover, as with the staff interviewees, contrasts were often drawn between the perceived apathy of current students and the more engaged behaviour of previous generations. For example, the Spanish government representative claimed:

'[H]istorically, yes, [students' political activity] was very important in Spain. But nowadays ... it's a very small percentage of those, that they're really involved in politics and in social problems and so on. The great majority, they're more fixed in their degree ... and they're not so worried about the other things.'

In explaining such views, there were some differences between the two groups of interviewees. Staff members across all six countries – but, perhaps unsurprisingly, not the policy actors – typically made reference to recent, market-led reforms of HE, suggesting that the entitlement and self-absorption on the part of students, which they described, was inextricably linked to processes of marketisation. The following quotation from a staff member in Danish HEI2_3 makes this point clearly:

'[T]he neo-liberal kind of regime has touched a lot of our students into being more compliant and more, 'It's not our responsibility, it's someone else who has to do it ... the other ones could do something'.

And then there's the service providing, so if you see the university or the school as someone providing a service, you don't feel responsibility to change anything, because they've got to do it.'

Staff also commented on the reduced time available for students to engage civically and/or politically – because of the increasing amount of paid work they had to do to be able to fund their HE, and/or as a result of reforms to incentivise quicker completion of their degree (Brooks et al, 2021a; see also Chapter 1). The following quotations are typical:

'They don't […] have time to be political, they do not have time to watch the news because they are so stressed about everything else. And I wish they could be more political, I see it as a … oh they should be the ones getting involved in politics, but when … like when should they do this? Between their working schedule and […] exams [what can] I expect from them?' (Staff member, German HEI2_3)

'I think students are very busy […] I mean they have a lot to study […] they have a lot of … practices, teaching, the lessons, the essays, exams! And then an increasing number of students are working, so that reduces the time to engage in, in movements.' (Staff member, Spanish HEI3_4)

Other explanations were also offered, and here there was more agreement between staff members and those involved in policy. For example, a number of interviewees believed that the composition of the student body had changed considerably over recent decades, and that this had had a direct impact on citizen-related activity. Echoing observations made by Klemenčič (2014) and Nissen (2019), they noted that the increasing diversity of the student body had meant that it was harder to identify common grievances and speak with a common voice. One staff member from Polish HEI2 claimed, "There is no such thing in Poland as students as a group who share political views; there are rather some individuals who try to take part in debates". Similarly, a Spanish staff member commented: "Young people are not important political actors in the society … they don't share values or identities, interests or platforms" (Spanish HEI1_1). Moreover, the Polish Student Parliament leader explained that his organisation specifically avoided campaigning on a large number of issues precisely because there was no common view among the student population.

Others suggested that 'non-traditional' students were less inclined to engage with broader social and political issues because they were more concerned with the material rewards of HE (as a result of the significant social and financial costs of attending – see Ball et al, 2002b) – or because of a belief that it is elite groups who tend to lead protests and other forms of civic engagement:

'[In the past, students tended to be] reasonably wealthy and you know they had loads of time to be [...] young and idealistic and ... go and march and all the rest of it, brilliant, lovely. It's a bit different these days! They're from different backgrounds, they've got you know, got their own problems to sort out.' (Staff member, English HEI1_2)

'I kind of miss the times when being a student meant being part of an elite that also sort of assumes the role of ... of agents that work for positive change ... and try to have an influence or to have an impact on [society], to influence it, in order to push it towards ... better ... solutions, outcomes. This was, this was very visible in Poland in the eighties, when the students were often ... the first to show up in, on street demonstrations for example, protesting against ... the old authorities. And right now, students don't seem interested in that anymore.' (Representative of Polish government)

Interviewees also asserted that students – along with people in general – tended to have a more individualised outlook on life, which militated against taking collective action. An English staff member (HEI1_2) contended that students' alleged lack of civic and political engagement was because "they think about issues on an individual level", while an interviewee from the same institution commented, similarly, "our culture now is not idealistic, it's quite self-orientated, I think – it's Thatcher's[3] legacy". Despite the interviewee here attributing individualism to a specific moment in UK political history, similar comments about a shift to more individually oriented cultures were made by staff members in Germany and Spain. (See also the discussion of individualism in Chapter 6.)

Others pointed to the impact of the wider social and political context, claiming that students were often disillusioned with the types of political engagement they saw around them:

'I don't see [students] as very much, how can I say, committed to politics. I mean we had a hard period with politics in Spain, so some of ... I mean many of us are a little bit fed up of you know ... maybe this government will do better, that's what I think. ... And somehow these issues with the corruption in the national government and everything is feeling of disappointment with politics.' (Staff member, Spanish HEI2_3)

'The students aren't politically active now, generally speaking. ... I think a lot of young people are disenchanted with politics.' (Staff member, Irish HEI2_1)

In explaining this disconnect between the views of students, on the one hand, and staff and policy actors, on the other hand, it is possible that the relative visibility of citizenship-related activity is relevant. Individual, non-formal actions are perhaps less likely to be observed by staff and other social actors than collective activities, and less likely to be formally recorded than turning out to vote in an election. In addition, in some of the staff narratives there are suggestions that pressing for education-related changes (such as improved turnaround times for assessment) and engagement with wider social issues are mutually exclusive. This is not a perspective that the students appeared to share. Moreover, as we have indicated above, unfavourable comparisons with previous cohorts of students sometimes seemed to be based on a misreading of political activity in the 1960s and 70s – and an incorrect assumption that in previous decades the majority of students had been involved in protests both on campus and off.

Whatever the reasons for this disconnect, it is certainly the case that, in general, we can see some stereotypical views of students being played out in the narratives of staff and policy actors. Indeed, although there is now a large academic literature on the ways in which young people in general, as well as students in particular, are politically engaged (for example, Vromen, 2003; Marsh et al, 2007; Vromen et al, 2016), views about their alleged apathy appear quite stubbornly engrained within the views of those interacting on a day-to-day basis with students (in the case of staff) and those formulating policy that directly affects the lives of students. There thus appears to be a high degree of continuity with previous research that has documented claims of youth apathy made by politicians, social commentators and others with social influence (Marsh et al, 2007; Klemenčič and Park, 2018; Bessant, 2020).

Conclusion

This chapter has highlighted a significant disconnect between the perspectives of students, on the one hand, and those of other social actors, on the other. In line with much of the extant literature on HE reform, the staff we spoke to tended to believe that, as a result of shifts towards more market-based HE sectors, students' interests had narrowed and, while they were often more aware of their rights, these were more likely to be articulated in an assertion of 'entitled consumerism' rather than a more rounded citizenship identity. They also believed that students' political activity and collective action had declined notably when compared to previous generations – a view that was shared by many of the policy actors we interviewed, and echoed in some (although not all) of the media texts.

Students, however, presented a very different picture – often constructing themselves and their peers as active citizens making a contribution to their communities (local and/or national, rather than global). While they tended to focus primarily on their responsibilities rather than their rights, such responsibilities were often framed, not in terms of conforming to social norms, but with respect to analysing critically the society around them as a first step towards effecting meaningful change. In this way, the students' views seem close to Biesta's 'subjectification' model. Students were also, however, aware that their own perspectives were not always shared by others in society, noting that their potential to contribute as political actors as citizens more broadly was often constrained by assumptions that they were not yet fully formed citizens able of articulating an informed and reasoned voice. We return to this apparent disconnect in Chapter 8.

Enthusiastic learners and hard workers

Introduction

A number of sociological analyses of European HE have argued that processes of marketisation and neo-liberalisation, enacted through various HE policies, have adversely impacted how students learn (for example, Moutsios, 2013). However, such claims have been subject to limited empirical investigation. Moreover, much of the empirical research on the marketisation of HE and its impact on students' engagement with their studies has focused on England, and there is a dearth of comparative studies exploring this topic across different European nations. Are the findings stemming from empirical studies focused on England applicable to other European nations? Are there similarities in how student learning is discussed by policy actors, the media, university staff, and students themselves? This chapter explores these questions.

We will begin by discussing how student learning was problematised in staff, policy and media narratives – often in line with the scholarship mentioned above. We will contrast this with students' own perspectives, highlighting how they placed considerable emphasis on their commitment to learning and claimed that they derived great enjoyment from engaging with the material on their course. We will also illustrate how students emphasised the hard work and effort they put into their studies, viewing this in largely positive terms. In doing so, we will problematise the construction of students – in scholarship as well as in some of our own data – as either focused on getting a degree certificate and job, *or* being passionate and driven learners, arguing that this is a false and unhelpful dichotomy. The chapter will then go on to illustrate how students felt that in policy, media and broader societal narratives, some students were viewed as being superior learners compared to other students, based on various perceived hierarchies relating to discipline of study and, in some cases, institutional affiliation. Finally, we will examine how social class inflected students' learner identities.

Are students passive and instrumental, or enthusiastic and driven?

Passive and instrumental learners: prevalent constructions of students

Scholarship about the instrumentalisation of learning at the HE level has a long history in the context of the US, with studies on the topic being published from the 1960s (for example, Clark and Trow, 1966). In the European context, in contrast, it is only more recently that this topic has attracted substantial scholarly attention, typically in relation to discussions of how policies of marketisation and neo-liberalisation have impacted the experience of being a student.

With respect to England, studies have illustrated how a raft of national HE policies position students as consumers, and HE as a commodity in which they will be willing to invest for personal gain (Naidoo and Williams, 2015; Brooks and Abrahams, 2018; Raaper, 2018). This is perceived as having had significant impact on student identities, pedagogical practices and relationships, curricula and learning outcomes (Molesworth et al, 2009; Nixon et al, 2010; Moutsios, 2013; Naidoo and Williams, 2015). An important theme in such studies is that students have come to see themselves as consumers and hence approach learning in an instrumental and passive manner. For instance, according to Molesworth et al (2009), the marketisation of HE in England has meant a shift in the mode of existence of students from *being* a learner to *having* a degree, and, as a result, contemporary students are primarily focused on learning what they need in order to do well enough on assessments to get a degree and secure a 'professional' job, rather than being driven by a desire for subject mastery and self-transformation. Research on European HE systems beyond England has linked similar trends to the Bologna Process and the establishment of the European Higher Education Area, which have been discussed by a number of scholars as being underpinned by a neo-liberal agenda (Amaral, 2008; Dobbins, 2011). According to Moutsios (2013), for instance, the Bologna Process has placed severe constraints on how learning takes place. As a result, he sees the contemporary university as being a far cry from the Humboldtian ideal of a university: a space marked by *Lernfreiheit* (the freedom of learning) in which students can engage in their studies guided by their own interests and free of any external constraints. While much of this scholarship has been based on a policy-level analysis, an emerging body of scholarship has explored the perspectives of staff and students themselves. Some of these studies have lent support to the arguments made above (for example, Nixon et al, 2010, 2018; Nielsen, 2015; Wilkinson and Wilkinson, 2020).

Echoing some of the arguments made in the studies described thus far, in all six countries in our study, a major theme in staff narratives was that, compared to past generations, students had become more instrumental in their approach to HE – both in terms of being more likely to see HE as a path to a job, and being less enthusiastic and engaged learners. While a focus on future jobs and careers was not necessarily discussed as a bad thing by all staff members, most were critical of what they viewed as being a more instrumental approach to learning on the part of many students, which was not always seen as being an outcome of an increased focus on jobs (as we will discuss in what follows). Staff described how rather than being self-directed learners who sought to explore their subjects in depth and learn for the sake of learning, contemporary students were more focused on tests and exams, and doing what they felt was expected of them in order to obtain a degree. Furthermore, most staff felt that it was important for students not to focus solely on their study programmes, but also to explore subjects outside the curriculum, and become involved in the wider life of the university, participating in extra-curricular activities and interacting with people from other disciplines and backgrounds (although they stressed that participation in these other aspects of university life should not be to the detriment of one's studies). However, they believed that contemporary students were much less likely to do this, and, as a result, the experience of being a student had become more circumscribed.

In some countries – supporting the scholarship described above – the perceived instrumentality in students' engagement with their studies was attributed to specific HE policies. For instance, in Germany and Denmark, the Bologna Process reforms, and national HE policies such as the Danish Study Progress Reform (see Chapter 1), respectively, were pinpointed. In both these countries, staff explained that changes to the pace and structure of degree programmes – often framed as a loss of academic freedom and flexibility in terms of being able to 'individualise' one's study programme, organise one's time as one wished, and study for as long as one wished – were responsible for shifts in how students viewed HE, and how they engaged with their courses and their HEI. The constraining of students' freedom and flexibility in this way was seen as making education less about *Bildung* and *Dannelse* – that is, education in a broader sense of self-development – and reducing the likelihood of students being driven by an interest in their fields of study and a desire for personal development. In Denmark, staff additionally discussed how national policies had brought about an increased focus on employability. Staff said that students were pressured to give back to society by quickly entering the labour market, and universities were incentivised to promote student employability (see also Jayadeva et al, 2021).

In England, in contrast, changes to the experience of being a student were attributed largely to the impact of high tuition fees on student behaviours and practices. Staff said that because of the large financial contributions that students had to make, they had come to think and behave like consumers who felt entitled to 'value for money' and a certain kind of education experience and outcome, rather than like learners pursuing knowledge for its own sake. In addition, staff believed that the high tuition fees that students paid had put pressure on them to think of their degrees as a path to employment. This, and the fact that a large number of students needed to undertake paid work to support their living expenses (leaving them with limited time to spend on their studies), was seen as further contributing to passive and instrumental learning practices among students. Some staff also discussed how they felt forced to adopt teaching practices primarily aimed at effectively transmitting set information, rather than engaging students as partners in the learning process, because of a pressure to ensure good rates of student progression and completion, and protect the university from being sued by dissatisfied students. This, too, was seen as reinforcing passive and dependent student learning behaviour.

Apart from specific HE policies, staff from all six countries discussed a number of other factors as contributing to an instrumentalisation of student learning. Several interviewees described how the school system primed students to think of their education instrumentally. For instance, an Irish staff member discussed how, at school, there was a "points race" to get into university, and students were trained to be exam-focused, rather than "Newman-esque"[1] in their way of thinking and operating (Staff member, Irish HEI2_4). According to some staff members across the six countries, for contemporary students, being a student was not as big an identity as it had been in the past, and the HEI was less of a key space in their lives. This was attributed to many students working alongside studying and also students having other opportunities and spaces for socialising. Such a perceived de-centring of the student role and the university from the lives of contemporary students – and an attendant fall in the time students spent on their studies – was thought to contribute to instrumental and passive learning behaviour, as well as limited student engagement with their HEIs. Finally, a few staff members discussed how massification had led to a rise in students with an instrumental approach to HE. For instance, according to a Polish staff member (HEI1_1), during her time as a student, fewer people had gone to university and these university-goers had been typically interested in learning for its own sake. She felt that at present, while there were still some students who were very engaged and interested in what they were studying, there were also a large number who were more focused on improving themselves for the labour market. Similarly, a Danish staff member observed that increased participation in HE had led to:

'a larger than average degree of students who are not here in pursuit of … of knowledge in the very true and beautiful sense, a lot more instrumental learners, a lot more […] students that are here to take exams in order to get a good job, to get a good salary, to buy a house in the suburbs and make a family.' (Staff member, Danish HEI1_2)

In contrast to staff narratives, in policy documents and interviews – particularly in Denmark, England and Poland – students were constructed as future workers much more than they were constructed as learners (see Chapter 5). In England and Denmark, especially, even when students were constructed as learners, this was mainly framed in relation to becoming equipped for the job market. Furthermore, in all six countries, student learning was problematised; similar to staff narratives, in policy documents and interviews too, students were often constructed as being dependent, passive and instrumental learners – people who learned by rote (Ireland), suffered from 'learning bulimia' (Germany), and memorised rather than questioned what they were learning (Spain). Such learning behaviour was sometimes presented as a problem specific to non-traditional students (see Chapter 7 for further discussion on this theme), while in other cases the HE system was faulted. However, unlike in staff narratives, in policy narratives, problems with the HE system were typically not seen as the result of the effects of specific policies but, rather, poor teaching and/or approaches to learning. For instance, according to the Spanish government interviewee and a representative of the Spanish HE leaders' organisation, the Spanish HE system was characterised by a focus on memorisation, and students were not taught to think critically and question what they were learning. Moreover, some Spanish policy documents claimed that students were not active and independent learners because the policies that have aimed at promoting student-centred learning have been poorly implemented, and staff had failed to engage students as active participants.

Thus, in line with some of the scholarship described above, in our staff and policy data, student learning was often critiqued as instrumental. Although it was not as big a theme as in our staff and policy data, in a number of the newspaper articles we analysed too, students were discussed as passive and entitled learners (see also Finn et al, 2021). We will now turn to the perspectives of students themselves. Were students mainly concerned with obtaining good grades, degree certificates and jobs, rather than being interested and engaged learners?

Enthusiastic and driven learners: students' own perspectives

As we will discuss in greater detail in Chapter 5, in all six countries, a number of students discussed how getting a degree would improve their career prospects or at least save them from unemployment. This theme was strongest in England and Ireland, where students were most likely to foreground career-related reasons for choosing to enter HE, and to discuss the purpose of HE as being related to securing employment. Nevertheless, this did not mean that students, including in England and Ireland, viewed and approached their degrees as merely a path to a degree certificate, job and income, or that they attempted to move through these programmes of study taking the path of least resistance.

Even when students foregrounded career-related goals for entering HE, many did not speak simply in terms of wanting to obtain a degree in order to get a well-paid job, but rather saw a degree as a path to entering a field or career that they were passionate about, and/or felt was a good match for their talents and interests (see O'Shea and Delahunty (2018), for similar findings in an Australian context). In many cases, students spoke enthusiastically about the field they wanted to enter, and the contribution they wished to make through this field. It was also not uncommon for students to see HE as an opportunity to *discover* their professional calling and figure out where their talents and interests lay.

There were also students who discussed entering HE in order to explore a particular subject in greater depth. For instance, two Spanish students described how they had enjoyed studying philosophy in school and now wished to study it at a "higher level", a Danish student described coming to university because he "just want[ed] to learn all there is to learn about history!", and a student from an English focus group described how he wished to "bath[e] in [his] subject". Even some students who were following courses that led to specific professions (for example, nursing) emphasised that they were very interested in the subjects they were studying (for example, illness, the human body) and were not *just* aiming at getting a job upon graduation. In discussing their interest in embarking on a detailed exploration of a subject through their degrees, a few students reflected on how university-level studies were *designed* to enable student-led in-depth learning, and this was what distinguished HE from school. For instance, a student from Poland observed that in the previous stages of education, students were mainly receivers of knowledge, but at university they were also researchers and discoverers of knowledge in a specialised area, and became part of a "community that's engaged with a particular field of study" (Focus group, Polish HEI3_1).

A number of students also described entering HE because of a desire to study and learn, framing this desire not in terms of a specific subject or field, but more broadly. For instance, students described how they were "thirsty for knowledge", "hungry for getting to learn something", and "addicted" to learning. Finally, across all six countries, some students said that they had entered HE in order to broaden their thinking and develop as individuals. Students spoke about how HE equipped one to acquire "another vision of the world", a chance to "discover yourself", "develop [oneself] as a person [...] and awaken concerns also", "challenge [one's] thinking", "expand [one's] horizons" and "evolve as a person". The kind of learning and development that students spoke of was not seen as happening exclusively through a study programme: some students also described the learning that took place through interacting with other students from diverse backgrounds, doing internships and other extra-curricular activities, and so on.

Many students did not frame their desire to explore a subject, learn and develop themselves in terms of increasing their employability – or, at least, not solely in these terms. Some noted that even if they were already assured an ideal job, and therefore did not need a degree for this purpose, they would still go to university because, as one student put it, "The process would really interest me, it is not just a case of obtaining a certificate" (Focus group, Spanish HEI3_1). Even when students foregrounded a desire to increase their employability, this did not necessarily mean that they did not also speak of enjoying their degrees and of being interested in their subjects, learning and personal development. The centrality of learning in students' identities also powerfully emerged from the plasticine models that they made to represent how they saw themselves. While a number of students made models of books, laptops, brains, trees and flowers to symbolise learning, knowledge acquisition and growth, there was a notable absence of models that foregrounded employment or more instrumental concerns (for more detailed analysis, see Brooks and Abrahams, 2021). Although students did not explicitly position themselves as 'co-producers' or 'partners' (Matthews 2018), many certainly appeared to view themselves as playing an active role in the learning process.

Further emphasising their non-instrumental engagement with their studies – or, at least, their belief that instrumental learning approaches were problematic – a few students complained about the instrumental learning behaviour of *other* students (sometimes unfavourably comparing contemporary students with previous generations of students) and attempted to distance themselves from such learners. For instance, one student observed:

'I think that in the current education system, yes, there is a typical student which is a student who comes here as a means of transit to the world of work and this, simply, is the [acquisition of] knowledge you will need in order to find a job which will support you. But I don't think that I, for example, am the typical student because I don't see … the university as being simply a tool required for work, rather a space of knowledge in which to create yourself … and to improve as a person.' (Focus group, Spanish HEI1_1)

Even more commonly, a number of students complained that *they* felt constrained in their ability to study, learn and explore their subjects in the manner that they wished. In Germany and Denmark, participants complained that while students in the past had had the freedom and flexibility to immerse themselves in their subjects and chart their own learning, contemporary students were under a great deal of 'performance pressure' as a result of reforms to speed up the time students took to complete their degrees (see Chapter 6). This, together with inflexible schedules and regular assessment, were spoken of as diminishing the richness of the student experience and negatively impacting learning. The following quotations are illustrative:

'The consensus is that you should finish your degree as quickly as possible and then enter the labour market as quickly as possible. It's no longer about assimilating a wide range of knowledge by adding several semesters that you don't need but that would help you grow as a person and broaden your knowledge, it's just important to get through as fast as possible.' (Focus group, German HEI1_2)

'[T]here has to be a purpose! That's the most important part, sort of in the political discourse, that we can't just, can't just get smarter [...] for the sake of getting smarter [...] Yeah, and it has to be measurable [...] you have to sort of be able to tick a box when, when ... with education.' (Focus group, Danish HEI1_2)

Here, the complaints of students in our study strongly resembled those of the Danish students interviewed by Nielsen and Sarauw (2017) and Sarauw and Madsen (2020); the participants in these studies are described as viewing changes implemented as a result of the Danish Study Progress Reform as restricting their possibilities for learning, impoverishing their experience as students.

In England and Ireland, while students did not complain about not having any discretion over the pace at which they had to move through their degrees, some complained that they were incentivised to focus mainly on assessments. For instance, an Irish student (Focus group, Irish HEI2_3) noted that while in the past ("like 600 years ago"), HE constituted people "philosophising" and learning in a room together, today it seemed to be mainly focused on enabling students to get good grades. She observed: "it's training you to get a piece of paper, it's training you to be an employee rather than to have a well-rounded education, which I think is what we should have". In Spain, some students from the two public HEIs in our sample believed that the quality of education was poor, which came in the way of them experiencing their studies as enriching and enabling of personal development. For instance, one student made a model of a "frustrated doll" to depict how she viewed herself:

'Well, mine is like a sad and frustrated doll, because I believe they have to change the teaching methodology that they use in class, it has to be more dynamic, different, not the typical one of coming here, sitting down, warming your seat and listening to all they tell you.' (Focus group, Spanish HEI3_3; see Figure 4.1)

Indeed, some believed that the poor quality of education in Spain contributed to Spanish students being viewed as inferior learners compared to or by students from other European countries. Finally, across all six countries, a

Figure 4.1: Person with their head bowed in sorrow and frustration

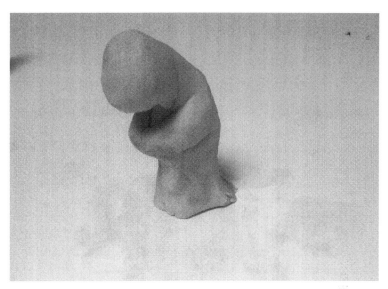

large number of students discussed and criticised how learning for its own sake, and knowledge for the sake of knowledge, were often constructed, by the people around them – and, in some cases, in political discourse – as a problematic goal for a student to have (we will return to this point later). Many described being advised by family and friends, as well as school career guidance counsellors, to choose study programmes with good job prospects and not to study something for its own sake. A number lamented how they received questions from family and friends about what they were planning to do *with* their degree and *after* their degree, and not many questions about whether they were enjoying the degree itself.

Our research thus joins a growing number of studies which have challenged the dichotomous manner in which students are often discussed within and beyond scholarship: as being either active, passionate and dedicated learners *or* instrumental, entitled, passive and interested only in non-academic goals. For instance, with respect to first-generation students in the US, Hurst (2010, 2013) and Grigsby (2009) have shown that it is possible for students to care about knowledge for its own sake while also wanting their education to improve their career prospects. In the context of England, scholars have argued that students exhibit varying levels of identification with a consumer identity (Tomlinson, 2017; Brooks and Abrahams, 2018), and that identifying as a consumer and/or having career-related motivations for doing a degree does not necessarily mean that students have become entitled and passive learners (Wilkinson and Wilkinson, 2020; Finn et al,

2021). Similarly, our research suggests that despite the fact that job or career-related concerns and motivations were prominent or foregrounded in many students' narratives – and despite some students discussing how their ability to learn in an explorative and open-ended manner was constrained by various factors (in some cases echoing staff narratives) – an interest in learning, personal development and bringing about positive change inform many contemporary students' decisions to enter HE and their experience of HE. Indeed, we would argue that framing only non-job-related motivations for entering HE as representative of an appropriate learner identity is elitist, especially in contexts of increased private investment in HE and uncertain labour market outcomes for graduates.

To a large extent, students' accounts of how they perceived and engaged with their studies contrasted sharply with how they are often constructed not just in scholarship, but also in the narratives of other key stakeholders, such as HEI staff and policy actors, who have considerable influence and impact over how universities operate. Nevertheless, student complaints about feeling constrained in their ability to learn in the manner that they wished, and their attempts to distance themselves from instrumental learning styles they felt were exhibited by some other students, suggest that there are some overlaps between how staff and students conceptualised what constituted good education and an appropriate learner identity. Moreover, while an 'instrumental' approach to learning was decried by staff and students across all six countries, there was some variation between countries in terms of how it was felt learning ought to take place at the HE level, which related to national traditions of HE (see also Brooks et al, 2021a). For instance, in Denmark and Germany, reforms that have restricted students' ability to determine the length of their studies and to prioritise their own time during their degrees – features that have long characterised HE study in these countries – were discussed as impoverishing student learning. Meanwhile, in the other countries in our study, where the right to prioritise one's own time or decide on the length of one's degree has not been normalised, students and staff did not discuss the fixed length of degree programmes as impinging on students' ability to learn in a self-directed and explorative manner.

Students as hard workers

In the plasticine models that students made to depict how they saw themselves and how they were seen by others, an important theme was the amount of hard work that being a student involved (see also Brooks and Abrahams, 2021). Many students made models of books and laptops to portray how they saw themselves as hard workers, and some also felt that they were seen in this way by those around them. Although several students emphasised how working so much could lead to stress, exhaustion and limited time for other activities

Figure 4.2: Student with laptop attached to head

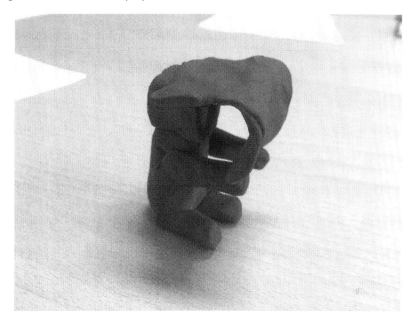

and responsibilities (see Chapter 6), most presented their busy student lives in positive or at least neutral terms. The following quotes are illustrative:

'That's me with a laptop! That's basically what I do all day, that's how I fall asleep, that's how I wake up! Basically I study, I programme, that's it, there's not much else and there's not much time for anything else.' (Focus group, Irish HEI2_3; Figure 4.2)

'My family, like my close family [...] are just baffled at the amount of time I spend in front of a screen, typing or reading and stuff, so ...! [...] So yeah, [I made a model of] my computer screen.' (Focus group, English HEI2_2)

It is possible that students' emphasis on their hard work was partly a reaction to wider narratives of them being lazy and societal discourses about the neo-liberal imperative to 'work hard' as frequently articulated by politicians and other policymakers (Littler, 2013; Mendick et al, 2018). In all six countries, a large number of students made models to depict how they were seen as lazy by people they knew, but also 'society', politicians and the media (see Chapter 7 for a more detailed discussion). Strikingly, this was one of the most prominent ways in which students felt they were seen by others. In line with students' perceptions, our analysis of policy documents and the interviews we conducted with policy actors showed that students were frequently constructed as not working hard enough. This was most explicit in Denmark, where a major theme in many policy documents was that students were not spending enough time on their studies, which was seen as especially problematic given that they were beneficiaries of the government (through the receipt of free education and maintenance grants). Indeed, the figure of the 'lazy' student has been used as a foil for introducing a range of reforms intended to encourage students to move through their studies at a faster pace (see also Brooks, 2021; Ulriksen and Nejrup, 2021). Similarly in Spanish policy narratives, various explanations were put forward to explain a supposed lack of hard work among students – from not being sufficiently encouraged by teachers to not feeling pressured enough by the cost of their education to put a lot of effort into their studies, given that they typically lived with and were supported by their parents. In contrast, in the English policy narratives, students were presented as being very hard-working precisely because of the pressure that they felt as a result of paying high tuition fees. Nevertheless, even here, an implicit contrast was drawn between those students who work hard and are thoroughly deserving of their degree outcome and others who have not shown such commitment and yet have been unfairly rewarded with a 'good degree' as a result of 'grade inflation' (Brooks, 2018b; see also Chapter 7).

Similarly, in the newspaper articles we analysed, a major theme was that a large proportion of students were not suited to HE and were not hard-working and committed to their studies. The presence of these supposedly inferior learners was often linked to the massification of HE. Such a framing of students was most pronounced in Denmark, but visible in the other five countries too (see Chapter 7). While, across all six countries, there were also a number of articles that presented portraits of students and their achievements, implicitly highlighting their hard work, only certain students – those studying STEM subjects (science, technology, engineering, mathematics) or management – were portrayed in this way (we will return to this point). In England alone, a few newspaper articles explicitly framed students as hard-working, in some cases almost as if to challenge a prevalent contrasting view. For instance, one article titled, 'Who says students are lazy!', offered a portrait of a very hard-working student who balances studies with running her own business, introducing the student like this: '[she] doesn't fit the modern student stereotype of all play and very little work' (*Daily Mail*, 12 October 2016).

Most focus group participants took exception to being constructed as lazy and did not see such constructions as being harmless. Many emphasised how such constructions made invisible the hard work that the majority of students invested in their studies (often outside of 'visible' contact hours), and the high levels of stress many experienced as a result of the demands of their study programmes, and having to balance these demands with paid work, internships and family responsibilities (see Chapter 6). Thus, our study participants did not seek to present themselves – or to be viewed by others – as 'effortless achievers', in order to demonstrate 'authentic intelligence' or portray an image of being 'cool', as has been documented in some other studies which have explored the relationship between learner identities and narratives of hard work and effort (for example, Jackson and Nyström, 2015). They also did not try to position themselves as 'stress-less achievers' or people who were cruising through their degrees, ably balancing academic and non-academic activities and pursuits (for example, Nyström et al, 2019). Indeed, some students (particularly at the more elite universities in our sample) rejected constructions of themselves as highly intelligent because they felt such constructions suggested that it was easy to be a student and failed to acknowledge their hard work. It is also important to note while some previous studies (for example, Brown et al (2016) writing about England and France) found that students at elite HEIs discussed hard work as being the defining feature of an *elite* education, we did not encounter much inter-institutional differentiation in narratives of hard work among our participants. Rather, across HEIs and countries, our study participants appeared to view hard work as part of a successful or, at least, legitimate learner identity.

We also encountered more sympathetic constructions of students. For instance, while some staff members were critical of students' lack of investment of time and effort in their studies, many were rather sympathetic towards students, noting the pressures the education system placed on them, and how hard most worked. In the films we analysed, too, students were largely portrayed as hard-working and driven (although some students more so than others). The theme of students as hard workers was especially foregrounded in the German comedy, *Wir sind die Neuen*. The film tells the story of three pensioners who move into a flat together, below a flat occupied by three university students. The pensioners are portrayed as fun-loving people, who like to throw parties and seek out new experiences. They are keen to befriend the students, whom they imagine would be similarly inclined, but soon realise that this is not the case: the students are extremely focused on their studies, want to be left alone, and immediately start complaining about noise from downstairs (see Appendix for further details). The plot of the film is intended to be humorous because it reverses the typical roles associated with pensioners and university students. However, this role reversal can also be read as a comment on how contemporary students are very studious and hard-working, and university studies are extremely demanding. There is also a suggestion that this was not always the case; one character, Thorsten, makes a comment blaming the previous generation for not having taken their studies seriously enough, which has led to a situation where contemporary students are given a restricted amount of time to complete their degrees.

In the next section, we will explore how a number of students felt that the manner in which one was seen by others – as either hard-working or lazy, impressive or useless – was mediated by the subject one studied, and, in some cases, by the HEI which one attended. We will also examine the impact of social class on students' learner identities.

A hierarchy of learners?

Hierarchies between disciplines of study

In student focus groups in all six countries, a major theme was that the manner in which one was viewed by others – 'society', the government, family, friends, other students – depended on the subject one was studying. Students from a range of disciplinary backgrounds discussed how those studying humanities or social science subjects were viewed as problematic, and inferior to students studying STEM subjects, for a number of reasons (see also Jayadeva et al, 2022).

First, according to students, humanities and social science courses were widely seen as being 'useless' and 'pointless' because they were not thought to lead to employment, or, at least, not to good careers (see also Brooks et al, 2021b). Many students discussed how, for this reason, prior to entering HE they had received advice from family, friends and their school career guidance counsellors to study a STEM subject, and had been strongly discouraged from studying humanities or social science subjects. Students who were enrolled on humanities or social science courses described how they were constantly confronted with questions, from their friends, family and even classmates following other programmes, about the value and legitimacy of their study programmes. For instance, a student from a Spanish focus group observed:

'[W]hen you go to a family meeting and they ask you about what you are studying and you say, "information technology", they say, "very good, very good money", but if you say, "sociology" or "social work", they ask, "Will it give you any opportunities?" [And you reply:] "Listen, why don't you ask me if I am happy doing my course or if I like it, instead of if it will give me opportunities or allow me to make money".' (Focus group, Spanish HEI3_2)

Similarly, a student in England, studying English and art, made a model of a bucket without a bottom to depict how she was viewed by her family and school friends as:

'doing a degree [that is] kind of pointless, like a bucket without a bottom! [others laugh] [...] the first question I get asked is, well what are you going to do with that? [agreement] And I'm like, ooh, don't

Figure 4.3: Bucket without a bottom

know. And they say, oh do you want to be a teacher? I'm like no. [...] And you can either see the judgement in people, or they just say it and say, well that, you're going to be in loads of debt, waste of money, you know just pointless.' (Focus group, English HEI3_2; Figure 4.3)

Another reason why some students felt social science and humanities courses were seen as useless was because the subject matter was thought to be not particularly valuable to anyone. As one Polish student noted: "Students of humanities and social sciences have the worst image. They are viewed as some kind of parasites and society would be okay without them" (Focus group, Polish HEI2_3). A few students felt that such negative stereotypes surrounding students of these subjects also stemmed from people simply not knowing enough about what these subjects involved and the kinds of jobs to which they could lead.

Students discussed how, apart from social science and humanities courses being viewed as useless, they were also considered to be less challenging than STEM courses, both because the subject matter was perceived as being less difficult, but also because these courses typically had fewer contact hours. As a result, students following such courses were thought to be not very intelligent and rather lazy. In Poland and Spain, particularly, students discussed how studying humanities and social science was seen as the last refuge of those people who were not talented enough to study STEM subjects but wished to enter HE. As one student put it, people were seen as studying humanities subjects "not by choice but out of necessity" (Focus group, Polish, HEI1_2). Similarly, a Spanish student noted: "In my experience of sixth form, the social [sciences] were for the stupid, this was being said all the time"

(Focus group, Spanish HEI1_1). In the plasticine models students made to represent how they felt they were seen by those around them, a number of humanities and social science students from all six countries made models of beds, bottles of alcohol, three Zs to denote sleep, and so on to depict how they were seen as lazy and hedonistic.

Students following humanities and social science courses spoke about how, in contrast, STEM students were viewed as being intelligent, hard-working, higher achievers and people with bright futures. This was discussed as being a product of STEM courses being widely viewed as challenging, valuable and leading to good careers. Many of our participants following STEM courses made models of books, graduation caps and spectacles, to portray how they were viewed positively, and often linked this to their subject of study. For instance, a medical student made a model of a pair of spectacles and a number of books to depict how she was seen by others and explained the model like this: "I have made a pair of spectacles and a lot of books [...] because if you study Medicine they see you as a clever girl who studies a lot, who will be a good medic, who will contribute a lot, who will cure people" (Focus group, Spanish HEI1_2).

While the humanities and social science students in our focus groups did not typically agree with the negative ways in which their disciplines were viewed, many expressed frustration at being positioned as inferior learners. Some students felt that the widespread valorisation of STEM subjects, together with the related view that a degree should lead straightforwardly to a specific career, led to many students choosing subjects that they were not interested in or well suited to study.

Particularly in Denmark, Poland and Spain, some students discussed how STEM subjects were promoted as the most worthwhile fields of study by both politicians and the media. Our analysis of policy and media narratives from all six countries do indeed demonstrate a valorisation of STEM subjects. In policy narratives in some countries, linked to the construction of students as future workers, was concern about whether students were choosing the 'right' study programmes. For instance, in several of the Polish policy documents, concern is expressed that students are picking the 'wrong' subjects – humanities courses (which are not seen to prepare them well enough for the labour market), rather than STEM courses which are seen as valuable in this regard (see also Stankiewicz, 2020). The expansion of the number of students opting for social science and humanities courses is discussed as 'the dark side' of massification (Polish speech 3). Recent reforms have aimed at providing students with more information about the relationship of courses to the labour market in order to enable them to make better decisions regarding subject of study. Similarly, recent reforms in Denmark have sought to direct funding away from courses with perceived low labour market relevance (see Chapter 1). In Spain, Germany, Ireland

and England, although such significant attempts have not been made to divert students into STEM study programmes, the importance and value of STEM subjects was still emphasised in different ways in policy narratives, most importantly through an emphasis on the importance of these subjects for the economy.

Furthermore, in a number of newspaper articles, STEM subjects were presented as valuable for the country (economic prosperity, international competitiveness) and the individual (good job prospects), and the popularity of STEM courses among students was celebrated – or, in some cases, limited student enrolment in such courses was problematised. Another category of newspaper article that we encountered was inspirational stories of students who had participated in various national and international competitions or made other notable achievements. Strikingly, the students focused on were almost always STEM students (or, in some cases, management students). The social sciences and humanities were the focus of just a few newspaper articles. These articles, published in Polish and Danish newspapers, focused on the fall in student numbers on specific humanities programmes, and the threat to these subjects as a result of policy reforms, respectively.

In the films and TV series we analysed, although the hierarchies between subjects were not a major focus, there were a number of references to the perceived superiority of some subjects over others. For instance, in the English comedy, *Fresh Meat*, Vod, a student studying for an English degree, downplays her good grades by suggesting that English is not a very challenging subject ("read some books, had some opinions. It's English, it's not hard"). In the German comedy, *13 Semester*, a student named Dirk observes that in order to be successful in the upcoming economics exam, a lot of hard work is needed – after all, it is economics they are studying, not social work. In the first episode of the Spanish drama, *Merlí*, one of the lecturers welcomes the new philosophy students by humorously remarking that a philosophy degree is the "official degree with no prospects", and references are made to the philosophy programme having a high drop-out rate (although the TV series itself takes pains to emphasise the beauty of philosophy and present the discipline in positive light).

Studies thus far have examined students' relationships to their subjects of study (for example, Bradbeer et al, 2004; Ashwin et al, 2016), and have shown that different disciplines have different pedagogical cultures, which can mediate students' understandings of their learner identities (for example, Nyström et al, 2019). However, what has been less studied is how students feel that their subjects of study are perceived by relevant others, and how such perceptions might mediate the manner in which they are viewed. Our research thus addresses an important gap, illuminating the extent to which the valorisation of STEM subjects, and an attendant problematisation of humanities and social science subjects – through HE policies, media representations and strongly entrenched societal stereotypes attached to different disciplines – can impact the experience of being a student.

Hierarchies between higher education institutions

In all the countries in our study, with the exception of Germany, some students also discussed how the HEI to which one belonged mediated the type of learner one was imagined to be by relevant others. This theme emerged most strongly in England. To some extent paralleling students' views about how one's subject of study mediated the manner in which one was viewed by others, English students discussed how the HEI a student attended might be seen as an index of their intelligence, work ethic and likely future success (see also Jayadeva et al, 2022). Regardless of the HEI they attended themselves, students discussed how everyone from politicians, to 'society' and 'the public', to many of their own friends and family members tended to view students studying at the top universities more positively. According to some students, the university one attended could even trump the subject one was studying, when it came to the way one was perceived by others. Students at what were perceived to be the 'top' universities were viewed as hard-working, especially intelligent and destined for success. Comments like these were typical:

'[T]here's this whole perception that I'm going to get a better job because I have a [name of university] degree.' (Focus group, English HEI2_2)

'I think, obviously, the students who go to like [names of elite universities], [politicians] kind of think, oh yeah, well they're going to potentially be in the government in a few years' time. [Agreement]' (Focus group, English HEI3_1)

Our participants also discussed how students at lower status institutions might be seen as lazy, hedonistic, not very intelligent, and, all told, less serious learners. For instance, one student from the high-status university in our English sample contrasted how students from her university were treated with respect, while those from the university in the city where she was from (a lower-status university) were seen as drinking and doing drugs, being rowdy and 'floating' through their time in HE (Focus group, English HEI2_1). This was a view also expressed by students from the less high-status institutions in our sample. For instance, one student reflected:

'I just think that, if I'm honest, I think society just now sees [...] especially universities that are not [...] the Russell Group universities

[…] I definitely think that people just see it as just, oh well, go from school straight into uni, there you go, just go and do an extra three years.' (Focus group, English HEI1_1)

Given the hierarchical manner in which students felt HEIs were organised in the national imagination (and beyond), some discussed the pressure they had felt to secure admission to a high-status HEI. One student said:

'So there's a lot more universities recently, and so there was a lot of pressure to be quite selective, like a consumer, and sort of affiliate with more prestigious brands of university […] I think there's a lot of pressure before going to university to make sure that you get yourself somewhere good, that's recognisable, that isn't just going to leave you [agreement from other students] sort of, people going like, who, where … where did you get that university degree from?' (Focus group, English HEI3_3)

In some cases, students described how they had chosen to study at their university, despite the fact that it was not one of the elite universities in the country, because it had offered a study programme that particularly interested them, but had then felt that they had to continually justify their choice of university to their friends and family.

A number of students from all three English universities problematised the construction of students from 'top' universities as superior to those from 'lesser' universities. Some students ridiculed how their admission to a high-status HEI had immediately transformed them in the eyes of those around them. Once again, such stereotyping of students based on institutional affiliation was not seen as harmless but as having material impact. For instance, a student from one of the less prestigious universities in our sample discussed how employers were willing to pay students from the 'classic universities' or 'Russell Group' universities more than they were willing to pay those who attended less prestigious institutions, not because the students in the former group possessed superior skills but because they were imagined to do so (Focus group, English HEI3_3).

The prominence of this theme in England compared to the other countries in our study is unsurprising, given the differences in how the HE systems of these countries are structured. England can be said to follow a 'neo-liberal model', where resources are concentrated in a small number of elite institutions such that there is a high degree of vertical or reputational differentiation between universities (Hazelkorn, 2015). In contrast, the HE systems in some of the other countries in our study, such as Germany, could be seen as characterised by a 'social democratic model' where all universities are supported to pursue high-quality teaching and research (Hazelkorn, 2015). Nevertheless, even in countries with ostensibly 'flatter' HE systems, some students discussed how

HEIs, and their students, were hierarchically ordered. While in England and also Ireland hierarchies were typically drawn between older and newer HEIs, in the other countries in our study, and also in Ireland, other axes of differentiation were also visible. For instance, in Ireland and Denmark, some students made distinctions between universities, on the one hand, and universities of applied sciences (Denmark) or institutes of technology (Ireland), on the other hand, and it was felt that university students were viewed more positively (see also Reimer and Thomsen, 2019, for some evidence of stratification in Denmark along the lines of university age and location). In Spain, students at elite private universities were sometimes discussed as being seen as superior to students from public universities, although some public universities were also discussed as highly selective and prestigious.

While hierarchies between HEIs were not a major theme in the staff and policy interviews, or in the policy documents and newspaper articles we analysed, they were referenced to different extents in the Irish drama, *Normal People*, and the English comedy, *Fresh Meat*. In *Fresh Meat*, one of the protagonists, the rich JP, an alumnus of the elite Stowe School, is presented as attending the fictional Manchester Medlock University because he could not get into a 'proper' university. In the Irish drama, *Normal People*, the elite status of Trinity College Dublin permeates the entire series. For instance, of the two protagonists, the affluent Marianne has always assumed that she would study at Trinity (just like her mother), while the other protagonist, working-class Connell, had never imagined that this would be an option for him, until he is encouraged by Marianne. At several points in the series, we see supporting characters, from Connell's hometown, express awe at the fact that Connell will be/is attending Trinity.

Social class

Social class mediated students' learner identities in various ways. This seemed to be especially pronounced in England and Ireland, where variations were apparent between how students from the different HEIs in our sample spoke about their reasons for entering HE. In England, students attending the lowest status HEI (HEI1) were more likely to discuss coming to university in relation to improving their job prospects, while the students in the elite university (HEI2) were more likely to foregrounded their intrinsic motivation to be at university, and their desire to study "for the love of it" as one student put it. Some students even explicitly distanced themselves from employment-related motivations. Similarly, in Ireland, students at the elite university (HEI3) were much more likely than the students at the two other universities to describe coming to university because they were interested in a subject, or wanted to expand their knowledge on a topic. However, unlike in England, they typically also discussed how the knowledge they had gained might be valuable for getting jobs they might want to do in the future.

To some extent, these institutional differences may be seen as mapping onto social differences. As discussed in the previous section, the HE system of England exhibits a high level of stratification compared to the other countries in our study. 'Research intensive' institutions (such as 'Russell Group' universities, and HEI2 in our sample) are richer, more selective and occupy higher positions in national and international league tables than HEIs which have more recently obtained university status (such as 'post-92' universities or HEI1 in our sample). A number of studies have highlighted how students from lower income families are more likely to attend lower-status institutions, while privileged students are over-represented in the intakes of higher-status institutions (Reay et al, 2010; Boliver, 2013). Our sample of students in England reflected this pattern. While the Irish HE system is arguably less hierarchically organised than in England (Hazelkorn, 2015), HEI3 is one of the most rich, selective and prestigious in the country and, of the three HEIs in our sample in Ireland, it had the most privileged student intake. The differences we observed in England and Ireland with respect to how students framed their reasons for entering HE could thus be attributed, at least to some extent, to their socio-economic backgrounds. For instance, previous studies have shown how, given the greater financial and social risks that undertaking a degree involves for them, students without a family history of HE are likely to emphasise future job opportunities rather than a love of learning for its own sake (Ball et al, 2002b). It could also be argued that because students from higher socio-economic backgrounds attending elite HEIs feel more confident about getting attractive jobs upon graduation, they are less likely to emphasise job-related motivations for entering HE.

In addition, other studies have highlighted how social class can be mediated by institutions, through drawing on the concept of 'institutional habitus'. Reay et al (2010) discuss how the institutional habitus of an HEI, specifically the learning environment and culture that characterise it, can impact the learner identities that its students develop. In their study of working-class students attending four different types of HEIs in England, Reay et al found that those at the elite HEI in their sample were most likely to develop a strong sense of themselves as successful learners, because they led lives that revolved around their degree programmes and the university as a physical and social space. Unlike students in the lower-status HEIs in their sample, who needed to undertake paid work alongside their studies, and typically lived with their families, students at the elite HEI were expected by the university – and were able – to devote themselves to their study programmes and university-related activities. Thus, being a university student was likely to become their primary identity, while the learner identities of the students at the lower-status HEIs remained fragile and in competition with their other roles and identities. Similarly, other research focused on first-generation students in the US, Canada, UK and Germany (Spiegler and Bednarek, 2013) as well as Australia (O'Shea and Delahunty, 2018) has highlighted how such students may view themselves as imposters, both because they do not feel entitled to attend university, and because they often have more limited engagement with their universities, as a result of working alongside studying and living off-campus. It is possible, then, that another reason the students at the elite universities in our sample in England and Ireland were more likely to foreground learning-related goals or motivations for entering HE, was because they saw themselves as successful learners, and their learner identities were their most prominent identity.

Related to this, staff in all six countries described how not all students could afford to focus completely on their studies because of the need to undertake paid work to support themselves or finance their education. Except for in Denmark (where students receive grants to cover their living expenses while studying), staff discussed how an important reason – but by no means the only one – for which many students worked was financial need. Staff described how not all students were able to access funding to support themselves because of limited funding options and, in some cases, because funding was tied to academic performance rather than need. While most staff members felt that balancing work with studies could be a valuable experience for students – especially if the job was related to one's field of study – they complained that many students, especially those from lower socio-economic backgrounds, were forced to work so much that their academic performance suffered.

These themes were also visible in the films we analysed. For instance, in the English comedy, *Fresh Meat*, the two most well-off students, JP and Oregon, are portrayed as people who did not need to worry about the kinds of jobs they would be able to find upon graduating, while this was a major concern for many of the other main characters. Furthermore, while Oregon is depicted seeking out work experience solely in order to build her CV, other less well-off characters are shown having to work in jobs unrelated to their courses in order to support themselves, and having to balance studies and work. In the Irish drama, *Normal People*, working-class Connell initially plans to study a course that would have good job prospects (law), until his girlfriend, Marianne, convinces him to study the subject in which he is really interested, English. At university, while Marianne and her friends are portrayed as not needing to work, and being able to spend all their time on their coursework and 'wider university experiences', Connell is shown working two different jobs (both unrelated to his degree) in order to support himself, until he manages to get a scholarship. In the Spanish drama, *Merlí*, the uncertain career prospects attached to a philosophy degree is a recurring theme. Of the group of philosophy students we meet, the most affluent, Rai, observes that he is the only person studying philosophy who does not have to worry about future prospects, since he is already rich. His interest in studying philosophy is revealed to be completely disconnected from employment-related interests. Thus, in media narratives too, social class was depicted as shaping students' experiences of HE.

Conclusion

In this chapter, we have attempted to illustrate how, despite prevalent constructions of students being instrumental and passive learners – visible in policy and media narratives of students, as well as in the narratives of staff members we interviewed – an interest in and commitment to learning and hard work was emphasised by most students. This emerged powerfully from students' narratives of their motivations for entering HE, but also from their complaints about various factors that constrained their ability to learn in the manner that they wished. We argue that such learner identities and an interest in more 'instrumental' concerns such as jobs and grades, are not necessarily mutually exclusive. Furthermore, we highlight how particular hierarchies – based on discipline, institutional affiliation and social class – appear to exert significant impact on the experience of being a student. Most notably, across all six countries, students following humanities and social science courses felt that they were viewed as inferior learners compared to students following STEM courses. Our findings also reveal some national variations; we show how institutional hierarchies and social class were experienced as mediating students' learner identities most strongly in England and Ireland, and how national traditions of HE strongly informed understandings of 'good learning' and 'good students'.

5

Future workers

Introduction

The discourse of human capital, which positions HE students as future workers and as a key economic resource, has been evident in various national and European policies introduced over the past two decades (Brooks, 2021; Keeling, 2006). At the institutional level, there has been a clear emphasis on adjusting study programmes to labour market needs, evident both on HEI websites (Bennett et al, 2019; Lažetić, 2019; Fotiadou, 2020) and in the ideas that circulate within university management (Boden and Nedeva, 2010). Students' perceptions of and identification with this discourse (especially in relation to notions of employability) have been studied previously (Tomlinson, 2007, 2010; Bonnard, 2020); nevertheless, broader cross-country comparative insights are yet to be made. In particular, the use of alternative contesting discourses by students and staff, which question human capital norms, have remained largely obscured.

In this chapter, we first outline how students are constructed as future workers within a dominant narrative of human capital development – evident in policies and, to a lesser extent, media narratives – in our six countries, and explore the degree to which this discourse is internalised by students and staff. Second, we identify how the future worker construction is reinterpreted by students within a strong discourse of credentialism; and, finally, we outline ways in which both students and staff discursively reject this future worker construction. In rejecting an understanding of 'future workers' based on human capital principles, students and staff draw on the concepts of vocation and *Bildung* to create alternative visions of the relationship between education and the world of work.

Discourse of human capital development

In the history of ideas, there are few with as much potency to shape global political discourse around education, economics and development as the idea of human capital. Although with much older intellectual roots (Brown et al, 2020), its modern conceptual and discursive underpinning is based on the theory proposed by economists Schultz (1961) and Becker (1975, 1993) (for a comprehensive overview see Brown et al, 2020). In essence, the theory is simple: it stipulates that education drives the marginal productivity of labour, and this marginal productivity then drives earnings (Marginson, 2019).

This economic theory has reshaped understandings of education at both the individual and macro-economic level. At the individual level, within human capital theory, the value of investment in education is defined in terms of the lifetime earnings of educated labour. Employers are understood to choose their future workers based on information about their skills and knowledge on the assumption that this will increase the productivity of their businesses. Consequently, students are encouraged to exercise rational choice and obtain skills and abilities that are desired by employers and which will therefore maximise their earnings.

Human capital theory asserts that, at the macro-economic level, investment in education not only triggers private enrichment, which leads to individual higher earnings, but also underpins national economic growth and development. This assumption has placed education and, in particular, *higher* education at the heart of economic policy in many developed and emerging economies (Brown et al, 2020). Education systems have been seen as key to producing human capital and thus enhancing workforce productivity and economic competitiveness. Universities, informed about the skills required in the labour market, have been expected to develop the right type of attributes and competencies in their students.

As a result of these ideological shifts, education has become 'economised', and discursively underpinned by the language of 'employability', 'skills', 'competition', 'entrepreneurship' and 'outputs', within an overarching framework of markets (Tomlinson, 2013). Reflecting this ideological shift, the functions of HE as a system of workforce training and preparation of future 'knowledge workers' in a 'knowledge economy' have come to be prioritised above humanistic and liberal purposes of, for example, developing critical and responsible citizens (see Chapter 3) or facilitating personal development (Chapter 2). From this perspective, students are seen primarily as economic resources who should optimise, in rational choice terms, their individual efforts in and aspirations for education – for the benefit of both their own economic prosperity and that of their national 'knowledge economy' (Tomlinson, 2013; Marginson, 2019; Brown et al, 2020).

Students as future workers within policy

The construction of students as future workers, informed by ideas associated with human capital, is clearly reflected in HE policy in our six countries – although with different emphases on particular elements of the narrative and different levels of presence (high in England and Denmark, slightly lower in Poland and Ireland and lowest in Germany and Spain). Chapter 2 provided examples of how this discourse was present in interviews with policy actors when they spoke about the transition of young people into the labour market, but it is equally present within the analysed policy documents.

The construction of students as future workers in line with the assumptions of human capital strongly infuses the English policy documents (Brooks, 2018b) and many interviews with English policy actors in which they emphasised skill formation as the primary function of HE. Furthermore, English policy documents present 'graduate outcomes' and 'the graduate premium' (that is, the extra pay received by graduates in work compared with non-graduates) as synonymous, and it is assumed that differences in graduate premiums depend exclusively upon variations in the quality of teaching and employment preparation offered by HEIs (Brooks, 2018b). In Denmark, the policy discourse (among government and business) is informed by the logic of human capital development even more so than in England, and constructs students as not sufficiently employment-focused, blaming both students and institutions for the overly long time students take to complete their studies (see also Chapter 7). The main emphases of recent policy initiatives in Denmark are the central regulation of the number of places made available for study, based on a labour market analysis (closing programmes with low graduate employment rates); incentivising completion of a degree within a prescribed period of time; promotion of internships; and the end of a legal right to transition straight from undergraduate to postgraduate study (see Chapter 1). These have been framed in terms of arguments about the importance of optimising generous taxpayer investment in HE. Moreover, there is a strong emphasis on matching more closely the supply of graduates to labour market needs, promoting entrepreneurship, building a strong 'employability' focus into curricula, and improving employment rates in subjects where it has been low (Danish speeches 1 and 2; Danish government document 4). Similar sentiments are expressed in Poland (although to a lesser extent than in England and Denmark). For example, Polish government document 3 declares the central aim of reform to be improving graduate employability because many students have chosen the 'wrong' subjects (humanities rather than STEM) and are not prepared for the labour market by the curriculum they follow. It calls for curricula to be co-produced with employers (as discussed in Chapter 4 in relation to discussion about hierarchies between disciplines).

In Ireland, instead of employers being presented as in need of/deserving high-quality graduates, there is a recognition that they benefit significantly from HE and therefore should pay a higher contribution to the costs of study (this argument is made explicitly in Irish government document 3). This can be linked to ideas within Irish policy about students helping to strengthen the national economy rather than deriving personal (financial and labour market) advantage. In Spain and Germany this type of discourse is, in comparison, much weaker. We found it only in the calls for employer involvement in curriculum design, and mostly in policy documents issued by relevant business associations.

We can thus see that the construction of students as future workers within policy, informed by ideas associated with human capital, has been most evident in the countries where neo-liberalism has strongly influenced public sector reforms (for example, England and post-Communist Poland), and also the smaller countries in which human capital is seen as a key competitive economic asset (for example, the Irish 'Celtic tiger' economy and the Danish 'knowledge economy'). In Spain and Germany, openly economically focused policy discourse about education has not been part of mainstream discourse, due to strong historical understandings of the role of HE in the education of responsible citizens for a democratic society (see Chapter 3). These cross-country differences also indicate the different ways in which HE is positioned as a public (or private) good.

Media discourse on students as future workers

Within the newspapers analysed in our project, 'students as future workers' were often discussed. However, there were notable differences across the papers – for example, this construction was most prominent in the German newspaper *Die Welt* and Polish newspaper *Rzeczpospolita*. The most visible theme, linked to this construction, and in line with the logic of human capital, centres on the topic of practical skills and experience. In the view of many media outlets, there is a shortage of such skills in the labour market, and HEIs are failing to cater for this need by providing too theoretical an education. This stance is illustrated in the following two examples of newspaper headlines:

'German students call for mandatory internships; Current preparation for a specific occupation is too short, according to the survey. University should follow more strongly the practice of polytechnics' (*Die Welt*, 27 October 2014)

'Students are not prepared to work in companies' (*Rzeczpospolita*, 8 September 2016)

When the issue of degree subject is discussed in the media, the construction of students as rational choosers typically underpins the discourse. Students are often called upon to make careful strategic and rational decisions based primarily on employment, career prospects and likely future earnings. This is a notably strong narrative in England and Poland. Nevertheless, in most newspapers there are also alternative discourses where the logic of rational choice is challenged and wider purposes of HE – not related to human capital development – are foregrounded (both for individuals and nations). This is particularly the case in Denmark, where there is much discussion about the government trying to limit student choice and focusing on only the economic benefits of study programmes; and in Spain, where the emphasis in the media is on lack of jobs rather than students making 'wrong' or 'irrational' choices. The following articles highlight the limits of rational choice logic when it comes to students' decision-making processes:

'Students do not know what they can become' (*BT*, 11 February 2015)

'Studying the future; You can make a career even in unusual subjects if important trends are identified' (*Die Welt*, 28 November 2015)

A variation of the construction of students as rational choosers, in the media, is the construction of disillusioned students who do not get the expected economic returns, despite having invested in their studies and made the 'right' choices. This is particularly strong in England in the context of tuition fees; however, similar examples can be found in newspapers in the other five countries. Within this type of article, such individuals are often perceived as future graduates at risk of unemployment, and institutions (and in some cases governments) are blamed for inadequately preparing them for the labour market.

'Students expect better jobs than they'll get, survey shows' (*The Guardian*, 26 June 2014)

'Too many people risk ending up with a useless education' (*Politiken*, 12 September 2016)

'A doctor [PhD] is poorer than an engineer' (*Gazeta Wyborcza*, 26 February 2014)

'70,000 graduates are working in jobs which do not demand any formal qualifications' (*El País*, 8 July 2014)

Student perspectives on their collective economic framing as human capital

Despite the strength of human capital discourse within policy and some newspapers, students rarely viewed themselves as a collective economic resource or as a part of an economic competitiveness story. However, when they did so, several notable cross-national differences appeared. We discuss these minority views in this section.

In Ireland, England and Poland, in contrast to the other three countries that will be discussed below, there was very little discussion of being understood as a collective economic resource.

In Ireland, when it *was* mentioned in focus groups, students tended to repeat dominant policy narratives about the importance of a 'knowledge economy' to a small country such as Ireland. Some Irish students understood the purpose of HE as creating capable and educated workers (Focus groups, Irish HEI3_3 and HEI2_1) and spoke of politicians seeing students as the future labour force (Focus group, Irish HEI2_2). Occasionally, this view was critiqued by some Irish students, commenting that the government focuses only on their economic value (Focus group, Irish HEI2_1). In England and Poland, this macro-economic growth discourse (emphasising benefit to the nation-state, for example) was less present than in Ireland, reflecting policy and media narratives in both countries where emphasis is placed on *individual* returns from HE, not those that might accrue to wider society. Indeed, the Polish students in our focus groups never discussed themselves in macro-economic terms. In England, on rare occasions when a macro-economic framing of students appeared, it was typically part of a criticism of politicians who were accused of viewing students as "a source of income for the future, we're the people who will be making the money for them" (Focus group, English HEI2_1) or, framed more positively, as a resource crucial for long-term economic stability (for example, the country needs "students who can earn a good deal of money to pay for social care for the older generations" (Focus group, English HEI1_2)).

In Denmark, Germany and Spain, a macro-economic framing of students was problematised by students, in some cases in very strong terms and with different rationales. Danish students felt that the policy reforms aimed at speeding up their progress through their degree made them feel more like workers-in-the-making, as the government was pushing them to get out of HE and into the labour market faster, so they could start paying taxes sooner. In contrast, they considered themselves as a resource for society on the basis of their critical thinking, not just their economic contribution: "I don't want to be a [resource] for industry, I want to be a [resource] for society" (Focus group, Danish HEI3_2). The main way in which Danish students talked about their role in society, with respect to the labour market, was in terms of them benefiting the country by becoming educated and making Denmark more globally competitive as a 'knowledge society' (deemed particularly important because of the country's small size). In this way, the connection with the labour market was usually discussed at a societal – rather than individual – level.

Interestingly, students also spoke of getting a free education and feeling that they should return this investment by working for society. Thus, Danish students did partially recognise and accept a macro-economic role, but this was typically discussed in collective and social democratic terms, with respect to giving back to society and the welfare state. They were not, therefore, reproducing an understanding of the future worker informed strictly by human capital theory.

Similarly, in Germany, although students acknowledged that they were indeed potential employees and employers, they believed that the emphasis of the state, and wider society, on them as future workers was a reductive view. They rejected the macro-economic construction of them as the future labour force (informed by human capital ideas) on humanistic grounds, asserting that the "human dimension is missing somewhat" when they are understood merely "as a machine in the economic system" (Focus group, German HEI3_3).

The most vocal criticisms of macro-economic framings of students as the future workforce came from Spanish students, who did sometimes position themselves as an economic resource but spoke about this in terms of exploitation and "working for the system" or, as evident in the excerpt below, just a "coin".

'Well, I think that right now we are a coin [a unit of currency] in that we are not being used but we are all going to facilitate others to make money, let's say. This is not going to be useful only to us but we are going to make money for others who are going to use us. This is what I think it is to be a student.' (Focus group, Spanish HEI3_3)

In similar critical tones, Spanish students discussed being seen by the country and politicians as a resource for the national economy, which is then wasted when highly skilled workers leave Spain because they cannot find jobs there (a view echoed by some staff). In this way, the (over-)optimistic discourse of human capital development reaches an ironic turn, faced with the harsh economic realities of graduate labour markets.

In summary, we saw in the previous sections that policy discourse and, to a lesser extent, media narratives in all our countries tend to construct students collectively as a macro-economic asset, in line with the economic theory of human capital development (although this is much less evident in Germany and Spain). However, staff and students (especially those in Denmark, Germany and Spain) tended to reject a macro-economic construction of themselves collectively as a future productive labour force. In the next section, we move to a more micro-level perspective to discuss the framing of students as rational choosers, in line with the logic of human capital theory.

Students' perspectives on themselves as rational choosers in search for high incomes

Within human capital theory-informed discourse, students are typically constructed as future workers and as individual, rational choosers who weigh up the costs and benefits of participating in education (Becker, 1993). Each student is seen primarily as a '*Homo economicus*' who makes decisions in a utilitarian and self-optimising manner to maximise their labour market potential (Tomlinson, 2008). They are held to prioritise higher earnings (graduate premiums) and/or better occupations with greater earning potential in the future. We have seen in previous sections that framing students' decisions in terms of rational choice is evident within policy and parts of the media.

In contrast, our focus group data indicate that it was relatively rare for students to discuss their own (individual) HE paths and biographies in terms of rational choices aimed at maximising incomes and career prospects (see also discussion in Chapter 2 on transitions to adulthood and in Chapter 4 on approaches to learning). Rather than pursuing instrumental choices in line with the assumptions of human capital theory, the HE decisions of many students across all six countries were very similar to what Hodkinson et al (2013) call 'pragmatically rational choices'. Rationales for study were typically structured around the options that they perceived to be available to them, and were closely bound to their inner learning biographies, that is, retrospective stories about learning and self-discovery (Tomlinson, 2008). They also acknowledged that their HE choices had often been influenced by peers and family, too. Typical of such narratives are students' comments about having "no other options than to go to university"; a belief that university is the "normal thing to do after school"; attitudes such as "it was taken for granted that you will go to university"; university as an "obvious choice", presumably "because that's just what you're expected to do, because everyone else starts studying"; and, finally, simply "I was raised in that manner" (see also Chapter 2). In many previous studies, such rationales have been described as characteristic of middle-class narratives about HE (Reay et al, 2009) although, in our data, as we explained in Chapter 2, we found little connection between socio-economic background and these kinds of statement.

While such types of narrative were the most common explanation of why the students in our research chose to pursue HE, other rationales were also given. For example, some participants explained their decision in terms of positional competition in the labour market (a 'need to stand out') and the belief that, for almost all occupations nowadays, one needs an educational credential (discussed below in relation to credentialist understandings of the 'future worker'). Others explained how they had decided to progress to HE because of a passion for a particular subject and/or the aim of following a specific profession (a vocation discourse). Equally, some students framed their decision to pursue HE as part of an individual personal and professional identity journey (consistent with the discourse of *Bildung*) (see also Chapter 4).

The rarest responses to the question of why our participants had chosen to embark on HE were those that were purely economic in nature and in line with the assumptions of human capital theory. Very few students justified their decision to study in terms of higher future incomes, for example, "better money in the long term" (Focus group, Irish HEI1_2) or "I just wanted a bigger pay rise, when I get my job!" (Focus group, English HEI1_2). In other rare instances where student narratives were aligned with human capital discourse, participants tended to focus on the concept of 'good jobs', understood as those that are well-paid or provide "enough money to move out of [the] house" (Focus group, English HEI3_2). Such comments were invoked to describe both their individual desires with respect to social mobility, and also their understanding of the purpose of HE. This extract from an Irish focus group (Irish HEI1_1) illustrates such economic rationalisations by students:

Focus group participant:	Yeah, it's very hard to get a job in this country if you don't have a degree. [agreement of the rest] And well it's like, you will get a job, but a well-paid job … Just, well, like, the price of living in this country is particularly high, so you really need a job that pays well to kind of have a good life.
Interviewer:	OK and that's, for you, college is the way to get that, is it?
Focus group participant:	Hopefully! [all laugh]

Such instrumental voices came primarily from focus groups in England and Ireland (and Denmark, to some extent) – and, in these countries, from students at institutions offering more applied studies. Laughter and humour often accompanied such claims, indicating a sense of discomfort. Such interventions can be understood as a means of students trying to distance themselves from a materialist narrative when they enact subjectivities promoted by the dominant policy discourse (Maguire et al, 2018). Such behaviour also perhaps hints at some implicit mistrust among students in public discourses about the economic value of their degrees. As we will see in the following section, this mistrust was very often linked to perceptions about increased positional competition and credential inflation – both of which were believed to make future work pursuits challenging.

Credentialist discourse

One of the major findings of our research is that European students do not internalise constructions of themselves as future workers in terms of the human capital discourse propagated by policy and parts of the media. However, with some national variations, they share a very credentialist understanding of HE and how labour markets function. In this section, we outline the key conceptual differences between human capital theory and credentialism.

In contrast to human capital theory, those adhering to credentialism view the labour market as based on the principles of occupational closure (Weeden, 2002), in which access to occupations is limited to holders of specific credentials. Authors such as Collins (1979) argue that the spread of educational credentials adds little or no value to individuals' human capital in terms of actual competences and skills, and explain the expansion of HE (and the consequent growth in credentials) as caused by the expansion of the middle classes, who have become involved in positional competition (Bourdieu et al, 1977; Brown, 2013). This explains both the growing pressure for individuals to acquire further credentials to access jobs, and the reduction of educational credentials to having primarily a symbolic value – merely a 'piece of paper' or 'a tick in the box'. As Tomlinson (2008) explains, 'instead of reflecting an increase in the skills and knowledge demands needed to *do jobs*, the upsurge in higher education credentials simply means that the stakes have been raised for what is needed to *get jobs*' (p 50).

Another characteristic of credentialist discourse is its understanding of the labour market in terms of screening and signalling theory (Spence, 1973; Bills, 2003), in which employers have difficulty recognising the actual skills and abilities of candidates due to an asymmetry of information (Spence, 1973). Unable to assess the productivity of potential employees, employers rely on proxies, signals and/or previous experience when recruiting. Educational credentials from different institutions serve as important signals for general abilities and a willingness to learn, but do not indicate actual concrete skills or abilities. Aside from educational credentials, employers may value other symbols including social characteristics (such as family background), appearance, letters of recommendation and previous experience (Weiss et al, 2014; Rivera, 2015).

Understanding the education/labour market relationship in terms of intensifying positional competition, constructs students, individually, as constant seekers of distinction and, collectively, as people forced to participate in fierce competition in a very congested labour market (Brown, 2013). In such markets, the value of credentials for the purposes of signalling and distinction has declined (Brown and Souto-Otero, 2020), and thus graduates are pressured to find other ways to stand out (higher degrees, better grades, extra-curricular activities, more experience on the CV, and so on).

Our study found very clear elements of a credentialist view of the relationship between education and employment among students in Europe when they were asked about the purpose of education, their individual goals, their labour market chances and their role as future workers. Given the massification of HE in most of our countries (with the exception of Germany) and the associated increased pressure in the graduate labour market felt by our respondents, a credentialism discourse is to be expected. This was, however, less present in Denmark, Germany and Poland than in Ireland, England and Spain – reflecting the fact that the former typically have more specialised degrees than the other three countries, with clearer routes into the labour market as a result (Teichler and Kehm, 1995; Teichler, 2009). In such occupationally specialised labour markets, concerns about credential inflation and social congestion are weaker than in less occupationally specialised and more flexible labour markets, such as in many Anglophone countries and Spain (Gangl, 2001; Müller and Gangl, 2003). Indeed, concerns were articulated particularly clearly within the Spanish focus groups, where perceptions about labour market congestion in the graduate labour market were heightened by the economic crisis and high youth and graduate unemployment (see Chapter 1).

In the rest of this section, we outline some forms that the credentialist discourse took among the students in our focus groups. They often discussed HE degrees as having been reduced to their symbolic values: a 'certificate' or 'piece of paper' needed for positional advantage in the labour market. This view of certificates as symbolic currency within positional competition is expressed through three different types of student narrative. The first narrative places emphasis on comparisons with people without degrees and the relative chance of success if one does not have a degree. The second narrative focuses on credential inflation, perceived in largely negative terms, and deemed to have been exacerbated by the behaviour of employers. Finally, the third narrative foregrounds the increased competition among students caused by credentialism and its perceived negative consequences.

Comparative chances of success without a degree

Students, particularly in Spain, Ireland and England, discussed university degrees as tools that give them a positional advantage in the labour market compared with people who do not have such qualifications. Acquisition of these tools was identified as one of the reasons for going to university. Focus group participants saw HE as something "to aspire to and which would improve their social status", allowing them to "have more advantages than other people who could not go to university and study" (Focus group,

Spanish HEI1_3). Students, especially in these three countries, often viewed credentialism as a rampant trend, remarking that many occupations that now require a university certificate did not ask for one previously (Baker, 2011).

Possible alternative paths to obtain useful credentials for the labour market, other than a university degree, were typically seen as not sufficiently rewarding or as undesirable in the positional competition by students in Poland and Spain. Options such as apprenticeships in Denmark, England or Ireland were barely even mentioned, likely because, in these countries, vocational training is already organised within specialised HE institutions (institutes of technology in Ireland, universities of professional studies in Denmark) or under-developed institutionally (England).

Credentials as ever-inflating 'pieces of paper'

When asked about the purpose of HE, students in Spain, England, Ireland and (in one focus group in) Germany typically expressed a credentialist understanding of HE – that is, they viewed it as a means of acquiring 'pieces of paper' which allow them entry to the labour market and thus the competition for jobs. Here, degrees are largely seen in terms of providing a positional advantage in the graduate market, similar to findings from previous research (Tomlinson, 2008). Again, in line with signalling theory, what is actually learnt at university is often described as not very relevant for labour market success. In this extract, for example, Spanish students describe credential inflation and discuss an ongoing scandal at one university that awarded a master's degree illicitly to a politician, which led to a wave of investigations into politicians' degrees. Again, humour and laughter show discomfort with the perceived necessity to pursue credentials in this way, while employers are largely blamed for this situation.

Interviewer:	What do you think is the purpose of university?
Focus group participant 1:	To obtain a piece of paper which says that you have studied something.
Interviewer:	To have a certificate.
Focus group participant 1:	There are so many of us. I believe there has been a fashion for getting a degree in general, so there has been a deluge of students and there comes a time when you have so many with degrees, that it doesn't matter if you've been to university or not these days, it's the most common thing in the world, so it has lost its value.

Focus group participant 2:	Now you have to have a master's degree, all the time higher qualifications, higher, higher. [Laughter]
Interviewer:	Are you describing a particular case? [Laughter]
Focus group participant 3:	The people who have finished [their degree] say to you, 'No, all that you learned at university doesn't count for anything, because when you start work you're like ... you haven't learned anything'. And you would think that if you have studied for four years, then when the day arrived to enter the labour market it would be of some use to you.
Focus group participant 4:	Then when you arrive to begin your work experience, they say to you, 'OK, go and serve coffee,' and you say, 'But what's this?'
Focus group participant 5:	And more so these days when a master's is worth more than a [bachelor's] degree, so it seems.
Focus group participant 6:	OK, recently I think they [master's degrees] have been devalued a little, above all those from the university of [name of the other university in their city], ha, ha, ha. [everybody laughs]. (Focus group, Spanish HEI3_1)

Similar examples can be found in England and Ireland, especially among students from lower-ranking institutions. A slight variation in the general narrative about credential inflation is evident in Poland and Germany, while it was least present among Danish students. In Poland, the discourse of wanting 'a piece of paper' was discussed more in terms of the characteristics of perceived 'instrumental' students who choose business degrees and social sciences over STEM subjects and students who 'don't care, they don't work hard'. In general, Polish students did not reduce their potential degrees to only pieces of paper, typically viewing them instead in terms of the skills, abilities and/or knowledge for which they have to work hard. In Germany, on the other hand, credentialism ("You just have to have the piece of paper", Focus group, German HEI3_3) is placed within the overall political and social ethos of the so-called 'performance society' (*Leistungsgesellschaft*), propagated by centre-right German governments as a German version of the ideal meritocratic society (Böhme, 2010). From this perspective, education and training efforts are valued highly as genuine symbols of merit and performance as long as they are formally certified so they can be verified by bureaucratic procedures in the public and private sectors. Within the 'performance society' ideal, individual merit and effort are almost always rewarded if properly certified in compliance with bureaucratic rationality. Consequently, people are encouraged to secure certification in every activity they do. As a practical consequence, in the German labour market it is quite usual for employers to request certification for every single item mentioned on a graduate's CV and application.

Positional competition and its consequences

To some degree in all our countries, there was a recurring perception in the focus groups that students are required to obtain HE degrees in order to stand out in the labour market, and that this includes competing for credentials:

> 'I think a little of it is credentialism for credentialism's sake, that is, "If you don't have a certificate, you're not going to get a decent salary," so it doesn't matter what you study. To study is a means of gaining entry to a group of people who can earn a little more than the people who haven't studied … I think they are all formalities, including a master's degree.' (Focus group, Spanish HEI1_3)

In the four countries where the credentialist discourse is strongest (Spain, Ireland, England and to some extent Poland), emphasis was placed on gathering extra value and distinction for HE credentials through participating in extra-curricular activities, optional projects and so on. This was seen as a way of 'standing apart' from other graduates with similar profiles and achievements: "You've got to have the degree but then you've got to have the bonuses on top of it as well" (Focus group, English HEI3_2). Student narratives in England were much more individualised than in the other five countries, with responsibility for obtaining these additional 'bonuses for the CV' seen as lying solely with students themselves. In other countries where this 'standing out' discourse was strong, namely Spain, Ireland and Poland, students viewed it more as a shared responsibility of both students and institutions.

In Germany, this issue is discursively framed around differences in the value of bachelor's and master's degrees, following reforms introduced by the Bologna Process (see Chapter 1). In particular, it is discussed in terms of the contested issue of whether a bachelor's degree is sufficient for competition in the labour market or whether a master's degree is required. Some students considered the bachelor's to be "half a degree" and felt that students "have to do a master's in order to make anything of yourself". At the same time, others stated that employers insist that students do not pursue an additional degree: "You don't really need a master's, it won't be of any use to you anyway. We'll teach you everything you need to know. And um, there's no point in doing a master's" (Focus group, German HEI3_1). Students felt that employers say this because they can pay less to those who do not hold such a qualification.

Increased positional competition has consequences in terms of interpersonal relations between students and levels of stress (see Chapter 6). Students in Spain and England reported very high levels of fierce and stressful competition – for higher marks in Spain ("You don't know the trauma I had") and for activities to add to their CV in England ("I felt a massive pressure to, you know, sort of make myself worthwhile for employers"): "I have noticed that there is a lot of competitiveness in the university, between the students, [who are not willing] to lend you their notes because [they say]; 'I want to have better marks than you and stand out more' ... it's like everybody looks after themselves and that's it" (Focus group, Spanish HEI3_3).

As we can see from the data presented so far in this chapter, the construction of students as future workers is strong. Nevertheless, students do not understand this construction in terms of the human capital approaches that dominate policy and some media discourses about HE. Instead, the majority of students – especially in England, Ireland, Poland and Spain – viewed the relationship between HE and work very much in credentialist terms. Becoming a future worker is thus seen not as something that automatically follows from personal investment in HE (as the human capital approach would suggest) but rather as an identity realised only through fierce positional competition, based on credentials and other symbols. The students we spoke to felt forced to participate in such competition, but uncomfortable about doing so – blaming employers for creating such conditions and institutions for not offering sufficient support to obtain the much-needed advantage.

Discourses of opposition: vocationalism and *Bildung*

Acts of discursive contestation of, and disagreement with, the dominant policy discourse can come in many forms. We have seen, for instance, that the discussion of HE in terms of human capital or descriptions of the pursuit of credentials were very often accompanied by humour and laughter (as well as sarcasm and irony) which can be interpreted as acts of 'everyday resistance' and a means of distancing oneself from aspects of reality that are considered disturbing (Scott, 2005 in Amoore, 2005). A sizeable minority of our student and staff participants go further, however, criticising contemporary policy constructions of students as future workers much more actively.

In these expressions of opposition to dominant discourses, staff and students rely on different discursive strands coming from non-economic ideas about education itself: those associated with vocation and *Bildung*. Here we outline these two major alternative discourses, which contest the construction of student as future worker. Both are based on the assumption that the understanding of students as 'future workers' has been hijacked by a pervasive narrative of human capital development, which foregrounds economic rationality. These contra-discourses see students as future workers guided by more internally driven values about life and work (vocation) or as a result of processes of self-development and self-realisation (*Bildung*); moreover, both emphasise the contribution of education to the public good and wider society, rather than to individuals.

Vocation

The term 'vocation' in the context of HE is a highly charged word, yet it implies a very specific understanding of the role of education and its links with the world of work. Originating from both Catholic and Protestant religious traditions, the ancient Greek concept of κλῆσις [klēsis] ('vocation' or 'calling'; in German *Beruf* or *Berufung*) was reinterpreted by Luther and Calvin in the sense of the spiritualisation of worldly activities, and subsequently politicised by Weber in *The Protestant Ethic and the Spirit of Capitalism* (Frey, 2008). The concept of a vocation is thus secularised and yet, simultaneously, the concepts of study, work and career choice are understood in terms of devotion and passion. Without this conceptual understanding of vocational pursuits, it is hard to comprehend fully the discussions about passion in our student focus groups – which were most prominent in Ireland, and then Poland, Denmark and England. In a vocational understanding of the world, individuals should find and then fulfil their own unique calling. Universities are places where one finds one's true calling and passion for a subject and/ or an interest in a profession (another Latin term with religious etymology). Alternatively, in the case that a vocation is found before entering HE, universities become places to obtain the necessary training and certification that enable that vocation to be realised. Moreover, the labour market is not seen as a place of competition but, rather, one where vocation becomes materialised in the form of a profession and, preferably, a lifelong career. Material rewards are of secondary concern.

This view occurs relatively frequently among students. For instance, in our focus groups in all countries, a vocal minority of students described their reasons for studying in terms of having a vocation in mind (teaching, journalism, urban planning, veterinary science and so on), or wanting to study for a vocation from a young age, for which a degree was a requirement. This is not always linked to a typical profession but could also be a passion for a specific subject: "I felt I had a vocation. I don't know, I felt it was something I had to do and I did it, I don't believe I have made a mistake.

... Yes, I wanted to study philosophy and I would like to dedicate my life to it" (Focus group, Spanish HEI3_1).

The vocational world view is in conflict with both human capital discourse (and its concept of the future worker as a rationally calculating economic resource), and credentialism (in which the future worker is one who wins a positional competition through the acquisition of numerous certificates and other symbols). Unlike these two perspectives, a vocational perspective sees value beyond mere material and/or positional gain. This is played out in our data. For instance, students asserted that viewing them as future workers was only a good thing "if you're doing something that you're really passionate about" (Focus group, English HEI3_2); that people who do not have this passion "end up hating it [their job] in the future and end up regretting it immensely" (Focus group, Irish HEI3_2); and that one should do "something that you like, because then you can get a job in it and it won't be a job, it will be something you like doing" (Focus group, Irish HEI2_2).

Along similar lines, students (particularly in Poland) were often critical of purely credentialist motives: "Somewhere at the end they want to get this piece of paper. ... It's all devoid of meaning. ... They don't become students because of some calling, because they decide on that, but because everyone else goes" (Focus group, Polish HEI3_2).

Similarly, staff also used vocational arguments to express their opposition to the construction of future workers as individuals who act opportunistically in the labour market and do not have a calling. They believed that such constructions encouraged students to focus solely on studying to secure a job, which then often divorced them from their passions – "they come away from their interests" (Staff member, Irish HEI2_1). One Polish staff member articulated her challenge to the construction of students as instrumental future workers clearly in vocationalist terms:

I think you should study, you should always study a course that you are interested in, not because perhaps I will find a job later on if I do a degree in this and that, because if you're not interested in what you do, you will never be good at it, in my opinion. (Staff member, Polish HEI1_2)

Although the vocationalist worldview foregrounds work as an important part of human existence, it reinterprets the construction of students as future workers. Within a vocation discourse, fulfilment through the world of work remains an essential aim, but this aim is understood as a passionate fulfilment of a calling or vocation. It is thus in clear opposition to the economic logic of human capital that sees students primarily as '*Homo economicus*'.

Bildung

One should not underestimate the role of education as a primary social institution (Baker, 2014), which not only follows the needs of the economy and wider society but redefines them with its underlying values and philosophy. Educational philosophy can shape understandings of student (and staff) identities and the roles they play both within universities and when they enter the world of work. One of these fundamental educational ideologies is centred around the German concept of *Bildung* (Danish *Dannelse*) that cannot be translated directly into English, but loosely means 'cultivation', 'edification', 'personal development', 'self-formation' or 'character formation' (see Chapter 1). This is a concept with both educational and political dimensions and has a very long history in European philosophy centred around the question of what constitutes an educated or cultivated human being (Biesta, 2002; Horlacher, 2015; Rømer, 2021). It is central to the Humboldtian university model and the pedagogical approach called *Didaktik* that underpins European continental teaching practice, from early schooling to university (Hopmann, 2007; Hudson, 2007; Hansen, 2008).

Students and staff, particularly in Germany and Denmark, used the ideology underlying the concept of *Bildung* to contest the discourse of student as future worker and related policies that seek closer alignment of education with immediate labour market needs. Inherent in *Bildung* is the idea that humans are beings with 'potential to become self-motivated and self-directing', while the task of education is one of bringing about or releasing this potential 'so that subjects become fully autonomous and capable of exercising their individual and intentional agency' (Edwards and Usher, 1994: 24–25) and do not unthinkingly conform to pre-set external social and economic expectations. (This has some similarities to the concept of 'subjectification' that we discussed in Chapter 3.) The Enlightenment answer to the question of what constitutes an educated or cultivated human being is not given in terms of discipline, society or morals – as an adaptation to an existing 'external' order (including the demands of the labour market) – but in the understanding of *Bildung* as the cultivation of the inner life, that is, the human mind or human soul: self-*Bildung* (Biesta, 2002). In the open-ended educational process of *Bildung*, people become world-wise by finding themselves and their place in the world (Rømer, 2021). The words that characterise this discourse, and that were also often mentioned in the focus groups, are 'personal development', 'growth', 'open(ing) minds', 'providing different angles', 'broad(ening) horizons', 'self-reflection', 'finding one's own path', 'personal journey', 'engaging (actively) with the world', 'whole person' and so on. We find these words in many of our students' narratives (see also the discussion about *Bildung* in Chapter 2 in relation to the growing up/being grown-up discourse in Germany and Denmark, and in Chapter 4 with respect to non-instrumental approaches to learning).

Given the strength of *Bildung* traditions, particularly in Germany and Nordic countries, it is unsurprising that the *Bildung* discourse was found in many staff reactions to the construction of students as future workers and in opposition to the perceived credentialist reality of 'studying just for a degree'. In most cases staff realised it is also an "old way of thinking" (Staff member, Danish HEI1_3) and an unrealised ideal that people do not necessarily follow in practice (Staff member, German HEI3_1). The *Bildung* discourse of contestation of the reductive 'anti-human', 'not transformative enough' future worker construction is almost always formulated in the 'Yes, but ...' or 'It is also ...' forms, as illustrated in these two extracts:

'But there's still a very strong sense between the students, also [within] academia in Denmark, but also on the political level of Denmark, that pursuing a university programme is also the shaping, shaping your personality somehow, in Danish we call it *Dannelse*. And that's also a role of, of university students. It's not only to learn the academic trade.' (Staff member, Danish HEI1_1)

'I do think education, higher education certainly as, yes preparing for a labour market, but also personal development ... When you look at the word "education" in the Latin original, it means to *educe*, to draw out. Not to stuff in! Not push forward, to draw out what is already there and to help develop that and unfold it. ... The labour market is part of what we're dealing with, but it's not all there is to being a student.' (Staff member, German HEI1_4)

The *Bildung* discourse and implied vision of education as personal development is also very visible in student narratives about the purposes of HE and when asked about whether they understood themselves as future workers. Again, similar to staff, *Bildung* discourse was strongest among Danish and German students and some students in Spain. Danish students spoke of becoming a 'better human' through HE and 'evolving', or described the purpose of education in Humboldtian terms – contending that societal development could and should be achieved through personal development (see also the discussion of the transition to adulthood in Chapter 2): "I think it [the purpose of HE] is to develop society! [agreement] Just keep growing and doing something new, yeah. Discovering new things. But just not for the society, only ... also for yourself, like personal development" (Focus group, Danish HEI1_3).

Similarly, German students saw university as a place to develop "as [a] person ... how a person defines him or herself and what their attitude is to the world" (Focus group, German HEI3_2). Spanish students in some cases (when not talking about credentialism) also explained the purposes of university as "cultivation and … personal improvement" (Focus group, Spanish HEI1_1).

Students, particularly those in Germany and Denmark, used *Bildung* discourses to criticise the construct of students as future workers and studying just to be a professional. One Danish student, for instance, used a tree metaphor (reflecting the various nature and plant analogies often used in the Enlightenment and *Bildung* philosophy):

> 'It's not just, OK, you're studying nursing so you're going to become a nurse and, you know, be valuable, and then if I don't do that, you know, I'm just trash. It's not like that, no. We're not just a bucket you can just fill up, we're still … We're like a tree, we can grow different ways, you know …! And no matter what, we'll be beautiful! Well, personal growth, you know, that's … a big thing.' (Focus group, Danish HEI2_1)

German students also used the idea of *Bildung* as self-formation to criticise attempts to shape HE in accordance with the need of the labour market, under the influence of companies:

> 'The important thing is that you're there to serve a commercial purpose and nothing more, that you're not studying to achieve something for yourself but for others, for the economy, and I find that really annoying because it's not my idea of studying, which is about forming and educating yourself.' (Focus group, German HEI1_3)

They felt also that the 'future employee' narrative stifles the intellectual development of people, and their creativity, with its focus on imminent labour market needs. One student, for example, stressed, "We are, or at least were, a nation of poets and thinkers … Of course, we still have a pioneering role intellectually … we also have the opportunity to aspire to individual achievements which promote ideas, irrespective of which facets prevail" (Focus group, German HEI2_3).

As we can see, the discourse of *Bildung* is a clear case of how rich educational and intellectual traditions can profoundly shape understandings of student and staff identities and can be used effectively to contest macro narratives of human capital development and related constructions of students as future workers.

Conclusion

This chapter has shown how the construction of students as future workers is important to all the social actors involved in our study. Within policy and, to a lesser extent, the media, future workers were understood in terms of human capital – and this was common across all six countries in our sample. This discourse was strongest in England, Ireland, Denmark and Poland – and weakest in Spain and Germany. (To some extent this reflects the wider welfare regime in the various nations. Neo-liberal ideas have, to date, been less influential in the HE sectors in Spain and Germany than in the other four nations.) Nevertheless, students mostly did not enact the prescriptions of human capital discourse. They did not position themselves as rational choice-makers seeking higher earnings, nor did they see their wider collective role as a national economic resource. Instead, they understood themselves as future workers in an almost procedural and formal way, viewing work and employment as a 'natural' next stage of their lives. Moreover, human capital discourse was critiqued by students for overpromising – offering prospects without any guarantee that they would be realised. Labour market realities were perceived, instead, in terms of an increasingly congested positional competition (Brown, 2013) based on credentials. Such perceptions were strongest in countries which have less occupationally and educationally specialised graduate labour markets (England and Ireland) or that have experienced devastating effects of economic crisis on youth employment (Spain).

We have also shown how both students and staff offered substantial critiques of an understanding of 'future workers' grounded in ideas associated with human capital. These critiques – underpinned by the concepts of vocation and *Bildung* – were evident in many narratives from staff and students, across all six countries. They were particularly marked, however, in Germany and Denmark due to specific deeply rooted cultural traditions about education in these countries. These counter-discourses emphasised the non-economic value of both education and work, and constructed students as future workers in more humanistic terms – guided by more internally generated values about life and work (vocation) – or as engaged in a process of self-development and self-realisation (*Bildung*). Both emphasise the public good contribution and societal impact of education and work, rather than individual gains. They thus represent strong indications that alternative policy realities are both possible and feasible in contemporary Europe.

6

Stressed

Introduction

In general, and as we have shown in various of the preceding chapters, the students who participated in our research saw themselves in largely positive terms, emphasising their enthusiasm for their studies, their willingness to work hard and their desire to contribute in an active manner to the society around them. However, such understandings were sometimes held in tension with a number of less upbeat constructions. Indeed, across the sample as a whole, students were often seen, by themselves and others, as stressed (often acutely) – with negative consequences for their academic studies and wider lives.

In this chapter, we explore this construction in detail, examining some broad trends that held across most of the six nations in our research. We also consider the exception of Poland, where there was a notable absence of any reference to stress or related conditions, and the curious case of Spain, where stress was discussed at length by students but not reflected at all in the narratives of other social actors. We first situate our discussion within the extant research on students' mental wellbeing (noting, however, the relative dearth of comparative studies in this area). Although stress, in itself, is not a mental illness and can sometimes have a positive impact, from a biomedical perspective, prolonged stress can increase the risk of mental ill health. Moreover, student stress is commonly viewed as impacting negatively on general wellbeing and is often conflated with mental illness (for example, YouGov, 2016). We then examine the prevalence of the construction of students as stressed across the dataset, showing that it was common in all countries apart from Poland. Following this, we explore the likely reasons for this prevalence, often drawing on the explanations offered by our participants. These include a range of immediate concerns – such as the need to juggle multiple commitments, the pressure to work harder and faster, and apprehension about moving from education into full-time work – as well as broader societal phenomena such as an increase in societal individualism and competition, and changes to social norms around disclosure of mental distress.

Understanding students' mental wellbeing

The mental wellbeing of HE students has become of increasing interest to policymakers and HE practitioners over recent years. There has been concern at the high prevalence of mental health problems (particularly depression and anxiety) among HE students as well as at their rate of increase (Storrie et al, 2010; Neves and Hillman, 2018; Duffy et al, 2020). There is less consensus, however, about whether students are more likely to suffer mental ill health than their non-student peers. While UK and Australian research has indicated that, on average, students had lower mental distress scores than the general population (Cvetkovski et al, 2019; Tabor et al, 2021), not all studies have reached the same conclusion (see, for example, Larcombe et al, 2016). Nevertheless, irrespective of whether the student population differs from the wider population in this respect, mental ill health affects a relatively large number of individuals – 20 per cent of all students involved in Auerbach et al's (2016) research reported mental health problems over a 12-month period – and has been shown to be associated with particular campus-wide problems. For example, Hirsch and Khan (2020) argue that the widespread sexual assault that has taken place within American universities can be considered both a cause and consequence of students' mental health struggles. While, as noted above, stress is not, in itself, a mental illness, the two are often closely bound together. For example, concern about the prevalence of mental health conditions has resulted in a wide variety of university-led interventions intended to build resilience and reduce susceptibility to stress, anxiety and the like (for example, Holdsworth et al, 2018; Pappa et al, 2020). Furthermore, both stress and mental health struggles are seen by some as part of the collective identity of being a university student (Ask and Abidin, 2018), reinforced through media discourse (Williams, 2011; Calver and Michael-Fox, 2021).

While much of the literature in this area tends to explain student stress and other potential threats to students' mental health and wellbeing by recourse to individual-level psychological attributes, a small number of scholars have employed a wider analytical lens and explored the impact of social, economic and institutional factors. Writing with respect to the US, Walsemann et al (2015) have argued that the taking on of loans to finance HE courses can have an adverse effect on students' mental wellbeing while, in Australia, Larcombe et al (2016) contend that caring responsibilities and hours available for study both impact on students' experiences of psychological distress. Bristow et al (2020) make similar arguments on the basis of their English research, arguing that students have been placed in new positions of vulnerability through 'the dominance of a moral economy within the university that emphasises neo-liberalism and competition' (p 93) and the structural inequalities that have been thrown into sharp relief by efforts to widen participation. They also suggest that changing cultural idioms of distress may be at play. They write: 'Explaining difficulties in terms of mental fragility and compromised wellbeing may be, we suggest, propagated and sanctioned by the very university policies designed to redress the problem' (p 97). Drawing on the concept of 'cognitive availability' (that is, the idea that an action, response or description becomes available to an individual when they are exposed to that idea), Bristow et al contend that the discourses used within HE institutions and broader society may encourage students to turn to psychiatric and psychological vocabularies to make sense of their university experiences. Here, there are parallels with those who have argued that students are increasingly positioned by the media, politicians and policymakers as vulnerable and fragile (Finn et al, 2021) and that this alleged vulnerability has driven a 'therapeutic turn' in education (Ecclestone and Hayes, 2009) (we discuss this further in Chapter 7). (See also the 'safetyism' mentioned in Chapter 1, in relation to putative 'culture wars'.)

Although these researchers have helpfully shifted the focus away from individually focused explanations to those that are more structural and/or collective in orientation, to date there are few studies that have explored the extent to which stress and other potential threats to students' wellbeing may vary across nation-state. Eskin et al's (2016) study is a notable exception but includes only three European countries in its sample and focuses solely on very severe psychological distress. Bregnbaek's (2016) ethnography of students attending two of China's top universities describes vividly the psychological strains experienced by this 'fragile elite' as a result of the pressure placed upon them by their parents and the state and does relate this to the specific national context, namely China's one-child policy (that was in place from 1979–2015) and the particular political system. Nevertheless, without comparative data, it is hard to draw any conclusions about the extent to which their stress and anxiety should be considered unique. The remainder of this chapter begins to fill this gap.

Stressed as common construction

As noted above, across our dataset, one of the most common understandings of students was as stressed. This was evident in all countries with the exception of Poland (considered below), although in Spain it was discussed only by students rather than the other types of social actor (explored in a later section of the chapter).

In some cases, this construction was bound up with contentions about the poor mental health of students more generally. This was particularly pronounced in England, where newspapers ran stories with headlines such as 'Bristol student deaths highlight campus crisis in mental health' (*The Guardian*, 26 November 2016), and 'Universities need to do more to protect students' mental health. But how?' (*The Guardian*, 22 September 2016), and the TV series *Fresh Meat* depicts Vod, one of the main characters, visiting a therapist at the university wellbeing centre. Moreover, a member of staff at one of the English HEIs in our sample claimed that it was important that HE taught students how to become more resilient, as so many of them had mental health problems – echoing Bristow et al's (2020) contention that the responsibility for responding to what it presented as a mental health 'crisis' in England often falls on the HE sector. Similar themes were prominent in Ireland, within the media in particular, emphasising the importance of universities in supporting students' mental wellbeing – evident in Connell's visit to the university counselling service in *Normal People*, and numerous articles on this theme in *The Irish Times*.

In other nations, while research participants typically talked about stress (and sometimes anxiety) rather than mental ill health, they were often describing equally serious conditions as those mentioned in England and Ireland. This is evident in the student focus group excerpts below.

'On my degree course they [students] are very stressed. The majority have a lot of physical problems ... because of the stress. In essence, actual illnesses caused by stress.' (Focus group, Spanish HEI2_2)

'Five of my friends have been to A&E [hospital accident and emergency department] and all of them were sent home after being told that what had happened to them was caused by stress. I think there is a real health problem in Spain related to stress and it is principally apparent in students.' (Focus group, Spanish HEI2_2)

'I was in the library recently a student literally collapsed ... it hit home because I was thinking "I've been in situations when I could have collapsed because I was feeling so stressed ...".' (Focus group, German HEI1_2)

In other cases, students described stress that was perhaps less severe but which nevertheless was prevalent and often had a significant impact on their lives:

'I'm kind of like sinking into the ground because I am always so busy and stressed.' (Focus group, Danish HEI3_3)

'My parents see me as ... being a little overwhelmed and lost – stressed and short of time.' (Focus group, Spanish HEI1_1)

Indeed, a Spanish student made a model with a fallen head (see Figure 6.1) and explained, "Its head has fallen because it's very stressed" (Focus group, Spanish HEI3_2).

Figure 6.1: Student with a fallen head

Assertions about the widespread prevalence of stress among students were also made frequently by staff and the media. The examples below represent only a small selection of such data from Denmark, Germany, England and Ireland:

'Half of the students at the University of Copenhagen are plagued by stress' (*Politiken*, 2 February 2014)

'Many of the students are reporting a lot of stress. ... They feel very stressed.' (Staff member, Danish HEI3_4)

'And what I unfortunately must say is that I think what … being a student right now means … being stressed a lot of times.' (Staff member, German HEI3_2)

Although there were a small number of exceptions (including some of the students' union leaders), policy actors were, in general, less likely than the other groups to whom we spoke to make reference to stress, anxiety and mental ill health on the part of students. This may be explained, in part, by a desire to emphasise the positive features of the HE systems for which they were responsible.

There was also no discussion of students as stressed by any of the social actors in Poland. Comparative studies within the field of health indicate that Poland has one of the lowest rates of mental health disorder in Europe (OECD, 2018). However, such rates may be related to greater stigma attached to reporting, and lesser awareness of, mental health concerns in former Communist countries (Winker et al, 2017; OECD, 2018; Doblyté, 2020). Indeed, Poland's approach to mental health has been criticised for failing to reduce the stigma attached to a diagnosis, and relying too heavily on medical rather than psychological or social solutions (Gierus et al, 2017; Szukalska, 2020). Such concerns may make it less likely for students to feel comfortable discussing stress in a focus group setting (because of its association with mental ill health), and for it to be a common cultural trope (see discussion of 'cognitive availability' below) drawn upon by the media and HE staff. The absence of this construction may also relate to some specific educational factors. Polish students differed from their peers in other countries by emphasising more frequently that there was nothing particularly distinctive about being a student (Brooks and Abrahams, 2021; discussed further in Chapter 8) – a view that can be explained with reference to the sharp recent increase in HE participation rates in Poland (see Chapter 1), and an ensuing societal view that now 'everyone' is a student (Brooks and Abrahams, 2021). It is perhaps unsurprising that, in such a context, student life is not seen as particularly stressful – as it is perceived to be a common pursuit that can be undertaken by most people.

In the remainder of the chapter, we return to those countries where students *were* commonly understood as stressed, to explore some of the explanations for this construction as articulated by our participants.

Juggling multiple commitments

One key source of stress, as identified by students themselves, and also other social actors, was what they believed to be the necessity to juggle multiple commitments. Despite their focus on studying hard (as outlined in Chapter 4), many of the focus group participants spoke of feeling like they were being pulled in different directions by the various activities with which they were engaged.

'I think it's very stressful to … both study and come to class and see my friends and, yeah, there's a lot of stressful things – you have to be social as well [as study] and you have to do some sport as well and all those things.' (Focus group, Danish HEI2_2)

'So, your part-time job at the café, or putting together a PowerPoint presentation, that's not at all stressful in itself. But with everything together, keeping an overall eye on it the whole time, I find that quite hard.' (Focus group, German HEI1_3)

This emphasis on juggling numerous commitments and the attendant stress is also articulated clearly in the English TV series *Fresh Meat*. One of the main characters, Vod, is forced to take up paid employment to support herself, while also attempting to have an active social life, and, at least sometimes, engage with her studies. First, she works as a hotel cleaner, which keeps her very busy and then, later on in the series, she struggles to combine her part-time job in a pub with the writing of her dissertation. In addition, in the Spanish TV series *Merlí*, an Argentine student, Minerva, is portrayed as suffering from stress because of her multiple commitments. In particular, she finds it hard to balance her time between her job at the university library (which is tied to her scholarship) and her studies.

The pressure to take on multiple commitments in this way was explained, by some students and other social actors, in terms of their understanding of HE as a time of transition (see Chapter 2), and expectations that they would have an active social life, engage in a range of extra-curricular activities and make friends for life. For others, it was more directly related to the need to earn money to finance their studies and/or living costs. Furthermore, some believed that, given the congested nature of the graduate labour market, it was necessary to take up a variety of activities beyond the classroom, to help distinguish their CV from others' (see also Chapter 5). In these accounts, we see played out the increasing importance of paid work to students across Europe, not only for funding one's HE (Antonucci, 2016), but also for developing the 'personal capital' required by many graduate employers (Brown and Hesketh, 2004). Staff and policy actors, who were more able to make comparisons between generational groups than students themselves, often asserted that the pressure – or requirement – to engage in paid work and other pursuits alongside studying had become particularly acute over recent years because of changes both to HE funding in several of the countries in our sample, and to the graduate labour market following massification.

It was believed by many of those to whom we spoke that feelings of stress, associated with juggling different aspects of one's life, were particularly common among those from less affluent backgrounds who often had to work long hours to be able to support themselves financially, as they had fewer familial resources to fall back on. This is illustrated clearly in the following excerpt from a Spanish focus group as part of a discussion about stress, studying and paid work: "[Affluent students] are never overwhelmed like the others who have to find the money to pay for their course, or those who depend on a grant from the ministry" (Focus group, Spanish HEI3_2). A small minority also highlighted that the stresses of juggling could be particularly acute for older students, too, echoing the findings of Larcombe et al's (2016) Australian study:

'Typically, those who are older and working and have family will experience more stress, just because of the time and life demands. Those who are ... younger and come from, maybe perhaps coming from more affluent backgrounds, meaning they may not need to work as much, or they have funding from the government because they qualify, or they might have stipends of some sort, that obviously eases their sort of ... at least these outside demands on, you know, making a living.' (Staff member, German HEI1_4)

We see similar themes being played out to some extent in media texts. The stress experienced by Vod in *Fresh Meat* is linked partially to her financial concerns, while in *Normal People*, Connell becomes stressed when he loses his job for the summer and is thus unable to pay his rent. Both characters come from low socio-economic groups and have no familial experience of HE.

Pressure to work harder and faster

All four types of social actor claimed that the stress and anxiety experienced by students were related, to some extent at least, to the increased pressure they faced, when compared to previous generations, to study harder and faster. This is a central theme of the German film, *Wir Sind Die Neuen*. As explained in Chapter 4, the drama revolves around a group of three students who share a flat, all of whom study extremely hard. As the film develops, their excessive studying is shown to have negative consequences for both their physical and mental health. Moreover, their behaviour is contrasted with that of their neighbours – three pensioners who shared a flat many years ago when they were students themselves, and have decided to reconstitute their living arrangements – and who now spend their time partying, relaxing and seeking new experiences. They end up helping their younger neighbours establish a more balanced life. Although a comedy, the film can also be read

Figure 6.2: Book

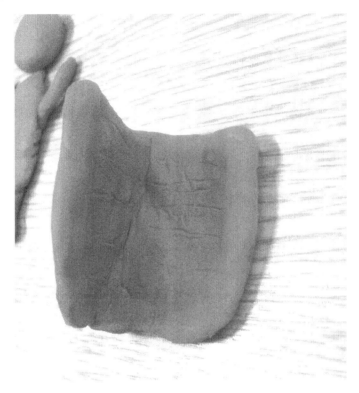

as a critique of the pressurised and stressful lives of contemporary German students (in contrast to the more laid-back approach taken by previous generations). The students we spoke to in our focus groups made links themselves between the pressure they felt to work harder and/or faster and their general health. The plasticine model of a book (see Figure 6.2) was made by a participant in an English focus group to represent how hard she felt she had to work all the time. She commented: "I just see myself as studying all the time because. ... My course is just so intense ... I thought university would be more fun. ... So yeah, it's just stressful" (Focus group, English HEI3_3). Similar comments were made in Germany and Spain. Indeed, in Spain, one focus group participant commented, "There are quite high levels of stress on any degree course" and "You can never rest, because you finish one day and, on the following day, it's 'Read this, read that ... prepare that, study for the exam'" (Focus group, Spanish HEI3_2).

In explaining what was often perceived to be a new pressure to work harder and/or faster, some respondents pointed to the impact of massification of HE. Various interviewees believed that because around half of each cohort was now progressing to HE, it was no longer enough just to have a degree – it had to be a good degree (see discussion of credentialism in Chapter 5) – and that hard work and long hours were required to achieve such a result. In England, this was thought by staff to be exacerbated by the high fees that students were paying; they needed a 'good degree' to demonstrate that their time at university had been worthwhile. These sentiments were also reflected clearly by the students themselves. For example, one English focus group participant commented, "If you're conscientious and want to gain a good degree out of it, then you are dragged into this sort of spiral of stress and deadlines" (Focus group, English HEI3_3). Moreover, in Denmark, staff remarked on the contradictory messages that were often communicated to students: on the one hand emphasising that making mistakes was an important part of the process of learning and, on the other hand, that, under current labour market conditions, high scores were very important.

In Denmark and, to a lesser extent, Germany, these pressures were explained in terms of recent policy changes that had required students to move through their studies at a faster pace. The reforms are both linked to the Bologna Process, although in Denmark they are typically referred to as the Study Progress Reform (see Chapter 1). While in general, the government officials we interviewed tended, unsurprisingly, to be supportive of recent policy initiatives, in Germany, even the government official remarked on the pressure experienced by contemporary students as a result of the Bologna reforms. He talked, for example, about a widespread belief in the prevalence of what he called 'bulimia learning', in which students raced through material as fast as they could, and then regurgitated it for the exam. Similar sentiments were expressed by the German students' union interviewee and German staff. For example, when discussing the impact of the Bologna Process, one German member of staff asserted:

'I have the feeling they are really like stressed, stressed because they want to reach their diploma, their bachelor degree in three years, and then they have the feeling, "Oh I have to be really fast now", so ... they don't relax. ... it's a little bit different when I was a student, yeah, it was like, "OK, you go to the university and you have maybe four and a half years"... but nobody cares if you need six years or whatever, so it doesn't matter, nobody talks about how long you did it. And now it's always like, oh the students are really in a rush.' (Staff member, German HEI2_2)

German students also made direct links between the stress they experienced and the requirement to move quickly through their studies: "There are days when I am feeling mega-stressed because of all the demands pulling on me from all directions ... and I've got to write my dissertation because otherwise I won't be in the recommended period of study" (Focus group, German HEI1_2).

Very similar sentiments were evident within our Danish data. Both Danish newspapers, for example, made direct links between the Study Progress Reform – and specifically the requirement for students to move more quickly through their studies – and stress and mental ill health. Articles on this theme include: 'Progress reforms destroys students' (*Politiken*, 1 June 2015); 'Students: it's a reform from hell' (*Politiken*, 19 November 2015); and 'Students fear more stress after the reform' (*BT*, 11 May 2015). The same connections were made by Danish staff and the representative of the Danish national students' union, and by many of the students who participated in the Danish focus groups. The following quotations are illustrative:

'[I]t's more stressful to be a student now because they have to complete [their degrees] more quickly.' (Staff member, Danish HEI1_1)

'The Study Progress Reform in Denmark ... it has put pressure on students to go really quickly through education ... [and has led to] many students feeling severe stress.' (Danish students' union leader)

'It's very stressful ... because I think society thinks we should run really fast, we should go through our study really fast, we don't have time to just focus on our work, on being good at it, we have to get fast.' (Focus group, Danish HEI2_2)

To some extent, the prominence of this theme in Denmark and Germany can be linked to what many respondents in these countries viewed as a significant shift away from a long-held belief that students should have discretion about how fast they move through their studies. Indeed, as we have outlined in previous chapters, Germany and Denmark, in common with many other countries in central, north and eastern Europe, have both been strongly influenced by the Humboldtian model of the university, which emphasises the importance of *Lernfreiheit* – the freedom to learn and the right to prioritise one's own time (Sarauw and Madsen, 2020). Affected by this, students have typically taken much longer to complete their studies in these two countries than in other parts of Europe. The challenges of adjusting to a new tempo can, as has been shown in other studies (for example, Shaw, 2001), be experienced as dislocating and stressful. While our Danish and German students were not necessarily accustomed to the tempo they felt ought to be an integral part of 'university time' (having recently left school), it appears that their *expectations* of what 'university time' should look like, based on national traditions of HE, led them to experience the lack of freedom to study for as long as one wanted, at the pace one wanted, as challenging (see Brooks et al (2021a) for a more extended discussion).

It is also possible that the perceived pressure to work harder and, in some cases, faster – and the stress and anxiety that often seemed to follow – are related to broader societal discourses about the neo-liberal imperative to 'work hard' as frequently articulated by politicians and other policymakers (Littler, 2013; Mendick et al, 2018), and which we discussed in Chapter 4.

Habitus disconnect

As we noted above, some scholars have argued that an increase in the stress reported by students is associated with processes of massification and, in particular, the greater difficulty of transitioning to HE for students from lower socio-economic backgrounds with no familial experience of university, when compared to their more privileged peers (Bristow et al, 2020). Although this is related to specific material factors such as the need to engage in paid work (discussed previously), it may also be associated with a 'habitus disconnect' – that is, a lack of fit between the dominant dispositions, assumptions and culture of the HE space, and that of such students' homes and families (Reay, 2017). This is a prominent theme in the TV series *Normal People*. Across the 12 episodes, we follow the story of Connell, a young man from a single-parent, working-class background who struggles with several aspects of the middle-class culture that surrounds him during his studies at Trinity College Dublin. In many of the episodes, Connell is depicted as stressed and anxious: he feels homesick, lonely and alienated by the institutional culture, and is very self-conscious about expressing himself in seminars and in front of his (upper middle-class) girlfriend's friends. Although the stress he faces in the series is also related to various financial problems, such as losing his part-time job and therefore being unable to pay his rent, the sense of cultural disconnection he experiences is brought out strongly.

Similar themes were raised within some of our focus groups. For example, a German student described her own difficulties at talking about her university experience with her parents, and linked them explicitly to feelings of stress:

'I come from a working-class background where nobody has an academic degree or the *Abitur* [highest German school-leaving qualification]. The awareness of what studying means, what it gives you, just isn't here; there's a complete lack of comprehension about why you might need it and, in particular, why I myself would. And I found it difficult to enter into a conversation with my parents on the subject, because there was just no basis there for it. They insisted emphatically on their opinion that it would be better to go out into the commercial world and earn some money, and it was always about earning money, not about the fact that I can enrich myself by learning something. [...] I found that really stressful.' (Focus group, German HEI1_3)

The stress associated with feeling unable to talk about university life with one's family was also articulated in Ireland:

> 'I'm the first one [in my family] to go [to university] ... and they're proud of me for going but I can't talk to them about it because they don't really know. ... They don't understand that I'm actually under a lot of stress and it's really hard. ... They just assume that I'm this genius who can do it all.' (Focus group, Irish HEI2_3)

In this extract, however, it is not the inability to talk to one's family that is seen as stressful per se but rather that the family does not provide a forum for discussing stress (and thus, presumably, helping to alleviate it) because of what the student felt was her family's lack of understanding of the pressures of HE and their incorrect assessment of her abilities. Nevertheless, across the dataset as a whole, such disconnects – and their impact on mental wellbeing – were described by only a small number of participants. More common was the belief that family background was related to stress through various material factors and, in particular, the level of economic resources to which students had access – which required the kind of 'juggling' discussed above.

Concerns about the future

A further explanation provided by our participants – albeit again a relatively small minority – for the stress experienced by students was related to concerns about the future, and primarily about securing a job.[1] Such concerns are played out in the English TV series *Fresh Meat*. Several of the main characters are portrayed as stressed and anxious as they come to think more about their lives after graduation: Howard is anxious about not being able to find a job because of what he perceives to be his poor social skills, while his house-mate Kingsley appears stressed when he discovers how difficult it is likely to be to pursue a career in the music industry. Similarly, Oregon, another central character, is portrayed as stressed after failing her final exams, disappointing her parents and not receiving a scholarship for postgraduate study.

For some of our focus group participants, concerns about future employment were linked to what they perceived to be greater competition between graduates as a result of massification (see also discussion of credentialism in Chapter 5). The plasticine model made by a participant in Danish HEI3_1, for example, was meant to represent competition for jobs, with the frame including a large number of highly educated people (see Figure 6.3). In describing this model, the student claimed there are "all these great candidates but there are no jobs for them, which kind of makes me a bit stressed and a bit worried for the future, which is why [the people in the model] are all a bit sad".

Figure 6.3: Frame containing candidates for jobs

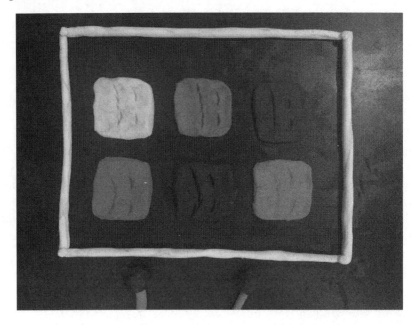

These concerns – and particularly the need to differentiate oneself from other graduates – often appeared to drive the 'juggling' described previously. In Spain, but not in the other countries, some participants spoke of their concerns about increased competition, not just from fellow nationals, but also from graduates from other countries competing in a global labour market. The representative from the Spanish HE leaders' organisation commented that he thought students felt under pressure "because of their knowledge about their future responsibilities and the uncertainties that global competitiveness is bringing to all sectors". Moreover, Spanish students talked explicitly about competition with students from other nations, and felt that they would be at a disadvantage because of what they perceived to be the poorer quality of their HE (see also Chapter 4). Participants in a Spanish focus group (HEI3_1), for example, spoke about the stress associated with following a course that they thought was overly academic in orientation, and would not provide them with the practical, transferable skills that they believed their peers in other European nations were receiving.

In some cases, this stress was exacerbated because of concerns about economic conditions more generally. Again, this was articulated primarily in Spain. In the following quotation, for example, a Spanish student describes the plasticine model (Figure 6.4) they made to represent what they perceived to be the very few job opportunities available in Spain and, as a result, the huge degree of competition:

Figure 6.4: Briefcase and tick within a circle

'I have made a briefcase which symbolises work, and a "tick", which represents good qualifications and grades. All is encircled but there's narrow opening. So, I see myself as one of the thousands of young Spanish people who work, who study, who get good results, but in the end we are all inside the same circle and there is only a narrow exit, so it is a competition, more, more and more, always more, it's never enough.' (Focus group, Spanish HEI3_1)

The prominence of this theme in Spain appears to be directly related to labour market conditions. Indeed, as we noted in Chapter 1, at the time of our data collection, graduate unemployment was considerably higher in Spain than in the other five countries in the sample. Only 77.9 per cent of Spanish graduates were in employment, compared to an EU average of 85.5 per cent (Eurostat, 2019b). All of the other countries in the sample were above this EU average (Eurostat, 2019b).

Societal individualism and competition

A relatively common theme across all our participants was that the stress experienced by students was not related only to factors specific to the HE system but to changes in wider society and, in particular the rise of competitive individualism. In one Danish focus group, a participant claimed, "I notice a lot of students get stressed – but then I notice that in every layer of society, so it's not only student-related" (Focus group, Danish HEI1_3). Several Danish students claimed that stress was experienced equally commonly by pupils at lower levels of the education system:

'In high schools they want to achieve really high[ly] and they get all stressed about it if they don't get an A.' (Interview, Danish HEI2)

'I think that just generally being stressed is quite normal for students in Denmark, even in high school.' (Focus group, Danish HEI3_1)

Many of the different social actors involved in the research believed that there was now more pressure on students to be academically successful. The staff we interviewed in Denmark, England, Germany and Ireland all spoke of this kind of pressure, with some making reference to what they saw as an unhealthy 'culture of performance' within which students (and others in society) were operating, and which often led to feelings of stress and anxiety if individuals were not confident about reaching their goals. Students in these four countries tended to espouse similar beliefs, recognising that a lot of the stress they felt was linked to the expectations they had of themselves, or those that they believed others had of them:

'Sometimes the stress can be just what you expect from yourself, and sometimes the stress can be what is expected from you.' (Focus group, Danish HEI1_3)

'I'm madly stressed out at the moment, under an awful lot of pressure, because I have such high expectations of myself.' (Focus group, German HEI1_1)

'It's hard work, it's really stressful, you're under a lot of pressure because if you don't finish your degree you'll feel bad, you'll feel like you've let people down, so there's a lot of pressure.' (Focus group, Irish HEI1_1)

This kind of reasoning is also reflected in some of the media data – with articles such as 'Student leapt to death after she didn't get a first' (*Daily Mail*, 28 January 2016) and 'Fight the massive focus on performance' (*Politiken*, 20 July 2015). The latter article presents a strong critique of what is perceived to be an unhealthy and limited understanding of what constitutes a meaningful life. Related to this was a sense, noted most commonly in Denmark, Germany and Spain, that students now more frequently compared themselves to others than had been the case in the past – and that this could also be contributing to feelings of stress and anxiety. Developing this theme, one student commented, 'It's very typical for students to be stressed and to be

… kind of intimidated by all the other students and all the super students' (Focus group participant, Danish HEI3_1). Similar observations were made by other respondents, including this German interviewee:

'The individual has got a much higher responsibility to … to prove that he or she organises his or her own life and studying in the most effective way, yeah and … if he or she fails, it's an individual problem. And that … produces stress. If you don't function well enough, it produces stress. If you haven't got enough time to study because you are doing a job besides studying, it produces stress. If you don't really know how to position yourself in society, it produces stress. […] Because the welfare state starts retreating … it's a very high grade of individualisation and the system, the competition has become stronger.' (Staff member, German HEI1_1)

These narratives echo various studies from across the social sciences that have argued that poor mental health tends to be more common in highly individualised societies in which ambition and aspiration are valorised, competition is encouraged, and inequalities are evident (Wilkinson and Pickett, 2010; Greenfield, 2013). There is certainly evidence to suggest that individualism has penetrated university campuses – affecting students' relationships with one another with respect to both their learning and their wider lives (Brooks, 2007; Phipps and Young, 2015).

Increased disclosure and 'cognitive availability'

As mentioned previously, some scholars have argued that the increased disclosure of stress, anxiety and other mental health problems among students can be explained, in part, by the increased societal openness about such issues, as well as 'cognitive availability' and changing cultural idioms of distress (Bristow et al, 2020). Such arguments were also rehearsed by some of the staff members in our research who spoke about changing attitudes towards disclosure of stress, anxiety and mental ill health. This quotation is illustrative of the perspective of a number of staff members in Denmark, England, Germany and Ireland:

'You know in the past, in the Irish context it was very much you didn't talk about it, you know. So if something was happening, if something was happening within your family, within your community, it was almost … kept there, you know. But now students … students know it's OK to say, I'm struggling. It's OK to say, well actually I'm not feeling good, or I feel mentally challenged, I feel weak, I feel that I need to talk to somebody, maybe they don't need to talk to somebody, but need to be encouraged to do that, you know. So it's, it's just ... I think from a mental wellbeing point of view, students are more keenly aware of the need to ... to look after their mental wellbeing, but also to express when they're not feeling well.' (Staff member, Irish HEI1_3)

Moreover, various media depict stress – alongside anxiety and other mental health concerns – as being 'normal' rather than a sign of weakness. This is evident, for example, in newspaper articles such as that published in *The Guardian*: 'Students: where to get help for your mental health' (4 April 2014) – which suggests that mental health problems are extremely common and likely to be experienced by a vast majority of students. It is also a recurring theme in *Normal People*, during which the two main characters, Connell and Marianne, both experience significant mental health struggles throughout the series. Although Connell's are linked to his class position (see earlier discussion), and Marianne's are related to her problematic family relationships, the frequency with which stress, anxiety and emotional issues are depicted across the 12 episodes tends to underline a sense that mental health struggles are common among students, and evident not only among those from low socio-economic groups.

Our data provide some evidence to support the 'cognitive availability' thesis – in that there is a good match between the views of students and those of other social actors in Denmark, England and Ireland (where mental health constitutes a prominent discourse) and in Poland (where there is no mention of stress by any actor). Moreover, there is also some explicit consideration of mental health as a new cultural trope by students themselves (echoing some of the points made by Ask and Abidin (2018) about stress being part of the collective identity of students), as the following quotations illustrate:

'I feel that society expects students to have a giant workload, to be sort of stressed, and we read about it all the time, all these students, how stressed [they are].' (Focus group, Danish HEI3_3)

'I get the feeling that stress is a term that is really overused and it crops up everywhere ... I think that in our generation and in our society here in Germany, it's on everyone's lips ... but I don't get the feeling that our stress levels are higher compared to people who only work or who are only doing an apprenticeship.' (Focus group, German HEI1_1)

Indeed, one participant in an Irish focus group went as far as to say that they believed claiming that you were stressed was an important part of a student identity, irrespective of what you actually felt. They asserted, "You tell them, 'Oh, like I'm so stressed', but secretly you've done your assignments and things" (Focus group, Irish HEI2_2).

However, our data also highlight some exceptions, which raise questions about the cognitive availability thesis. First, in Germany, students tended to be positioned as stressed more frequently by the media and staff than by students themselves (although some students did talk about the stress they felt, as the preceding discussion has shown). It is possible that this disconnect can be related to a lingering sense of stigma about talking about such issues, as German students were the only ones to mention explicitly taboos about mental ill health: "Oddly, we haven't really spoken about it [stress] at all. Perhaps because it's still something of a taboo" (Focus group, German HEI1_1). Second, in Spain, although stress was mentioned frequently by the students in our sample, there appeared to be no strong societal discourse. It was mentioned very rarely by staff members, by only one policy interviewee (and in this case very briefly) and not at all by the Spanish newspapers (despite a strong emphasis on the material concerns of students). The apparent lack of societal discourse can perhaps be explained by the enduring importance of the family in the Spanish context. Family care remains important in the treatment of mental ill health in Spain (Marqués and Navarro-Pérez, 2019), in common with other countries with a Mediterranean welfare model (Stein et al, 2015), while the family is also seen as a crucial means of support for HE students more generally (Lainio and Brooks, 2021). In this context, it is perhaps unsurprising that stress, anxiety and other mental health issues are not individualised nor (implicitly) positioned as the responsibility of students themselves as they often are in Denmark, England, Germany and Ireland. This explanation does not, however, explain why the students who participated in the study spoke so readily, and in such stark terms, about the stress they were experiencing. Taken together, the Spanish data suggest that, while 'cognitive availability' may influence student perspectives in some nations, it is not, of itself, an adequate explanation for all the stress described by students. Instead, it appeared that, for Spanish students, a high degree of pessimism about their future employment and the pressure of having to juggle paid work alongside study in order to survive financially, provoked severe feelings of stress, irrespective of wider discourses and cultural tropes.

Conclusion

In this chapter, we have shown how, despite the construction of students across Europe as citizens (Chapter 3) and enthusiastic and hard-working learners (Chapter 4), they were also commonly understood as stressed by staff members and the media, as well as by students themselves. While this is not identical to the mental 'fragility' discussed by Finn and colleagues (2021), it was often associated with broader concerns about students' mental health. Participants typically believed the prevalence of stress among students was a relatively new phenomenon, linked to both HE-specific issues (such as massification and imperatives for students to move more quickly through their studies) as well as broader societal trends including heightened individualism and competition.

In developing our analysis, we have highlighted various possible social causes for stress (such as the perceived pressure to work harder and faster, and the need to juggle multiple commitments), and also emphasised the role played by social constructions. Indeed, while this particular construction was very common in the data, its absence from Polish focus groups and interviews suggests that national norms (for example, about the acceptability of disclosure of mental health struggles) continue to pattern the ways in which HE students are understood. Nevertheless, its prevalence among Spanish students but not among Spanish staff or in Spanish newspaper articles or films emphasises the limits of the 'cognitive availability' thesis – as well as differences in understanding of students between social actors in a single nation-state.

7

Threats and objects of criticism

Introduction

Issues concerning threats and risks have been extensively explored in youth studies. In such discussions, youth is often described as a risky period during which young people might pose a threat to social stability and/ or to themselves (for example, Dwyer and Wyn, 2001; France, 2007). In this chapter, we focus on the notions of threat and risk within HE settings specifically. On one hand, discourses of risk and threat with respect to HE students echo those documented in youth studies, especially when the perceived threat is associated with a failure to transfer existing values and social conventions to the next generation (Fyfe and Wyn, 2007; Jones, 2009). On the other hand, they also represent something of a departure from them – where the discourse of threat is associated with questions about the academic qualities of students, in the context of the massification of HE and an increasingly heterogeneous student body. This chapter explores the ways in which students are constructed as a threat or object of criticism – with respect to the quality of education, and to society more broadly. While these constructions differ across and within the six countries, we argue that behind these constructions are assumptions about an 'ideal' or 'implied' student, to which those who are criticised are seen as not conforming.

The extant literature on idealised notions of students has explored a range of desirable attributes with the aim of identifying the expectations students face when entering academic and disciplinary communities (Llamas, 2006; Ulriksen, 2009; Wong and Chiu, 2020). These are brought together in Ulriksen's (2009) and Wong and Chiu's (2019) concepts of the 'ideal' and 'implied' student. Idealised notions of students have been shown to underpin various HE-related myths, such as 'more means worse' (an increase in the number of students lowers academic standards), 'traditional student' (a homogeneous category to which the majority of students belong), and 'millennial student' (self-interested and emotionally fragile) that tend to dominate the popular and academic literature, and contribute to perpetuating a discourse of 'moral panics' about students (Macfarlane, 2020; Finn et al, 2021; Sykes 2021). Furthermore, a relatively large body of literature has critically analysed different power relations and discriminatory practices generated and maintained through the notion of the 'ideal student', as well as associated myths that define academic cultures and pedagogical practices (for example, Leathwood, 2006; Hurst 2013; Loveday, 2016; Burke et al, 2017). Our aim in this chapter is not to analyse the different characteristics attributed to the 'ideal student', but rather to show that constructions of students that position them as threats and objects of criticism are consistently based on images of 'implied' or 'ideal' students divorced from the existing socio-political context, as well as biased in terms of (although not exclusively) social class, generational disparities and false stereotypes. While the notion of the 'ideal' or 'implied' student can be associated with many of the other constructions discussed in the earlier chapters, in this chapter we use this notion as an analytical lens to show how it frames what are deemed to be acceptable and legitimate ways of being a university student (Ulriksen, 2009).

The chapter proceeds as follows: we first explore three constructions of students articulated by media, staff members and policy actors that position students as a threat and object of criticism. We start with the construction of students as 'lazy and incompetent' – evident across the dataset – and associated with massification of HE and a discourse about a 'loss of quality'. We highlight the image of the 'independent learner' behind this construction, and discuss its consequences for an increasingly diverse student population. In the second section, we show how students' political activism is constructed as a threat to 'free speech' and democratic society in newspaper discourses. We discuss how political acts are delegitimised by linking them to the image of the 'snowflake student' in England and Ireland, and to violence in Spain. The third section examines how students' lifestyle choices and expectations are placed under scrutiny and associated with generational disparities in the narratives by staff members and policy actors. In analysing the similarities and differences across these narratives, we show that the image of the 'ideal student' is linked to one in the past, in the future or abroad. In the final section we turn to students' own perspectives to explore their perceptions of how they are seen by other social actors, and consider the consequences of the critical constructions for the lived experiences of students.

Lazy and incompetent students lacking academic abilities

In the context of mass HE, debates about who can be a student and who cannot, and whether opening up HE for the 'masses' has resulted in a loss of quality and declining academic standards, have been ongoing for several decades (for example, Morley, 2003; Leathwood and O'Connell, 2003; Macfarlane, 2020). In this section, we show the continuing prevalence of these debates evident in the construction of students as 'lazy and incompetent' across the six countries and different strands of our study: in the media, policy documents, and in the interviews with policy actors and staff members.

Across many newspapers, the quality of the student population was discussed in several articles – often linked to points about the growing size and diversity of this population. In a number of articles in the German newspaper *Die Welt*, *The Irish Times* and the Polish paper *Rzeczpospolita*, students are criticised for lacking the interest, skills or intellectual capacity to study at the required level and, for instance, being 'more interested in the screen of a mobile phone than what the lecturer says' (*Rzeczpospolita*, 27 January 2015). In some articles, academics are interviewed who explain how the larger and more socially diverse student body has changed the demands and nature of their work: with teachers having to spend more hours teaching basic skills, such as writing, for example. In one article in *The Irish Times*, an academic expresses their concern about these changes, and contends that accepting too many less academically inclined students has led to a 'dependency culture' (30 January 2016). These accounts of students as not working hard enough, unable to meet the academic demands of the university and not interested in learning were common to many of the newspapers and were typically seen as a threat to the academic and intellectual ethos of the university. However, these discourses were not equally evident across the countries. They were most prevalent in the Danish newspapers, where the harshest language was also used. In Poland, Germany and Ireland, a number of articles were dedicated to the topic, whereas in the English newspapers only a few texts touch upon it, and in the Spanish newspapers it was largely absent.

In the English newspaper, the *Daily Mail*, the positioning of students as a threat to a high-quality education is associated with the discourse of grade inflation. Several articles report, in a rather sensationalist manner, the problem of grade inflation, suggesting that not all those students who receive a high grade deserve it. Instead, as the quotations below indicate, grade inflation is seen a consequence of the marketisation of HE, and HEIs are criticised for rewarding students with high grades, regardless of the students' 'profile', in order to compete in the market:

> Record numbers of top degrees are being handed out amid suspicions universities are lowering standards to boost their reputations and attract students. (*Daily Mail*, 17 January 2014)

> Research last year suggested one in six [universities] – including Oxford, Exeter and Warwick – were awarding more firsts and 2:1s than would be expected based on the profile of their students. (*Daily Mail*, 16 January 2015)

Even though this criticism is directed at the HE providers for inflating grades, Finn et al (2021) argue that the figure of the student implicit within this discourse is that of a passive consumer and entitled learner. In the extant literature, the construction of 'student as consumer' is often discussed as a problematic shift away from what HE and students used to be (Molesworth et al, 2009; Nixon et al, 2018; Macfarlane, 2020), suggesting that consumer and learner identities are mutually exclusive. While other scholars have challenged this claim as unproductive and creating a false dichotomy (for example, Hurst, 2013; Budd, 2017; Finn et al, 2021; see also our discussion in Chapter 4), media discourse tends to reinforce the norm of the 'ideal student' as detached from a consumer identity.

As mentioned earlier, the construction of the 'lazy and incompetent' student is most prevalent in the Danish newspapers, and the language used here is notably harsh – for example, students are labelled as 'lazy' and 'stupid'. It is often academics and sometimes fellow students, interviewed by journalists or writing opinion pieces, who are most vocal with these views. However, as the headlines below illustrate, these are picked up by journalists, and circulated in newspapers more broadly:

'More students are not suited for university.' (*BT*, 27 March 2015)

'This is how we put an end to the stupid and lazy [student].' (*Politiken*, 7 April 2015)

In many of these texts, a dichotomy between students who should belong to the university and those who should not is articulated. Those who do not belong are alleged to be lazy, unmotivated and even stupid, and positioned as a risk to high-quality education. For example, in the following quotation, an academic interviewed for an article entitled 'Many students do not understand the least bit' suggests that there is a group of students who should not belong to the university because they are not only 'incompetent' but also unwilling to learn, and not serious and independent learners:

There is just one group that should never have been at university. It is stupid students who would rather have teaching that is entertaining and does not contain so many formulas and such things [...] If they are lazy and do not want to work, they should not be at university [...] we must raise the bar for access, in order not to damage those who actually belong at university. (*Politiken*, 21 March 2015)

The presence of 'incompetent' students at the university is depicted as a threat to the value of university education, and this is then seen as a legitimate reason to exclude such individuals from certain activities or from the university altogether. For example, an academic interviewed in the Danish newspaper *BT* suggests that 'unwilling learners' should not be allowed to complete course evaluations because 'to be heard, you must know what you are talking about' (18 March 2015). Likewise, the exclusion of 'incompetent' students from the university is justified in terms of preserving the 'academic elite of society', to use the words of one student who wrote an opinion piece (*Politiken*, 16 April 2014). In other texts, it is justified with respect to the high cost of HE to the taxpayer (for example, *Politiken*, 1 April 2016).

In contrast to the Danish newspaper narratives, the interviewed staff members in Denmark disagreed with this view of students but they did, however, acknowledge that these discourses are common in the Danish media, and are shared by some of their colleagues and policy actors. Indeed, there are strong parallels in the Danish policy documents with the media discourses. In the Danish government documents, in particular, students are seen as too numerous and not of sufficient quality, as well as too slow and not putting enough effort into their studies (Danish speech 1, Danish government document 2) (for more detailed analysis, see Brooks, 2021). In the policy documents as well as in the newspapers (as mentioned earlier), criticism of students is linked to the welfare support students receive (free education and grants), making claims such as 'Tax-funded higher education is a unique privilege' (Danish government document 1). The problematisation of students in the Danish context, then, can be at least partly explained by the HE funding model, whereby tuition fees and education grants are covered by the state (see Table 1.1). For students, these discourses remind them of their responsibilities as 'good' citizens, and question whether they are all equally deserving of welfare (Van Oorschot, 2006).

When turning to our interview data from staff members and policy actors, we can see similar patterns to that within the newspapers. Some of our interviewees talked about the 'loss of quality' and associated an assumed decrease in the academic quality of students with the increased diversity of the student population. Many of our interviewees in principle advocated for an inclusive university and placed high importance on equality in opportunities to study, yet some of them commented on how, in comparison to the past, there has been a decline in the quality of students. For example, one Polish staff member (HEI2_2) estimated that nowadays a third of the student population has 'no ability' to be even an average student. In a similar vein, a Spanish staff member was critical of students lacking the knowledge or skills needed in university, asserting that "they don't know how to write ... they lack basic skills ... the most basic ones!" (HEI1_3).

A number of staff members and some policy actors also highlighted how the more diverse student body poses challenges to traditional teaching and learning methods. Some staff members explained, with a sense of disappointment, how they had had to lower the difficulty level of their teaching in order to cater for a more diverse body of students. The following quotation from an Irish staff member illustrates this:

'If you have, you know ... 25 per cent of your individuals who the university environment really, really suits, and then you have 50 to which it's kind of, you know, they're somewhat ambivalent, and 25 per cent who aren't, that is going to kind of, you know, change the overall ethos in terms of engagement. And as a lecturer, you have to lecture to the median in your class. Whereas if you have a group of, you know, ... very bright students, you know, you will change how, the material how you deliver it, perhaps the pace at which you deliver it, and you can challenge them more, you know, so that does influence it.' (Staff member, Irish HEI2_4)

What we can see in the accounts from staff members is that some students are viewed as not well suited to university; they are viewed as lack an appropriate level of academic competence, thus lowering the standards of teaching. Associating this 'loss of quality' with the expansion and increasing diversity of HE, as well as referencing 'past students' as being of higher quality, implies that it is the 'new entrants' who are seen as a risk to high-quality education. While staff members did not explicitly state who the 'new entrants' are, some policy actors in Denmark, Germany and Poland were more specific. They claimed that it was especially students from 'non-academic' families who had more passive approaches to learning and a more instrumental view of education. This was seen as problematic because these students struggled to 'adapt' to academic expectations and preferred to do 'something more hands-on' or were driven more by a desire to establish a professional career than contribute to societal change. One Danish policy actor suggested that the increasing diversity of the student population might be leading to changes in what it means to be a student:

'And I believe also the universities have some anxiety or feel that, that I mean that we risk going from being students to being more like pupils in the way that when you have that ... greater intake of students, you also have a broader ... they have a broad social background and different backgrounds and some of them might demand more ... more teaching and ... and perhaps more structured teaching, instead of that you have to take responsible yourself for your learning ... but there is a, maybe there is a shift from the ... original meaning of student, as I see it.' (Representative of Danish HE leaders' organisation)

Here, the original meaning of a university student is held to be associated with responsibility and independence – qualities that students from non-academic backgrounds are believed not to possess. This distinction is present not only in the quotation above but also in the examples discussed throughout this section. The 'lazy and incompetent' student, whose suitability for university studies is often questioned, is described as unwilling or incapable of independent learning, not interested in academic knowledge and, in general, less academically inclined. Simultaneously, it is suggested that the competent student is independent, motivated, hard-working, and naturally academically able. While such statements make transparent some of the expectations of the 'ideal student' (Wong and Chiu, 2019), they leave other aspects of this ideal profile hidden. In fact, many have argued that the image of an 'independent learner' is inherently masculine, western, white and middle class, which, in the era of mass HE, does not apply to a large number of students (Leathwood, 2006; Reay et al, 2010; Bathmaker et al, 2013). In other words, describing the 'ideal student' primarily in terms of their approaches to learning means treating them as an 'unspecified body', without considering their 'access to power, privilege and opportunity structures' (Danvers, 2018: 558). The 'incompetent student', then, appears to be understood as inherently 'deficient' in the university setting, lacking the cultural knowledge and skills that determine good academic performance (Yosso, 2005; O'Shea, 2015; Loveday, 2016; Burke et al, 2017). With an increasingly diverse student population, constructing the competent student in these terms may help perpetuate discourses that reward privilege and exclude those who do not meet the qualities of the 'ideal' from being seen as truly belonging in HE.

Students' political activism as a threat

In Chapter 3, we showed the ambivalent representations of students as political actors across our dataset. We also discussed how students' political activism was not always depicted in a positive light in the media. In this section, we extend this analysis by exploring the ways in which newspaper narratives position students' political activism as a threat to academic ideals, and to society more broadly. Interestingly, discourses of threat in relation to students' political activism were not evident across all the countries in our study. Instead, they were prominent only in England, Ireland and Spain (we will return to this point later). Furthermore, what was considered as a 'threat' was also played out differently in these three contexts: in England and Ireland, students were constructed as 'over-sensitive and immature' whereas in Spain, students were seen as posing a threat to the university and society through violence.

England and Ireland: over-sensitive and immature students

Over recent decades, the term 'snowflake' has increasingly been linked to the contemporary student population in the Anglo-American context, with young people denounced as overly sensitive and unable to deal with oppositional ideas (for example, Bloom, 1987; Furedi, 2017; Lukianoff and Haidt, 2018). These accusations are commonly associated with particular forms of protests, such as 'no-platforming' (a protest against or a decision not to provide a platform to a speaker representing ideas that are deemed to be harmful), or practices such as 'trigger warnings' (warning of possibly distressing material) and 'safe spaces' (space for discussion without the threat of violence, harassment or hate speech). While the discourse of 'over-sensitive and immature students' was evident in both newspapers in England and Ireland, perhaps unsurprisingly, this discourse was most pronounced in the English right-wing tabloid, the *Daily Mail*. In many articles students are labelled as the 'snowflake generation' who are demanding 'safe spaces' and 'trigger warnings' (see also Chapter 3). An extreme degree of concern or even rage is expressed at this image of the student, for example suggesting that students are 'the new fascists' (20 November 2015) or that 'they can't handle the truth' (20 February 2016). Students and the forms of protests they engage with are seen problematic as they are believed to threaten the essence of the university as a place for free speech and debate:

> I would argue that it is this fixation with safe spaces and trigger warnings that is helping to erode the traditional liberal ethos of our universities. In place of openness, there is now internal policing of thoughts and words. Sadly, those age-old principles of challenge and debate are being replaced by the new censors. (*Daily Mail*, 31 October 2015)

The image of the 'snowflake student' as a threat is also presented in the Irish newspapers. Here, the risk students are seen to pose expands from the space of the university to society more broadly. Similar to the *Daily Mail*, political acts such as 'no-platforming' or ensuring 'safe spaces' are problematised because they are seen to produce 'thin-skinned graduates' who are unable to 'deal with the rough and tumble of the ordinary outside world' where it is normal to 'be offended occasionally' (*The Irish Times*, 5 May 2016). In these statements, students' attempts to engage with and initiate discussions about power and injustice are ignored and the focus is shifted instead to the threat students are seen to represent. A good example of how the content of the message is ignored is in the *Irish Independent* where the agenda of the campaign 'Rhodes Must Fall' (a movement based at Oxford University aiming to decolonise university buildings and curriculum) is interpreted in the following way: 'Looking at his [Cecil Rhodes] statue was far too triggering for our Generation Snowflake' (*Irish Independent*, 5 April 2016).

What is notable in the newspaper discourses is that, first, students' political activism is reduced to expressions of emotional sensitivity rather than recognised as a legitimate form of political action (see also Finn et al, 2021). By neutralising students' political agency, students are framed as a threat to the existing traditions of the university and society. Second, the voices heard in these texts are exclusively figures of authority – academics, journalists and political actors – whereas students' own voices are rarely included. This allows these authority figures to dominate the discussion and represent students' motivations as 'censorious, separatist, and contrary to the pedagogical values of the University' (Waugh, 2019: 160).

In the other English newspaper, *The Guardian*, the discussions about this topic are more analytical and subtle, and also include students' voices. In contrast to the discourses presented above, the topic is framed in terms of politics. This is evident in the following quotation from a local students' union leader who is commenting on safe spaces:

> There are lots of prejudices in society: racism, sexism, homophobia, transphobia … Students are not shielded from these in their day-to-day lives, and, in some cases, they experience them a lot. So why not try to make the campus environment a bit more progressive, and different from those negative, prejudicial experiences? (*The Guardian*, 10 March 2016).

Nevertheless, despite this invitation to consider students' actions as a form of political discussion, advancing social justice and democratic ideals, it is presented only as one possible interpretation of students' actions. The other interpretations offered in the article are about students being 'less mature' than previous generations, and that students' actions to make the university a more inclusive environment are a consequence of the emergence of the 'therapeutic university' which treats students as 'vulnerable subjects'.

The constructions of students as overly sensitive and vulnerable subjects reflect wider debates about a 'therapeutic culture' that is seen to foster cultural decline and enable new practices of social control (Wright, 2008). For critics of the 'therapeutic culture', vulnerability is problematic because it is held to turn young people into 'anxious and self-preoccupied individuals rather than aspiring, optimistic and resilient learners' (Ecclestone and Hayes, 2009: i; see also Chapter 6). This therapeutic framing can further depoliticise student movements – when action is linked to mental fragility and framed as a cultural problem, rather than paying attention to the social, structural and economic problems that motivate these movements (Leaker, 2020). Furthermore, the portrayal of students as vulnerable and fragile creates an expectation of an 'ideal student' with a certain degree of resilience to enable them to thrive and achieve their potential (Waugh, 2019). As is evident in the newspaper discourses, the 'snowflake generation' is depicted as lacking resilience and positioned as a threat to traditional ideals of academic debate. In this way, particular forms of protest come to be seen as a cultural problem. Labelling other forms and spaces of communication (such as safe spaces) as censorship 'naturalises the dominant voice of the institution while pathologizing the alternative' (Hill, 2020: 5; see also Ahmed, 2015).

Spain: students as a violent threat

In Chapter 3, we noted the prevalence of the representation of students as political actors in the Spanish newspapers; for the most part, students' political activism is depicted in positive or neutral terms in the newspapers (as well as in the Spanish television drama *Merlí*). However, in a number of newspaper articles, a starkly different image of students is drawn. Similar to the discourses discussed earlier in the English and Irish contexts, Spanish students are criticised for 'shutting down the debate' and devaluing democratic principles. In both papers, *ABC* and *El País*, this discourse is articulated by constructing students as a violent threat.

In the two newspapers this representation is related to a single event (although not the same one). Several articles in *ABC* cover a student protest aiming to stop a local politician teaching at the University of Lleida. Students are reported to have called the politician a 'fascist' and criticised the People's Party (a conservative Christian-democratic political party in Spain) that she represents. Similarly, a number of articles in *El País* report a protest against two influential conference speakers in the Autonomous University of Madrid whom students accuse of corruption, abuse of power and widening inequalities in Spanish society. In both cases, students are portrayed as a violent threat:

> [S]ome students burst into her class, insulting her and threatening her [...] Since then ... Manso [the local politician] travels to the university with a triple escort [...] It was in this kind of atmosphere that Manso fulfilled her commitment to her students yesterday afternoon. There were no incidents, but there did exist a certain air of defeat. A sense of abandoning one's principles in face of threats from the violent. (*ABC*, 24 May 2016)

> About 200 violent demonstrators, many of them with their faces covered with masks and hoods, have forced the suspension of a conference which was to be given this Wednesday at the Law Faculty of the Universidad Autónoma de Madrid by ex-president of the government, Felipe González, and the president of Group PRISA [Spanish media company], also editor of El País, Juan Luis Cebrián. (*El País*, 19 October 2016)

In these texts, and in other articles regarding these events, it is not explained what kind of violent acts the students are accused of. Moreover, the voices of the students participating in the protest are not included in the articles. Whereas the articles in *ABC* are written by journalists, in *El País* academics, other students and authority figures also express opinions about this event, claiming the students to be a threat to free speech. For example, the protest is judged severely as 'a total contradiction of democracy'.

Even though students' political activism in the Spanish papers is not reduced to expressions of emotion, as in the English and Irish papers, they are portrayed as a threat to 'free speech' and 'open debate' on campus. The discourse of threat questions the legitimacy of the protest and positions the student activists on the edges of acceptable forms of political engagement (Gagnon, 2018). Moreover, through positioning the protest and the students as violent, an image of them as out of control and 'mindless' is constructed. Ahmed (2014) argues that the labelling of protests as 'mindless' is used when 'we don't want to hear what is it that they [protesters] are saying' (p 165). Indeed, in the newspaper discourses, the actions of the protesters are depicted as 'mindless acts' in opposition to 'free speech'. Only the violence is discussed; no space is given to the voice of the protesters.

The discussion presented in this section shows that in all three countries the reports focus on political activism that is about students' demanding *change*, but it is framed as a threat to 'free speech'. It is important to ask whether small groups of students raising awareness about injustices and aiming to make campus environments more inclusive really constitute a threat to free speech and democracy as the newspaper discourses suggest. As mentioned, this framing is problematic because by labelling student activism as censorship, students' own messages remain unheard. Moreover, media representations also suggest that students exert substantial power within the university – typically ignoring the considerably greater power wielded by politicians, media moguls and university leaders (Leaker, 2020). It appears, then, that by framing student protests as a threat to 'free speech', wider power imbalances are concealed.

While it is impossible to provide a conclusive explanation for the prominence of the construction of political activism as a threat only in these three countries of our study, we can speculate about some possible reasons. In the case of England and Ireland, the discourse of the 'snowflake generation' can be seen as part of broader debates related to identity politics and 'culture war', originating in the US (for example, Lukianoff and Haidt, 2018; see Chapter 1). It has not been as widespread (at least at the time of our analysis) in the campuses of continental Europe. The 'violent acts' reported in the Spanish newspapers, on the other hand, can be read in the context of broader social movements in Spain over the last decade, in which students have played a leading role (in the anti-austerity protests as well as the mobilisations for independence in Catalonia) (Zamponi and González, 2017) – rather than linked to identity politics. In that sense, these events can be understood as part of 'traditional' left-wing student politics where independent groups protest against the ideologies particular political figures represent. The political orientation of the newspapers also has a role to play: *ABC* as a right-wing paper and supportive of the conservative views of the People's Party, and *El País* as a long-standing supporter of the former prime minister Felipe González. In light of the stark differences between the English newspapers in the tone used when reporting about 'over-sensitive and immature students', we can see that, at least in the case of Spain and England, the political orientation of the newspaper appears to inform how students are talked about.

Lifestyle choices and expectations: a generational criticism

Alongside being criticised for their political activity, students were also appraised negatively for their lifestyle choices and expectations of the future – and compared unfavourably to previous generations. This was particularly evident in the interviews with staff members and policy actors in Denmark, Ireland, Poland and Spain. Although this was a much less prominent theme than the one discussed previously – and many staff members and policy actors also expressed sympathetic and positive views about students (see Chapters 4 and 6; see also Jayadeva et al, 2021) – it tended to be articulated in three main ways, which we outline below.

Students prioritising materialistic lifestyles

The first way in which students' lifestyle choices and expectations were criticised, evident across the four countries, was with respect to their assumed materialism and independence. Some staff members made judgemental comments about students' desire to be independent, especially when seen as aspiring to sustain a materialistic lifestyle. For example, staff members criticised students for what they perceived to be their decision not to engage fully with their studies but, instead, work and earn money to fund a certain lifestyle. The following quotation is illustrative:

> '[C]ompared to when I started teaching, I would say ... the majority of my students do some type of part-time work. A large portion of those students are doing it so that they can support themselves with having a good car, with having ... access to smartphones, with the ability to go on their holiday ... So they kind of want to do it all, they want to have the lifestyle, and they want to be a student, and sometimes their being a student can suffer because they want to have the lifestyle.' (Staff member, Irish HEI1_1)

In this quotation and in other similar accounts, students' (alleged) materialistic values are compared to the interviewees' experiences of the past: either their own experience of being a student or their experience of former students. Gabriel (1993) has noted that nostalgic accounts and yearning for the 'good old days' should be understood not as an objective description of the past but rather as an idealisation of it in light of the discontents of the present. In that sense, and following Ylijoki (2005), these nostalgic laments can be seen as 'a form of institutional remembering and forgetting' (p 560), maintaining and transmitting the 'moral order' of the academic field. Thus, our interviewees' references to the past do not necessarily mean that the 'past student' was better than the current one, but they do imply that the 'ideal student' is a serious learner dedicated exclusively to their studies (Brooks, 2018c), and that this is incompatible with a materialistic lifestyle.

In one narrative in Denmark, criticism of students' lifestyle choices was linked explicitly to the welfare benefits they receive (free education and study grants), reflecting some of the earlier discussion in this chapter. The interviewee from the employers' organisation believed that Danish students were quite spoilt, and did not realise how lucky they were to have these benefits. She questioned whether the independent and 'adult-like' lifestyle that state benefits enable are essential for students, for example in terms of being able to travel for holidays and living in apartments rather than dormitories:

'[S]tudents expect not to live in a dormitory, we've not built dormitories so that they … I mean you could also say we're going to build all these dormitories and then you live there for five years, and then you get an apartment afterwards, you don't have to have the, you know living standard of … the equivalent of a graduate, you know, you're a student, and that's for a limited time of your life.'

Here, there is no explicit reference to the past; however, it is implied that it is the current generation of students who are 'privileged', although students in Denmark have enjoyed state benefits for a long time. By linking negative views of students to the welfare they receive raises questions, as discussed in the first section of this chapter, about whether students are seen as deserving of these benefits and the lifestyle they enable. According to Van Oorschot (2006), beneficiaries of welfare who are considered as likeable, grateful, compliant and conforming to set standards are seen as more deserving than those who do not fit this description. Indeed, the interviewee's comments that question the necessity of such a high level of independence while a student, position students as 'less deserving' as they do not appear to exhibit 'ideal' dispositions. In contrast to the nostalgic laments discussed earlier, the focus here is perhaps on the 'ideal *future* student': one who is more efficient, modest and grateful.

Poland and Spain: millennial students and the desire for an easy life

The second lifestyle-related criticism, prominent only in Poland and Spain, was that students' current and future expectations were unacceptable and they desire an easy life. This was seen as a generational characteristic and compared to the interviewees' own experiences during the Communist regime and Franco's dictatorship. A few staff members explicitly labelled the current generation as 'millennials', 'Y' or the 'me me generation', seen as valuing materialistic lifestyles and having an easy life. For instance, a Polish government official asserted that students' expectations of having a good job and a high salary after graduation were unacceptable. He explained how students should instead work from the bottom up, like he had to do in the past when he had started his career as a cleaner. Similar narratives were expressed by staff members where students' assumed 'easy life' was also contrasted with their own experiences under previous political regimes:

'You know I was born in Communist time, so at the beginning, when I was a child, everything was so hard to get. OK? I need to earn my own money to buy the small Lego set, it was so wonderful. And now they, it's so easy to have everything today. It's so easy. There are so many opportunities. [...] They [students] think they should be given this and this and this. [...] Entitled, they feel entitled. [...] sometimes you need to ... be positioned in worse condition to feel that ... no, it's not that everything is fine all the time. And maybe they, they had no chance to feel it.' (Staff member, Polish HEI3_3)

In these nostalgic comparisons, students are homogenised as 'millennials' – a universalistic notion of a generation that tends to overlook social conditions and individual subjectivities (Woodman and Wyn, 2015). Indeed, in the staff members' articulations of the 'difficult past' in comparison to the 'easy present', it is assumed that because some older forms of structural conditions and stratification have changed, it has resulted in universally better social conditions (Woodman and Wyn, 2015). Thus, not only do possible 'newer forms' of inequalities between and within generations remain hidden, but the construction of students as 'entitled' and 'having an easy life' underpins a mythical student of the past as the 'ideal' (Finn et al, 2021: 193).

Ireland and Spain: dependence on family members

In the third type of criticism, emphasis is placed on current students' lack of independence, because of particular familial relationships. This theme was prominent only in Ireland and Spain where some of our interviewees believed that families treat students in infantilising ways, which prevents them from becoming mature and independent. They asserted that as most students live with their parents, they can avoid responsibility and are more needy and less independent than before. For instance, one Spanish staff member was furious about what he saw as over-protective parents dealing with university administration on behalf of their child.

In other cases (and as we noted in Chapter 2), Spanish students were compared with other European students. Indeed, the familial dependence of Spanish students was contrasted with what some staff members and policy actors saw as the more independent nature of students in other European countries, such as Germany:

> '[In] most cases they are financed by their parents, I mean in some cases, these young people work, but I wouldn't say, my perception is not that this is the majority at all. Unlike I mean other countries are different. ... Because maybe a person that works in another country, in Germany for instance, and is very self-aware of how much it cost to go to university, how much he has to work to afford to study, maybe he's more self-aware of everything, and he's more focused at the end of the day.' (Representative of Spanish HE leaders' organisation)

Especially among the policy actors, differences from European peers were explained in terms of students' engagement in paid work, and their living arrangements. Spanish students' dependence was thus seen as a consequence of their lower propensity to work alongside their studies, and their assumed preference for living with their parents rather than alone or in dedicated student accommodation.

Similar narratives were also articulated in the Irish context, however only by the policy actors. Parents were sometimes seen as having too much influence on their children's choices, and treating them in an over-protective way more generally:

> 'I suspect that ... politicians and large sections of Irish society ... still see them as sort of barely grown-up children. ... And they still need to be herded around and looked after to the n'th degree, which is understandable, and Irish mothers are notorious ... for mothering their children to death, you know, as opposed to saying, right you're off, here's your handkerchief, wipe your own nose.' (Representative of Irish HE leaders' organisation)

In narratives such as these, there is little mention of how structural factors impact how students live their lives. In both countries, for example, tuition fees and grants are based on family income rather than treating students as individual citizens in their own right (Lainio and Brooks, 2021). Furthermore, both countries have a long history of strong familial relationships embedded within the Catholic tradition (Reher, 1998), which is not noted by our interviewees.

Comparisons of the Spanish students' level of independence relative to their European peers also speak to the broader discourse of Europeanisation in Spain. Moreno (2013) maintains that due to the long international isolation of Spain, becoming a developed European country is regarded as essential for the modernisation of the nation-state. Therefore, he argues, Europe and Europeanisation have had a substantial impact in the formation of domestic policies. As pointed out in Chapter 1, the aspiration to become European is also an essential part of education policies; according to Bonal and Tarabini (2013), policy discourse in Spain emphasises the importance of following the educational reforms already implemented by other European countries in order to improve the 'peripheral' position of Spain within Europe (see also Brooks, 2021). In contrast to the 'ideal student' being one in the past or future, the imaginary 'ideal student' here is the one who is located abroad: the 'independent European student'.

Taken together, these three different narratives about students' lifestyle choices and expectations criticise students for failing to adhere to the values that are expected of them. As our discussion has shown, it is not only the values of previous generations, but also those associated with 'welfare state deservingness', and ideals adopted from abroad. These articulations all tend to overlook the structural, cultural and political circumstances shaping young people's lives, and instead seek to legitimate an image of a student influenced by the interviewees' own understandings of what constitutes an 'ideal student' (see also Hurst, 2013; Wong and Chiu, 2019; Jayadeva et al, 2021).

Students' perspectives: contesting constructions and the power of stereotypes

So far in this chapter we have discussed three constructions of students that position them as a threat or object of criticism, outlined in the data from media, staff members and policy actors. In this last section we turn to the focus group discussions with students to examine their perceptions of how they felt 'others' (media, politicians, staff members, the general public as well as friends and family) see them. We show that our participants were aware of many of the critical constructions of them, and also discussed other stereotypes that they believed were common. Students were not only aware of these constructions and stereotypes, but also highlighted various harmful consequences these have on their lives.

Denmark: students under surveillance

The discourses constructing Danish students as incompetent and lazy, as well as those that question their deservingness of state benefits, were widely discussed by the Danish focus group participants (see also Jayadeva et al,

Figure 7.1: Dollar symbol and clock

2022). They believed that they were viewed by the media, government and general public as lazy, privileged and a financial burden on taxpayers, and as 'ungrateful students' who spend the money they receive 'wrongly' on cafés, partying or travelling. The Danish students also talked about how they were seen as an expense and even a waste of money. This was associated with what they felt was a growing sentiment in the country that the educational grants students receive ought to be reduced and that students should contribute financially to their own education. For instance, one participant made a plasticine model of a ball and chain to depict how students were viewed as an expense and a burden. Another student made a dollar symbol and a clock (see Figure 7.1) and explained, referring to the Study Progress Reform (see Chapter 1), how students were seen as an economic burden – reliant on welfare and taking too long to finish their degrees.

Students talked about the harmful mental effect these negative constructions had for them. Reflecting the discussion in Chapter 6, a number of students described how they felt criticised for not working hard enough to deserve their educational grants, and that this scrutiny was stressful and placed huge pressure on them. For instance, one student illustrated this by making a model of an eye to represent how students felt that they were under surveillance. Focus group participants also talked about how they had to respond constantly to these negative and inaccurate constructions:

'I feel like I have to defend myself all the time, I have to always ... answer for the different stereotypes and different ways that society or the public debate or the [government] speaks of ... And it just, like it's really frustrating that they don't actually acknowledge the amount of work that you actually put into it and ... yeah, everything that you do to get your education ... the work and the stress that you go through.' (Focus group, Danish HEI3_3)

While the policy reforms in Denmark have had material consequences for students' lives (for example, less time to complete their studies and a reduction in grants) (Sarauw and Madsen, 2020), the focus group discussions show how the image of students as lazy and privileged articulated by policy actors and circulated in the media also have a profound impact on students' everyday experiences. In the quotation above, for example, the student expresses frustration at the public not recognising the hard work that studying entails. As discussed in Chapter 4, this positioning of themselves as hard workers can be seen as a direct response to the negative constructions that students believe others have about them (see also Brooks and Abrahams, 2021).

Spain: peripheral and marginalised students

Earlier in the chapter, we discussed how some staff members and policy actors referred to the 'European student' as a point of reference in conceptualising the 'ideal student' in Spain. Spanish students also articulated this framing of Europe as reference point – not, however, imposed by actors in Spain but by others outside Spain. This was especially evident in the plasticine models: some students made models to depict how Spanish students were viewed by the European general public and students as inferior to students from other European countries (see also Jayadeva et al, 2022). For instance, one student made a model of 'a pile of shit' and explained:

'I've tried to focus on the view [of] the European general public [of] the Spanish situation. I think most of them knew some information about the corruption [...] and all the social conflicts and the crisis, and everything is quite negative. I think [...] that European students tend to think that Spanish students are like different [from] the real [European] students. ... Basically they think Spanish students are something to be maybe protected and [to be] tak[en] away from the really bad situation in their country. [...] it's that my international friends think that you have to want to get out of Spain, maybe because [it] is a complicated situation for work.' (Focus group, Spanish HEI2_1)

While students did not appear to be aware that staff and policy actors compared them to the 'European ideal student', the discourse of Spain as peripheral is also strongly present in their own accounts of how they believe they are viewed internationally. Even though students did not necessarily agree with the view they thought other Europeans have, the construction of Spanish students as somehow 'lacking' in relation to a more 'developed' Europe still appeared to have an impact on them.

Spanish students also recognised the media representation of students' political activism as a threat. Several focus group participants described this view as inaccurate and argued that conservative newspapers in particular often frame political activity in terms of the disruption students are claimed to cause:

'I think the more conservative media see us as a kind of threat, a force for radical change, that we want to set the world ablaze, that's to say, when the conventional conservative media print a story you always see things like, "The gatherings of students who want to sabotage a meeting of something or other".' (Focus group, Spanish HEI2_2)

Students found this kind of sensational reporting manipulative and problematic because it emphasises *what* students have done at the expense of *why* they have done it. In many respects, students' accounts of not being heard reflect what was discussed earlier in reference to Ahmed's (2014) argument – that is, that calling protests 'mindless acts' serves to obscure the message protesters want to deliver.

Interestingly, media representations of students' political activism as a threat were not discussed in the focus groups in England and Ireland. Perhaps the lack of discussion about this topic shows that the discourse about the 'free speech crisis' on campuses is largely imposed from outside the university rather than seen as a problem by the HE actors themselves (Leaker, 2020). Indeed, in England (as we noted in Chapter 1), studies have found little evidence of censorship taking place on campus or students being in favour of limiting freedom of speech (Grant et al, 2019; Finn et al, 2021). Regardless of this evidence, the UK government has recently decided to appoint a 'free speech champion' to monitor and sanction (when necessary) universities for violating free speech regulations (Tidman, 2021). This act speaks to the understanding of 'free speech' as an ideological tool, used by a range of political and other groups to justify statements, behaviours and policies (Leaker, 2020).

Hedonistic and nuisance students

Focus group participants in all six countries identified other negative constructions of how they felt others saw them, which were not dominant

Figure 7.2: Student holding a bottle of alcohol

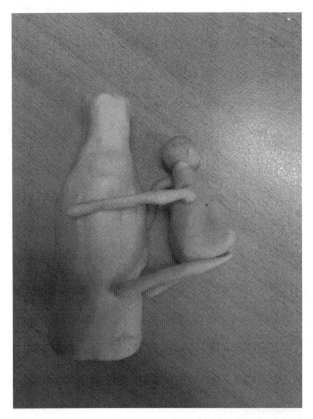

themes across the data from other actors in this study. A recurrent theme among students was that they felt that society largely perceives them as hedonistic and a nuisance: drinking and partying a lot, making noise in the local neighbourhoods and having plenty of free time (see also Jayadeva et al, 2022). This view was often depicted in the plasticine models – including a drinking glass and a pint or a bottle of alcohol (see, for example, Figure 7.2). Indeed, students across the focus groups believed that a stereotypical perception of students is that they drink all the time, and are thus seen as having an 'alcohol problem'.

Students also described how a common image of a student among the general public (and sometimes friends and family) is that of 'a carefree student' who has an enormous amount of free time and spends most of their day sleeping late instead of working hard. Students across the countries felt that these perceptions are mostly a cliché, and critiqued them as stereotypical and inaccurate. For example, and similar to the contestations by Danish students discussed earlier, many Spanish students felt that the view of them having an easy life and not studying hard was far from the reality, and instead, described how they work and study '24 hours a day' (see Chapter 4). Especially in

England and Ireland, but also in the other countries, students often blamed media (newspapers, films and television) for this misrepresentation:

> 'I don't think it's right to assume that like every one of us in this room like does drugs and constantly drinks and things like that, but the media like to play a part and be like, this is what they were doing and this is all they do all the time. And they don't realise like the hard work that we've got to do and things like that.' (Focus group, English HEI1_2)

In the media strand of our study, this representation of students was a dominant theme only in the English data, in the TV series *Fresh Meat* and *Clique*, and in the tabloid the *Daily Mail*. In the two TV series, partying and (heavy) drinking are normalised as part of student life as many of the activities students are depicted as engaging with involve alcohol consumption (and sometimes also drugs) in various social settings. Also, a number of articles in the *Daily Mail* represent students as 'party animals', evidenced in the following headline: 'Boozing games, bin bag outfits … Our finest young students at play!' (5 May 2014). The prevalence of these representations in the English media data can perhaps explain why English and Irish students spoke about media misrepresentations more often than students in the other countries. Furthermore, aligned with students' comments above, many previous studies have suggested that the media often represent students as party animals and living hedonistic lifestyles (for example, Hubbard, 2013; Tobolowsky and Reynolds, 2017; Calver and Michel-Fox, 2021).

Scholars have maintained that, due to the hegemony of drinking culture, reproduced even through university marketing, students who do not drink experience derogatory labelling, which can have a negative impact on their social identity (Andersson et al, 2012; Robertson and Tustin, 2018). Indeed, focus group participants talked about how the 'partying student' was often seen as a 'norm' that shaped their experiences. Students, mainly in England and Ireland, spoke about the pressure to conform to the norm of drinking and partying. They shared their experiences of not being considered an 'authentic student' and looked down upon if they did not drink alcohol and go out partying. For instance, one student said: "I'm told I'm a shit student because I don't drink" (England, HEI1_1). Regardless of students contesting the image of a partying and drinking student, here we can see the power of the stereotype in constructing the 'norm'.

Students discussed how these negative stereotypes also have implications for how they are treated by other people. In England, for example, one student explained how the stereotype of the drinking student led to the trivialising of student problems by dismissing them as alcohol-related. Similarly, Polish students mentioned how it can be hard for students to find accommodation, as some landlords do not even consider renting to students because of stereotypes about wild behaviour. A prevalent theme among students studying in smaller cities and towns in Ireland and England was the relationship with local citizens. Students felt that because of media misrepresentations, local people see them as a nuisance, which is then often used as a reason to blame students for all possible noise, mess and unfortunate events. Students explained how this has also led to a 'not-in-my-backyard' phenomenon, as local people put together petitions to prevent student housing being built in their neighbourhoods.

The evidence from our student participants, presented in this section, suggests that negative constructions and stereotypes are not only producing 'false images', but also functioning, to some extent at least, as a *subjectifying force* (Bhabha, 1983; see also Tyler, 2013), in that the discourses have various negative implications for students' lives and experiences. However, by resisting and contesting the stereotypes, students can also be seen to detach from them and reconstitute themselves as 'subjects of value' (Tyler, 2013: 214). Students repeatedly emphasised the realities of student life, and especially the hard work they were putting in, which can be seen as a response to criticism and an attempt to (re-)establish the value of being a student.

Conclusion

In this chapter, we have analysed three constructions of students that position them as a threat and object of criticism – often associated with the expansion of HE and the emergence of an increasingly diverse student population. We have shown that what underpins these critical constructions are images of an 'ideal' or 'implied' student, of which those who are criticised are viewed as falling short. We have suggested that the criticisms are explained by different factors, including assumptions about welfare 'deservingness' in Denmark; identity politics in England and Ireland; the legacy of dictatorship and Communism in Spain and Poland, respectively; and strong familial relationships in Spain and Ireland. We have concluded that the idealised images tend to reinforce understandings of students that are exclusionary, and which overlook structural, cultural and socio-economic factors that can have a significant impact on being a student. Furthermore, we have shown the ways in which the critical constructions produced and mediated by social actors can have direct and material effects on students themselves. The power of stereotypes is not only in producing and disseminating 'false images', but also in the harmful consequences these can have on students' lives, and the limited subjectivities made available to them.

8

Conclusion

Introduction

The preceding chapters have presented six key ways in which HE students have been understood by policy actors, the media and HE staff – as well as students themselves – across Europe. Some of these, such as the construction of students as future workers (Chapter 5) and political actors (part of the discussion of citizens in Chapter 3), have been prominent themes in the extant literature on students, as discussed in Chapter 1. Others, however, are newer and have been much less well examined in relevant scholarship – for example, conceptualising students as hard-working and enthusiastic learners (Chapter 4) and as stressed (Chapter 6). Moreover, our discussions of students as 'in transition' (Chapter 2) and as threats or objects of criticism (Chapter 7) develop themes that have been well-rehearsed within youth studies (for example, Dwyer and Wyn, 2001; Lesko, 2012) but not necessarily within research on HE specifically. Taken together, the various constructions discussed in the earlier chapters provide important new knowledge about how HE students are understood.

The conceptualisations that we have discussed in *Constructing the Higher Education Student: Perspectives from across Europe* may appear to some extent contradictory. For example, the upbeat and optimistic accounts of student life described by our focus group participants in Chapter 4, where we focused on students as enthusiastic learners and hard workers, can seem in tension with their positioning as stressed and as threats and objects of criticism, which we discussed in Chapters 6 and 7, respectively. In general, however, the constructions that emerged from our student data appeared broadly coherent and consistent, notwithstanding some of the differences between countries that we discuss in subsequent sections of this chapter. In relation to the example above, for instance, students noted how the stress they experienced (Chapter 6) was often related to the hard work they were putting into their studies (Chapter 4). Moreover, they resented being criticised as lazy (Chapter 7) primarily because they were working so hard. Indeed, a picture emerges across the six preceding chapters of students who consider themselves to be rounded individuals, committed to their academic work, who are developing personally, and as citizens – and not mere 'economic resources'. They are often, however, under pressure – feeling stress and aware that they are sometimes conceived of as a threat by others and/or not taken seriously as contributors to civic and political society. The contradictions and disconnects that *are* evident are largely between the views of students, on the one hand, and those of other social actors, on the other. This is a key finding of our research, which we discuss further below.

In this final chapter, we draw together arguments from the previous chapters and explore some cross-cutting themes. We first consider the distinctiveness of a student identity. Implicit in most of the discussion in the book so far is an assumption that there is something distinctive about being a student, and how students are understood has social consequences. However, we draw on data from Poland to note that this distinctiveness is not necessarily played out in the same way in all contexts. The chapter then moves on to explore the extent to which dominant constructions across and within nation-states were similar, engaging with the debates introduced in Chapter 1 about the degree of homogenisation of HE across Europe, and the extent to which nation-states can be considered 'coherent educational entities'. We suggest that there are also other important axes of difference to consider – beyond national boundaries and type of social actors – related notably to academic discipline, HE institution, and students' social background. The chapter subsequently explores the impact of constructions, maintaining that they are not merely of academic interest, but have direct and material effects, before looking to the future and considering how *Constructing the Higher Education Student: Perspectives from across Europe* can help to inform a future research agenda.

The distinctiveness of a student identity

In most cases, our research participants were able to identify what they considered to be distinctive features of a student identity – and it is these data that we have reported in the preceding chapters. Moreover, a student identity was considered to be a significant one – whether related, for example, to the process of becoming an active citizen or political actor, as explored in Chapter 3, or the object of societal criticism, as covered in Chapter 7. Nevertheless, it was notable that this view was not shared equally in all contexts. Indeed, as mentioned in Chapter 6, in Poland, there were a number of students (albeit a small minority) who believed that there were few characteristics, if any, that differentiated them from the population more generally. For instance, one focus group participant made a plasticine model of a 'regular person' to depict what being a student meant to them (Figure 8.1), explaining, "I've made a regular person [for my model] because I think that every student is just a regular person and the fact that you are attending university doesn't make you special in any way" (HEI2_3).

Other Polish students focused on particular characteristics that they had, which had no obvious connection to being a student. One explained, "I have

Figure 8.1: Regular person

made a person [in plasticine] because I see myself as an outgoing person and someone that needs other people to feel good and I am always at the centre of attention" (HEI2_3). This kind of comment was wholly absent from the focus groups in the other five countries where, typically, all participants considered that there was something specific about being a student, even if the nature of this differed. This lack of distinctiveness was also evident in the media data in Poland: there were relatively few newspaper articles that covered student-related issues specifically, and no TV shows or films that featured students prominently.

The Polish data can, perhaps, be explained by considering changes to the HE sector over the past decade. As noted in Chapter 1, Poland differs from most of its European neighbours by the sharp rate of increase in HE participation that has occurred over the past 30 years. In 1989, for example, only ten per cent of each age cohort progressed to university, whereas now the comparable figure is about 50 per cent. While the current level is not significantly higher than in many other European countries, the rate of increase has been notably steeper. This may have led to a perception among some Poles that now 'everyone' is going to HE and it is no longer associated with any special social status. A survey conducted in Poland indicated that 78 per cent of those interviewed believed that 'everyone can study' (Kwiek, 2018: 20) – perhaps linked, not only to the sharp increase in the percentage of each cohort progressing to HE, but also the ease of accessing most courses, even those in prestigious universities, because of policies of 'almost open access' (Kwiek, 2018: 21). In addition, it is possible that the prevalence of paid work alongside studies, in the lives of many Polish students, affected their perspectives. Although the level of student employment in Poland is similar to that in some of our other countries (Eurostudent, n.d.), the apparent belief among the population at large that a degree has low labour market value (Kwiek, 2018) may encourage students to foreground their worker identity rather than that associated with their studies. Indeed, research that has asked students (who have engaged in paid work during their studies) whether they identify primarily as a student or worker has indicated that the percentage choosing the latter is high in Poland (48.4 per cent, compared with 25 per cent in Ireland and only nine per cent in Denmark, for instance) (Eurostudent, n.d.).

Nevertheless, it is important to note that not all Polish students shared this view. As mentioned above, they constituted only a relatively small proportion, and many of their peers *were* able to identify features that distinguished students from other people – as has been evident from the discussion in the preceding chapters.

Increasingly similar students? The impact of the nation-state

Significant commonalities across nations

As explained in Chapter 1, one of our main aims in this book has been to engage with debates about the extent to which HE across Europe has been converging as a result of specific policy measures, such as those associated with the Bologna Process and the European Higher Education Area, as well as through neo-liberal globalisation more generally.

As will have been evident from the book so far, our research has revealed some important commonalities across the six nations in which we collected data. For example, Chapter 2 demonstrated the widespread view that HE constitutes an important rite of passage, which is now considerably more accessible to students from a range of different social backgrounds than in the past. Chapters 2, 4 and 5 all emphasise that many students from across Europe position themselves, to some extent at least, as future workers, even if they reject the ideas about human capital that underpin this construction within policy (Chapter 5). Nevertheless, in most cases, they object to being seen by others as *only* future workers; instead, they value the opportunity to become committed learners (Chapter 4), develop personally (Chapters 2 and 5), and learn how to effect change in the world around them (Chapter 3). In contrast to some assumptions in the extant literature, the majority of the students involved in our research saw no contradiction between being focused on securing a job post-graduation (and thus seeing HE as a transition to employment – see Chapter 2), and valuing various non-instrumental aspects of their HE experience. Thus, understanding oneself as preparing for the labour market was not necessarily seen as incompatible with being an enthusiastic learner and/or an active citizen.

These commonalities, across Europe, in how students understood their own role as students, were reflected in their views of how they believed they were seen by others. Common across the six countries was a sense that they could be marginalised as a result of being seen as 'in transition' or 'not a fully formed adult' (Chapter 2) and only a *future* citizen (Chapter 3) by policymakers and other social actors – and that being criticised as being lazy and/or a threat to society could have material impacts on their everyday lives (Chapter 7). Indeed, there were also clear commonalities across the nations in the views of others – and how, in many cases, these contrasted with the views of students themselves (this is a key point we return to below). As evidenced in Chapter 3, HE staff and policy actors typically did not view students as citizens – comparing their political activity and other forms of civic engagement less favourably to previous generations. Similarly, in Chapter 4, we showed how HE staff and policy actors across Europe tended to view students as instrumental in their approach to learning, apparently not recognising the enthusiasm that was so key to the students' accounts. The positioning of students as objects of criticism was also common across the six nations, as Chapter 7 demonstrates, with students frequently positioned (by HE staff, policy actors and the media) as lazy, incompetent and/or a threat to society.

Enduring national differences

These significant commonalities have, however, to be set against the various differences, by nation, that we have documented in some of the chapters. These suggest that despite arguments about the homogenisation of the European HE space, constructions of students remain, to some extent at least, inflected by national distinctions. In this section, we discuss some of the national-level differences reported in previous chapters and examine some of the likely causal factors.

As the preceding discussion has made clear, some national differences can best be explained with reference to relatively long-term historical and cultural trends. In several chapters we have noted the enduring influence of the Humboldtian model of HE in some of our nations, particularly Denmark and Germany. In Chapter 2, for example, we showed how German students tended to view their 'transitional status' in rather different terms from their counterparts in other nations. Influenced by the Humboldtian concept of *Bildung*, they did not see HE as a discrete stage of life, very different from those before or after, but as part of a process of ongoing personal development and change that would be lifelong. Similarly, as noted in Chapter 4, in their understanding of themselves as learners, Danish and German students, but not their peers elsewhere, placed considerable importance on being able to determine for themselves the pace at which they studied – associated with the Humboldtian idea of *Lehrnfreiheit* (the freedom to study – see Chapter 1). The most explicit invocation of Humboldtian principles is in Chapter 5, where we have argued that German and Danish students drew on the concept of *Bildung* as a means of resisting what they perceived to be dominant economistic policy discourses. Instead of endorsing the model of the student as an accumulator of human capital, they emphasised the importance of HE for personal development and the inculcation of critical dispositions. We have also suggested that, in England, there remains strong cultural attachment to the 'residential' model of HE – where students move away from the parental home for their studies. Although, in practice, a large number of English students now choose to 'commute' to their local HEI, the residential ideal remains strong, as Chapter 2 has evidenced. Indeed, in this chapter we demonstrated how English social actors, more so than those in other countries, tended to place considerable importance on HE as a time for learning to live independently, away from the parental home.

National differences can also be explained by different HE policies implemented in the various countries in the sample, and the principles underpinning them. To some extent these map on to the different welfare regimes discussed in Chapter 1 (see in particular Table 1.1). For instance, in Chapter 5, we contended that the 'future worker' construction was most closely aligned with ideas about human capital development within policy in the countries where neo-liberalism has had greatest purchase. Different mechanisms for funding HE, underpinned by different principles and values, also inform some of the national variation. For example, in Chapter 7, we argued that Danish students, in particular, were criticised by the media and policy actors for not always being 'deserving' of the welfare benefits they received – through their study grants. Although students in most other countries were also 'objects of criticism', only in Denmark (with the most generous student support system – see Table 1.1) was this couched in terms of 'welfare deservingness'. Moreover, as we outlined in Chapter 2, in those nations where all or most students paid fees (England, Ireland and Spain), students (and other social actors) were more likely to see their transition to the labour market as a matter of personal investment and benefit than in the other three countries. In Denmark, Germany and Poland, in contrast, greater emphasis was instead typically placed on societal contribution and benefit (see also the discussion of societal contributions in Chapter 3). Such differences are likely to be related both to the payment of fees (or not) and also to wider social norms about the purpose of HE – principles of public good are typically articulated more frequently and explicitly in systems that have retained public funding models. The extent to which national HE policies have promoted vertical differentiation of institutions is also significant, as some constructions – particularly those related to learners and learning (see Chapter 4) – differed by institution. Such differences were most marked in England, which has the most hierarchical system in the sample, underpinned by long-standing market-based policies encouraging institutions to compete against one another (McGettigan, 2013). (We discuss this further below.)

While the values and principles underpinning HE policy are clearly important in explaining some of the national differences in constructions of the student, so too are other aspects of social policy and state provision. We discussed this in Chapter 2, with respect to differing perspectives on students as 'in transition'. Specifically, we suggested that, in Spain, because of long-standing traditions of 'familialised social citizenship' (Chevalier, 2016) whereby parents have been held responsible for the support of young adults, HE is less commonly seen as a distinct period of preparation for adulthood – not least because many Spanish students remain living in the parental home throughout their degree programme. This can be contrasted with the position in Denmark, where many students have already transitioned to independent living before embarking upon their degree, facilitated by state support that is underpinned by assumptions about the importance of 'individualised social citizenship' (Chevalier, 2016).

In Spain, the emphasis on familial dependence is also bound up with wider debates about Europeanisation. As we discussed in Chapter 7, Spanish students were criticised by various (Spanish) policy actors and staff members for being less independent than their peers from other European nations – with German students held up as an example of the 'ideal independent student'. Moreover, Chapters 4 and 6 documented how some Spanish students believed that the quality of the education they were receiving was lower than that available elsewhere in Europe, and led to them being viewed as comparatively inferior learners, with worse employment prospects than their peers elsewhere in Europe. Implicit in such claims is a sense that Spain has much to learn from other European nations, echoing the argument of scholars such as Bonal and Tarabini (2013) (discussed in Chapter 1) that Europeanisation is often presented within Spain as a route to social and economic development and a means of becoming 'real Europeans' (see also Moreno, 2013; Brooks, 2021).

National norms relating to health and health policy are also relevant. In Chapter 6, we explained how Poland differed from the other five countries in the sample with respect to the absence of any discussion of stress – by students or other social actor. This may relate to the points made previously in this chapter about the 'student' not being seen as a distinctive a social identity in Poland when compared to the other countries – and thus students not perceived as being under more pressure than any other members of society.

However, it seems likely that it can also be explained, to some extent at least, by national norms about disclosure of mental ill health and psychological distress. As we noted in Chapter 6, there remains considerable stigma attached to such disclosures in Poland (likely related to its Communist past), which differentiates it from many of its European neighbours.

Some national differences can also be related to the economic situation at the time of our data collection. As we explained in Chapter 1, graduate unemployment was considerably higher in Spain than in the other five nations when we conducted our research (see, for example, Table 1.5). Although stress was widely reported across our sample (see Chapter 6), it was most closely related to students' concerns about their future employment in Spain, with participants remarking on what they believed to be the small number of opportunities available to graduates. Moreover, in Spain – but not elsewhere – students feared competition with graduates from other European countries, further emphasising a sense of being on the periphery of Europe, and comparing poorly to other Europeans, mentioned above.

Finally, it is likely that some of the national differences outlined in the preceding chapters can be explained by various shorter-term factors. For example, it is possible that particular reforms – that had been recently implemented at the time of our research – may have informed some understandings. In Denmark, for example, the construction of students as 'lazy' can be linked to policies of massification (see Chapter 7), while the Danish students' emphasis on their 'hard-working' nature (Chapter 4) can perhaps be read as a direct response to what they perceived to be a critique of them, within policy, as moving too slowly through their studies. Indeed, during our period of data collection in Denmark (most of which was in 2017–18), the Study Progress Reform (see Chapter 1), originally introduced in 2014, was still being embedded in the Danish HE system, and courting considerable controversy. Similarly, the very rapid expansion of HE in Poland between 1989 and 2014 may, as we have suggested above, have played into the sense among some students (although not all) and the media, that there is now relatively little that is special about being a student. It will be interesting to explore whether these views persist once these reforms in Denmark and Poland are fully embedded and normalised. Indeed, very recent research on the identities of Danish HE students has not highlighted issues to do with hard work and commitment to learning (Gregersen et al, 2021), suggesting that some constructions may be relatively malleable in nature even in the short term.

Degree of convergence *within* nation-states

Alongside examining the extent to which understandings of HE students were similar across different European nation-states, our research has sought to explore the degree of convergence *within* individual nations. Although various scholars have noted differences by stakeholder in, for example, policy perspectives (for example, Ashwin et al, 2015), there is also a tendency – perhaps informed by methodological nationalism (Wimmer and Glick Schiller, 2002) – within both research and practice to assume at least some degree of national homogeneity in numerous aspects of HE.

Nevertheless, as the preceding discussion in this chapter has already highlighted, our research indicates that there were relatively few examples where constructions of students were shared by all of the social actors in our study (policy actors, media, HE staff as well as students themselves). One exception is the understanding of students as stressed, discussed in Chapter 6. Students were viewed in this way by all social actors in all countries apart from Poland (where stress was not brought up in any of the interviews or documents – see discussion above) and Spain (where it was brought up only by students). Understanding students as preparing for work was also relatively common across all social actors. However, as we argued in Chapter 5, this was played out in different ways, with students in some countries drawing on ideas associated with vocation and personal development to critique constructions of the 'future worker' informed by human capital, and others emphasising the importance of credentialism.

More common – as will have been evident from much of the discussion in the previous six chapters – were differences in perspective by type of social actor. The most pronounced differences were between the perspectives of students, on the one hand, and media, staff and policy actors, on the other. For instance, in Chapter 3, we showed that while students, across all our six countries, considered themselves to be active citizens, committed to bringing about social change, staff and policy actors tended to see them, in contrast, as more passive, and often politically disengaged, while the media commonly took a more ambivalent view. Similar patterns were played out with respect to understanding students as learners, as outlined in Chapter 4. A prominent theme among HE staff across all six countries was that students had become more instrumental in their approach to learning, and less likely than previous generations to become involved in the wider life of the university. In some countries this was ascribed to particular policies such as the Study Progress Reform in Denmark, the impact of the Bologna Process in Germany, and the introduction of very high tuition fees in England. Policy actors tended to position students primarily as future workers rather than learners. However, they also sometimes problematised students' approaches to learning, with some commenting, for example, on their reliance on memorisation and rote learning – typically attributing this to poor teaching rather than specific policies. In contrast, students understood themselves as enthusiastic and motivated learners. Interestingly, while staff tended to believe that an overriding focus on employment, on the part of students, had driven out a commitment to learning, students themselves often saw the two as entirely compatible. As we argued in Chapter 4, even when students foregrounded issues related to their future employability in the focus group discussions, this did not mean they were not also interested in their subjects and stimulated by the new knowledge they were gaining. Indeed, in Chapter 5, we contended that students were involved in acts of everyday resistance to what they saw as their positioning as economic resources by policy actors, by drawing on discourses of 'vocation' and self-development (associated with the concepts of *Bildung* and *Dannelse*) as opposed to human capital.

Chapters 4 and 7 also emphasised significant differences between social actors in the extent to which students were conceptualised as hard-working (with respect to their studies). In these chapters we demonstrated that the construction of the 'lazy' and 'entitled' student was a common trope among the media, HE staff and even, in some cases, policy actors. This contrasted quite starkly with the centrality of 'hard work' to students' self-conceptions – evident in both the focus group discussions and many of the plasticine models made by the students (see Chapter 4). Moreover, students were typically aware that they were not seen as hard-working by others – and believed that such negative views often had substantial consequences. The conceptualisation of students as a threat, discussed in some detail in Chapter 7, also brings into sharp relief differences in perspective between students, on the one hand, and staff, policy actors and the media, on the other – despite some national differences in how this threat was perceived. Again, students were aware of such differences – and able to articulate what impact they believed they had. We return to this discussion below.

Finally, in Chapter 6, while in most countries – as noted above – there was a high degree of similarity between social actors in their construction of students as 'stressed', Spain provided an interesting exception. Here, while stress was a very prominent theme in the student focus groups, it was almost entirely absent from the media (the newspaper articles as well as the TV series and film we analysed), policy texts, and our interviews with policy actors and HE staff. As we explored in Chapter 6, this disconnect raises some questions about the 'cognitive availability' thesis – that is, the idea that the increase in students (and others) reporting psychological distress can be explained, at least to some extent, by the prevalence of discussion about mental health in wider society (Bristow et al, 2020). We suggested that the lack of wider debate about student stress and mental health in Spain may be related to social expectations that problems are resolved within the family (see discussion above about 'familialised social citizenship' in Spain). Moreover, students' pessimism about their future employment (in light of the high level of graduate unemployment) and the pressure many experienced through juggling paid work and studies provoked severe feelings of stress irrespective of the wider societal discourse.

Evidence such as this suggests that nations should not necessarily be seen as 'coherent educational entities' (Philips and Schweisfurth, 2014), at least with respect to how HE students are understood. There are clearly some important disconnects between the perspectives of students themselves and those of other social actors. In explaining these differences, it appears that, in some cases, critiquing students is effectively a means of critiquing broader phenomenon. For example, in Chapter 4, we suggested that although staff and students had radically different views about the extent to which students were enthusiastic learners and hard workers, staff were typically sympathetic to the position students found themselves in, and believed that their instrumental behaviour was a direct response to the policy environment around them. Oversimplifying perspectives – for example, constructing students as solely instrumental future workers, and viewing commitment to both learning and employability as mutually exclusive – can be seen as an attempt to convey the gravity of their concerns more clearly. Indeed, as Tight (2013) has argued, recourse to simplified metaphors is often essential to the way we think, and can help us evaluate our own understanding of social processes. Criticisms of students were also, in some cases, linked to broader generational critiques. This is evident in Chapter 3, where we described how numerous stakeholders compared contemporary students unfavourably to what were held to be their more politically active counterparts in previous decades. Similarly, in Chapter 7, we discussed how current students were criticised for their materialist lifestyles – with unfavourable comparisons again drawn with previous generations. The disconnects, documented throughout this book, between the views of students and others, suggest also that there is often a lack of knowledge of the realities of the lives of contemporary students – evidenced in staff members' ignorance of the enthusiasm with which students approached their studies (Chapter 4), various actors' lack of awareness of students' commitment to change society for the better (Chapter 3), and the absence of any societal debate in Spain about the apparent high levels of stress experienced by many students (Chapter 6). While such disconnects cannot be easily changed, they do speak to a pressing need at least to increase the voice of students in public debate across Europe.

Other axes of difference

So far in this chapter, we have explored the extent to which conceptualisations of students differ by nation-state and specific social actor. There are also, however, other axes of difference apparent in our data – in particular, differences by academic discipline, HE institution, and students' social class, which we focus on in this section. It is important to note, however, that these are not entirely unrelated to the points we have made above – indeed, some of the patterns we report here were evident across most or all of the six countries in the study and so feed into the discussion above about commonalities across nation-states.

First, in a small number of areas, there were significant differences by the discipline students were following. As we noted in Chapter 3, social science students were often more politically engaged and interested than their peers from other disciplinary backgrounds, and so were more likely to position themselves as significant political actors. In addition, in Chapter 4 we discussed in some detail how students believed that the type of learner they were thought to be (by others) was often closely related to their subject of study. In general, students from all disciplinary backgrounds held that those enrolled in STEM courses were viewed as superior learners to those in the arts and humanities – because of assumptions about likely employment outcomes, the difficulty of courses, and the inherent value of particular subjects. Students from all six countries expressed similar views about the ways in which academic discipline inflected perceptions of students. Moreover, in Denmark, Poland and Spain, in particular, our analysis of policy texts and newspaper articles demonstrated how the valorisation of STEM subjects was also played out in public discourse.

Second, alongside discipline, institution attended was also associated with differences in constructions of the HE student. In various cases, however, it is hard to disentangle the influence of HEI from that of social class: in many countries, students from privileged backgrounds are considerably more likely to attend prestigious universities than their peers without a similar level of social advantage. Thus, it is likely that a lot of the differences between HEIs evident in our data are related to differences in their social class profile. (It is also the case that our use of focus groups with students – rather than individual interviews – prevented us from analysing perspectives at an individual level, sensitive to a participant's social class.) In Chapter 2, we noted that students from some of the most prestigious HEIs in the sample were more likely than their peers at other HEIs to conceptualise the 'transitional' nature of HE as part of a familial tradition. Similarly, in Chapter 3, students attending the more prestigious universities in England and Germany were more likely to be optimistic about their future political influence than their counterparts at other institutions in the same country. The students to whom we spoke – but not the staff or policy actors – also believed that the type of learner one was held to be was affected by HEI attended. In Chapter 4, we noted that students typically thought that those attending what were perceived to be 'top' universities were thought to be 'better' learners, while those studying at lower-status institutions were more often seen as lazy, hedonistic and not committed to learning. Although such views were most common in England (the sector that has the most vertically stratified system – see Chapter 1), they were also evident in nearly all other countries, even those with much 'flatter' systems, with much less pronounced status differences between institutions.

Differences by social economic status were also discussed explicitly by some of our respondents, independent of the points made above (in which institutional status can be seen as something of a proxy for social class composition). For example, as we discussed in Chapter 4, staff in all six countries commented on the fact that not all students had equal capacity to devote themselves completely to their studies – because of the need, in many cases, and particularly among those from lower socio-economic groups, to engage in paid work alongside their degree programme. This differentiation was also a theme in various of the analysed TV series and films. Similarly, in Chapter 6, we documented how this need to work alongside studying was felt to contribute to the widespread stress experienced by students. In addition, Chapter 6 highlighted how, in some cases, a sense of 'habitus disconnect' was believed to exacerbate feelings of stress – for those students who had moved from low-income families into the predominantly middle-class milieu of the university. Finally, in Chapter 7, we argued that while socio-economic status was rarely mentioned explicitly in constructions of students as threats or objects of criticism, it was often a strong implicit theme. Indeed, we suggested that the 'incompetent' students, identified by a range of social actors in many of the six countries, were often assumed to be those who have gained access to HE as a result of massification – and were thus less likely to have a family history of degree-level study. Moreover, we contended that discussions (among policy actors, HE staff and the media) about 'loss of quality' within the student body were often linked (implicitly and sometimes explicitly) to having a more socially diverse intake.

Impact of constructions

As we explained in Chapter 1, examining how HE students are understood is important, as it can generate new knowledge about the extent to which we are witnessing homogenisation of HE across Europe and the degree to which nation-states can be seen as distinct and coherent educational entities – feeding into significant academic debates (for example, Slaughter and Cantwell, 2012; Dobbins and Leišyté, 2014; Sam and van der Sijde, 2014). It can also, however, enhance our awareness of the day-to-day lives of students as how they are constructed – by the media, policy and HE staff – can have material consequences (for example, Tran and Vu, 2016). Indeed, as Bacchi (2000) has argued, with respect to policy understandings in particular, governments do not respond to problems 'out there' but commonly construct such problems through the very policy proposals that are offered as solutions. This perspective draws on a materialist view of language in which words are understood as doing more than naming things; they impose limits on what can be said and whose voices are viewed as legitimate. For example, as outlined in Chapter 4, some of the students who took part in our focus groups believed that the construction of them as lazy made invisible the hard work they put into their studies, the high levels of stress some experienced, and the challenges – for a considerable number – of juggling paid work alongside their studies. Chapter 7 explored these impacts in more detail, arguing that pervasive negative constructions of students can act as a 'subjectifying force' (Bhabha, 1983). For example, Danish students reported feeling under surveillance, and thus having to constantly defend themselves and reassert their identities as committed learners; Spanish students believed the impact of their political activity was minimised because of the ways in which the media focused on the type of action taken (that is, the violence sometimes used) rather than the reasons for the action; while English students reported that problems they faced were often trivialised or dismissed because of assumptions that they must be alcohol-related. In addition, students from Poland described how they had had problems finding accommodation because of prevalent stereotypes of the 'hedonistic' student. We have also suggested (in Chapter 4) that the ways in which constructions of students are sometimes inflected by discipline – and in particular the privileging of STEM subjects – can have direct impacts on students. Those not enrolled in STEM disciplines reported feeling like 'lesser' students, and were often worried about their future.

In Chapter 6, we considered explicitly the relationship between societal discourses and students' perspectives, in our discussion of 'cognitive availability' – with respect to stress and mental health specifically. Although we drew on data from Spain to show the limits of this theory (noting that while students discussed stress a lot, this was not reflected in wider societal discourses), we also presented evidence that, in a small number of cases, students themselves thought that widespread assumptions that students would inevitably experience considerable stress *did* affect how students understood the challenges they faced in HE. These participants believed that they and their peers readily drew on vocabularies related to stress and anxiety as they were so widespread.

It is likely, also, that the constructions reported in this book will have had various effects of which students will have been unaware. For example, it is possible that assumptions by staff that students are largely instrumental and passive in their approach to their studies (as documented in Chapter 4), could contribute to them adopting classroom practices and pedagogies that may be ill-suited to students' actual needs and motivations. Moreover, assumptions about students from lower socio-economic backgrounds being in some ways 'less competent learners' (as discussed in Chapter 7), may also affect pedagogical practice, as well as potentially labelling such students in a damaging manner. At a more general societal level, the assumed generational differences evident in some of our data – for example, relating to political commitment and civic activity (noted in Chapter 3) and the alleged increase in materialism (Chapter 7) – may reinforce social division, and make inter-generational solidarity more difficult to achieve.

However, while we have strong evidence from our study that some conceptualisations do have significant impacts on students themselves, our data also indicate quite clearly that students are not passive recipients of wider societal understandings – and have considerable capacity both to recognise how they are seen by others and to resist particular constructions. This has been evident in the discussion above and preceding chapters, where we have explained how students were conscious of the ways in which they believed they were seen by others and were able to articulate how they thought these were at odds with their actual experiences, behaviours and motivations. We have also discussed some specific cases of resistance. This is perhaps most evident in Chapter 5, when we explored how students often drew on ideas associated with vocation and self-development (typically discussed in terms of *Bildung* or *Dannelse*) to oppose their framing as solely economic resources. In this way, they were able to resist dominant policy discourses, which often conceptualise students primarily as human capital. Similarly, students' assertion of themselves as enthusiastic learners and hard workers can be read as a clear rejection of their construction as instrumental, passive and, in some cases, lazy learners by many staff and policy actors (discussed in Chapters 4 and 7). In this way, our research reinforces Clarke et al's (2007) contention that political subjects are not 'docile bodies'; rather, they should be considered as reflexive subjects who can contest how they are constructed in policy, sometimes offering their own redefinitions. It also articulates with a growing body of work within higher education studies that has shown that policy constructions are not often translated straightforwardly into student subjectivities (for example, Nielsen, 2011; Tavares and Cardoso, 2013; Tomlinson, 2017).

Looking to the future

We hope that *Constructing the Higher Education Student: Perspectives from across Europe* has provided a detailed and informative insight into how HE students are understood across Europe, showing that while there are some key similarities in such conceptualisations, there are also crucial differences – most notably between the perspectives of students, on the one hand, and those of other social actors, on the other. We have also demonstrated that, despite homogenising pressures exerted through the Bologna Process and the establishment of a European Higher Education Area, as well as more general trends towards massification and marketisation, understandings are also affected by specific national cultures, histories and policy trajectories.

Despite the breadth of our research, there are some student experiences that we have not been able to explore in this book. For example, we chose to focus on only undergraduate students, to keep the project a manageable size – but acknowledge that the experiences and perspectives of and about postgraduates may be considerably different. Moreover, our focus on only domestic students (again, for reasons of manageability) clearly excludes international students, who constitute an important and sizeable population in several of the countries in our sample. Extant research would suggest that how they are constructed is likely to be significantly different from domestic students (for example, Sidhu, 2006; Lomer, 2017; Brooks, 2018a, 2018b). Similarly, for logistical reasons we collected data in only six countries. While our country choice captures well some key dimensions of difference in the continent (see Chapter 1), we cannot expect the constructions discussed here to be evident in other nations, even those within Europe. Future research could usefully consider patterns in other nations, as well as constructions of both postgraduates and those who cross national borders for HE.

Charting the stability of understandings over time would also constitute a worthy subject of study. Above, we have suggested that the constructions we have identified are influenced by various long-term factors (such as national cultures of education) as well as a range of shorter-term factors (such as particular policy initiatives). It would be interesting to see how these play out in the long term. Will some of the national differences we have outlined here become less prominent if nations move further towards a market model? Or will new differences between nations emerge, based on local political, economic and/or cultural factors? Moreover, other shifts in the HE landscape – that have taken place since our data collection – may come to exert a significant influence on conceptualisations of students. Since we conducted our interviews and focus groups, the UK has left the EU (and, as a result, the Erasmus+ mobility scheme) and the COVID-19 pandemic has hit. Both of these could potentially have a significant impact. With respect to the former, it seems likely that any impact on understandings of what it means to be a student will be felt most acutely in England (rather than the other five countries in our study). Although none of our English participants constructed themselves as 'European' during the focus group discussions, such positioning among students in general may become even rarer with reduced opportunities to study or work in mainland Europe, as a result of the UK's withdrawal from the Erasmus+ scheme. Moreover, the absence of any discussion of students as Europeans in English policy documents, which we have explored elsewhere (see Brooks, 2021), seems likely to continue.

At the time of writing, the medium- and long-term impacts of COVID-19 on HE are still unknown. Nevertheless, if there is a substantial shift to greater use of online learning, as a result of experiences during the pandemic, this may raise important questions about the extent to which understandings of what it means to be a student revolve around assumptions about a communal, embodied experience. Such ideas are touched upon briefly in our discussion of students as 'in transition' – but are likely to be thrown into sharp relief by greater reliance on virtual interaction and pedagogy. We would suggest that charting change in understandings of students is important – not only as an intellectual endeavour – but because of its implications for both policy and practice within higher education: to engage with students effectively, as a policymaker, member of HE staff, or even a member of the public, it seems critical that we comprehend *their* perspectives on the world, and *their* understandings of what it means to be a contemporary HE student.

Appendix

Table A.1: List of all analysed policy documents, with labels used in text

Label	Reference
Danish government document 1	Expert Committee on Quality (2015) *New Ways & High Standards – the committee on quality's final reform proposals for Danish higher education.* (Available in English)
Danish government document 2	Ministry of Finance (2016) *A Stronger Denmark – a more robust SU system.* (Translated from Danish)
Danish government document 3	Ministry of Higher Education and Science (2016) *Strategy for Research and Education concerning the Arctic.* (Available in English)
Danish government document 4	Ministry of Education and Research (2017) *Education and Research Policy Report*, June 2017. (Translated from Danish)
Danish speech 1	Tornaes, U. (2016) *Education is key to freedom.* (Available in English)
Danish speech 2	Pind, S. (2017) *Our future universities.* (Available in English)
Danish speech 3	Pind, S. (2017) *The key to a happier future.* (Available in English)
Danish speech 4	Pind, S. (2017) *More cooperation between universities and business.* (Available in English)
Danish employers document 1	DEA (2015) *Student financial aid and student behaviour in the Nordic countries.* (Available in English)
Danish employers document 2	DEA (2016) *What does working during a degree mean for completion of higher education?* (Translated from Danish)
Danish employers document 3	DEA (2017) *Perspectives on the government's proposed SU reform.* (Translated from Danish)
Danish employers document 4	DEA (2017) *How do we train for the future labour market? Strengths of the Danish education system.* (Translated from Danish)
Danish union document 1	DSF (Danish National Union of Students) (2014) *Our education – our solutions.* (Translated from Danish)
Danish union document 2	DSF (Danish National Union of Students) (2015) *Progress reform problems.* (Translated from Danish)
Danish union document 3	DSF (Danish National Union of Students) (2016) *New taximeter system focusing on quality and social mobility.* (Translated from Danish)
Danish union document 4	Akademikerne (2016) *Analysis of the labour market for graduates.* (Translated from Danish)
English government document 1	Department for Business, Innovation and Skills (2016) *Success as a knowledge economy: teaching excellence, social mobility and student choice* (Cm 9258), London, DBIS

Table A.1: List of all analysed policy documents, with labels used in text (continued)

Label	Reference
English government document 2	Department for Business, Innovation and Skills (2016) *Higher Education and Research Bill: factsheet*, London, DBIS
English government document 3	Department for Business, Innovation and Skills (November 2015) *Fulfilling our potential: teaching excellence, social mobility and student choice*, London, DBIS
English government document 4	Competition and Markets Authority (2015) *Higher education: undergraduate students: your rights under consumer law* CMA33(a), London, CMA
English speech 1	Jo Johnson (Universities Minister): *Higher education: fulfilling our potential*, University of Surrey, 9 September 2015
English speech 2	Jo Johnson (Universities Minister): *Teaching at the heart of the system*, Universities UK annual conference, 1 July 2015
English speech 3	Jo Johnson (Universities Minister): *The student journey – from teenage to middle-age*, 9 June 2016, Regent's University London, Higher Education Policy Institute's Annual Conference
English speech 4	Jo Johnson (Universities Minister): *Universities UK annual conference 2016*, 8 September 2016
English employers document 1	Confederation of British Industry (2016) *CBI response to the 2015 higher education green paper – fulfilling our potential: teaching excellence, social mobility and student choice*, London, CBI
English employers document 2	Association of Graduate Recruiters (2016) *Association of Graduate Recruiters (AGR) response to 2015 Higher Education Green Paper consultation*, London, AGR
English employers document 3	National Centre for Universities and Business (2016) *A year in review 2015–16*, London, NCUB
English employers document 4	National Centre for Universities and Business (2016) *State of the Relationship Report 2016*, London, NCUB
English union document 1	University and College Union (2016) *Higher Education and Research Bill: Public Bill Committee. Written evidence from the University and College Union*, September 2016
English union document 2	University and College Union (2011) *High cost, high debt, high risk: why for-profit universities are a poor deal for students and taxpayers*, London, UCU
English union document 3	National Union of Students (2013) *A manifesto for partnership*, London, NUS
English union document 4	National Union of Students (2015) *Quality doesn't grow on fees*, London, NUS
German government document 1	Federal Ministry of Education and Research (BMBF) (2017) *Internationalization of education, science and research: strategy of the Federal Government*, March 2017. (Available in English)

(continued)

Table A.1: List of all analysed policy documents, with labels used in text (continued)

Label	Reference
German government document 2	Kultusminister Konferenz (KMK) (2016) *Education in the Digital World Strategy*. (Translated from German)
German government document 3	Kultusminister Konferenz (KMK) (2015) *Admission to university and admission to higher education for applicants who are not able to provide proof of the university entrance qualification obtained in their home country*, December 2015. (Available in English)
German government document 4	Federal Ministry for Education and Research (2017) *Education and research in figures 2017*, May 2017. (Available in English)
German speech 1	Thomas Rachel (Parliamentary State Secretary, Federal Ministry of Education and Research) (2017) *For good education in Europe: a successful Erasmus programme*, 31 March 2017. (Translated from German)
German speech 2	Thomas Rachel (Parliamentary State Secretary, Federal Ministry of Education and Research) (2016) *Escape and study: a record*, 17 November 2016. (Translated from German)
German speech 3	Thomas Rachel (Parliamentary State Secretary, Federal Ministry of Education and Research) (2016) *Education, participation, integration – Erasmus+ and refugees*, 19 April 2016. (Available in English)
German speech 4	Thomas Rachel (Parliamentary State Secretary, Federal Ministry of Education and Research) (2016) *Europe 2030: united we stand*, 25 February 2016. (Translated from German)
German employers document 1	BDA (Confederation of German Employers' Associations) (2017) *Education in 2030: the educational policy position of employers*, March 2017. (Translated from German)
German employers document 2	BDA (Confederation of German Employers' Associations) (2014) *International potential for Germany's future*, July 2014. (Translated from German)
German employers document 3	BDA (Confederation of German Employers' Associations) (2013) *University funding: holistic, transparent and performance-oriented*, April 2013. (Translated from German)
German employers document 4	BDA (Confederation of German Employers' Associations) (2012) *Bologna @ Germany*, July 2014. (Translated from German)
German union document 1	FZS (Free Federation of Student Unions) (2016) *Refugees and university*, 29 January 2016. (Translated from German)
German union document 2	FZS (Free Federation of Student Unions) (2017) *Press release of the LAK BaWü to the demonstration against study fees on 13.01.2017*, 11 January 2017. (Translated from German)
German union document 3	GEW (Trade Union for Education and Science) (2017) *Education in the migration society: think further!* 9 May 2017. (Translated from German)

Appendix

Table A.1: List of all analysed policy documents, with labels used in text (continued)

Label	Reference
German union document 4	GEW (Trade Union for Education and Science) (2017) *Education funding. Think further: growth, inclusion and democracy. Why more money needs to be spent on education and where it should come from*, 25 January 2017. (Translated from German)
German union document 5	GEW (Trade Union for Education and Science) (2017) *Education in a digital world*, 10 May 2017. (Translated from German)
Irish government document 1	Department of Education and Skills (January 2011) *National Strategy for Higher Education to 2030*, Dublin, Department of Education and Skills
Irish government document 2	Higher Education Authority (April 2013) *Report to the Minister for Education and Skills on system reconfiguration, inter-institutional collaboration and system governance in Irish higher education*, Higher Education Authority
Irish government document 3	Expert Group on Funding for Higher Education (July 2016) *Investing in national ambitions: a strategy for funding higher education*, Dublin, Department of Education and Skills
Irish government document 4	Higher Education Authority (December 2016) *Higher Education System Performance 2014–16 Second Report*, Dublin, HEA
Irish speech 1	Seán Ó Foghlú (Secretary General, Department of Education and Skills) (2014) *2014 Higher Education Colleges Conference*, 11 April 2014
Irish speech 2	Jan O'Sullivan (Minister, Department of Education and Skills) (2014) *Irish Universities Association Funding Symposium*, 29 September 2014
Irish speech 3	Jan O'Sullivan (Minister, Department of Education and Skills) (2015) *Union of Students in Ireland Congress*, 24 March 2015
Irish speech 4	Seán Ó Foghlú (Secretary General, Department of Education and Skills) (2016) *European Access Network Jubilee Conference*, 30 May 2016
Irish employers document 1	Irish Business and Employers Confederation (2009) *Consultation on the Strategy for Higher Education. IBEC Submission*, June 2009 Dublin, IBEC
Irish employers document 2	Irish Business and Employers Confederation (2014) *IBEC submission to Higher Education Authority on the National Plan for Equity of Access to Higher Education 2014–2017*, Dublin, IBEC
Irish employers document 3	Irish Business and Employers Confederation (2015) *National Skills Strategy 2015–2025*, Dublin, IBEC
Irish employers document 4	Irish Business and Employers Confederation (2016) *Department of Education and Skills Statement of Strategy 2016–2018*, Dublin, IBEC
Irish union document 1	Union of Students in Ireland (2016) *The Student General Election Manifesto*, USI

(continued)

Table A.1: List of all analysed policy documents, with labels used in text (continued)

Label	Reference
Irish union document 2	Union of Students in Ireland (2016) *Position paper on the funding of higher education*, USI
Irish union document 3	Irish Federation of University Teachers (2013) *Defend the university – launch address by Jens Vraa-Jensen*
Irish union document 4	Irish Federation of University Teachers (2014) *IFUT submission to Government Working Group of Higher Education Funding*
Polish government document 1	Ministry of Science and Higher Education (2005) *Law of higher education – justification*, 2013 amendment. (Available in English)
Polish government document 2	Ernst and Young Business Advisers and The Gdansk Institute for Market Economics (2010) *Higher education development strategy in Poland to 2020* (Report prepared for the Polish government). (Available in English)
Polish government document 3	Ministry of Science and Higher Education (2011) *Higher education reform.* (Available in English)
Polish government document 4	Ministry of Science and Higher Education (2016) *The law on higher education: ten key issues (that need to be addressed through the Act 2.0 Preparation for a New Act on Higher Education process).* (Translated from Polish)
Polish speech 1[1]	Ministry of Science and Higher Education (2016) *Minister of Science announces more changes in science and education*, 19 September 2016. (Available in English)
Polish speech 2	Ministry of Science and Higher Education (2016) *Minister of Science announced the establishment of the National Agency for Academic Exchange*, 26 October 2016. (Available in English)
Polish speech 3	Ministry of Science and Higher Education (2016) *Gowin: massification is the dark side of education in the field of social sciences*, 28 November 2016. (Available in English)
Polish speech 4	Ministry of Science and Higher Education (2017) *Gowin: the model of mass higher education has become outdated*, 21 April 2017. (Available in English)
Polish union document 1	PSRP (Students' Parliament of the Republic of Poland) (2016) *Student rights and duties (training information).* (Translated from Polish)
Polish union document 2	PSRP (Students' Parliament of the Republic of Poland) (n.d. but about 2016) *Acknowledgement of effects of learning.* (Translated from Polish)
Polish union document 3	Council for Higher Education and Science and Solidarity (ZNP and NSZZ Solidarność) (2017) *Request to guarantee conditions for sustainable development in higher education and science.* (Translated from Polish)

Table A.1: List of all analysed policy documents, with labels used in text (continued)

Label	Reference
Polish union document 4	Council for Higher Education and Science and Solidarity (ZNP and NSZZ Solidarność) (2017) *Opinions on the assumptions made in the submission by AMU/Kwiek.* (Translated from Polish)
Spanish government document 1	*Organic Law of 2001* – with updates. (Available in English)
Spanish government document 2	Ministry of Education, Culture and Sport (2012) *The socio-economic contribution of the Spanish university system.* (Available in English)
Spanish government document 3	ANECA (National Agency for Quality Assessment and Accreditation of Spain) (no date given, but assume 2012/13) *Strategic Plan 2013–16* (but later extended to cover 2017 as well). (Available in English)
Spanish government document 4	Ministry of Education, Culture and Sport (2016) *Strategy for the internationalisation of Spanish universities 2015–20.* (Available in English)
Spanish speech 1	Jose Ignacio Wert Ortega, Minister of Education, Culture and Sport (2012) *Minister of Education, Culture and Sport's speech at the ceremony to mark the start of the university year, in Madrid* (26 September 2012). (Translated from Spanish)
Spanish speech 2	Jose Ignacio Wert Ortega, Minister of Education, Culture and Sport (2014) *Minister of Education, Culture and Sport's speech at the ceremony to mark the start of the university year, in Toledo* (30 September 2014). (Translated from Spanish)
Spanish speech 3	Íñigo Méndez de Vigo y Montojo, Minister of Education, Culture and Sport (2016) *Minister of Education, Culture and Sport's speech at the ceremony to mark the start of the university year, in Cáceres* (3 October 2016). (Translated from Spanish)
Spanish speech 4	Íñigo Méndez de Vigo y Montojo, Minister of Education, Culture and Sport (2016) *Minister of Education, Culture and Sport's speech at the ceremony to mark the start of the university year at the National University of Distance Education* (6 October 2016). (Translated from Spanish)
Spanish employers document 1	Fundación CYD (2015) *Annual Report 2015: executive summary.* (Translated from Spanish)
Spanish employers document 2	Fundación Universidad-Empresa (FUE) (2012) *Entrepreneurial education: services and programmes of the Spanish universities.* (Available in English)
Spanish employers document 3	Fundación Universidad-Empresa (FUE) (2012) *Entrepreneurial education: best practices Spanish universities.* (Available in English)
Spanish employers document 4	Fundación Universidad-Empresa (FUE) (2015) *Guidelines establishing and effectively running student/graduate internship programmes* [jointly written with other national organisations]. (Available in English)
Spanish union document 1	CREUP (Public Universities' Students' Union) (2015) *Learning centred student.* (Translated from Spanish)

(continued)

Table A.1: List of all analysed policy documents, with labels used in text (continued)

Label	Reference
Spanish union document 2	CREUP (Public Universities' Students' Union) (no date given, but accessed June 2017) *Government, governance and university autonomy.* (Translated from Spanish)
Spanish union document 3	Central Sindical Independiente y Sindical de Funcionarios, Sector de Enseñanza (CSI-CSIF) (2015) *Definitive Education Policy Paper.* (Translated from Spanish)
Spanish union document 4	Federación de Trabajadores de la Enseñanza de la UGT (FETE UGT) (2017) *9 March 2017 strike against cuts in the university, university counter-reforms and job insecurity.* (Translated from Spanish)

Table A.2: Brief description of all higher education institutions, with labels used in text

Country	HEI label	Brief description
Denmark	HEI1	Older university, established pre-Second World War
	HEI2	University college with a vocational focus
	HEI3	Younger university, established post-Second World War
England	HEI1	Low-status university, focused mainly on teaching
	HEI2	High-status 'research intensive' university, belonging to the Russell Group
	HEI3	Mid-status university, focused on both teaching and research
Germany	HEI1	University of applied sciences
	HEI2	Large, old and prestigious university
	HEI3	Mid-sized university, established post-Second World War
Ireland	HEI1	Institute of technology
	HEI2	Less prestigious university
	HEI3	Prestigious university
Poland	HEI1	University established pre-Second World War
	HEI2	University established post-Second World War
	HEI3	Large technical university
Spain	HEI1	Public university, established post-Second World War
	HEI2	Private university
	HEI3	Public university, established pre-Second World War

Table A.3: Plots of the analysed films and TV series

Country	Name	Plot summary
England (or UK)	*Clique*	*Clique* is a psychological thriller that follows the lives of a group of students at Edinburgh University. It had two seasons, both of which feature the same leading character, Holly, but in two separate stories. In season one, Holly's best friend gets drawn into the elite clique of 'alpha-girls', which is led by a popular economics professor who runs a programme called the 'Solasta Women Initiative' (linked to the private bank Solasta Finance that she owns with her brother). This programme provides highly competitive internships for talented female students. Behind the well-intentioned programme, Holly discovers a highly corrupt corporate environment controlled by men who exploit the young women mentally and sexually with fatal consequences. In season two, Holly is in her second year at university when she encounters an elite clique of young male students who are involved in running an alternative media website, which is led by a confrontational former academic with right-wing views. The young men play an active role in producing material for the website – for example, about over-sensitive 'snowflake students' – as well as inviting a controversial speaker to interrupt an event organised by a feminist student movement called 'Women Rise'. The boys' clique is concerned about the oppression of men, claiming that feminism frames all men as murderers and rapists. The series revolves around topical themes present in young people's lives within and outside the university context: identity politics, feminism, patriarchy, misogyny, sexual abuse and corruption.
	Fresh Meat	*Fresh Meat* follows the lives of six university students at the fictional Manchester Medlock University in England. The six students – Howard, Vod, Oregon, JP, Josie and Kingsley – end up living together in a house share after missing the application deadline for campus accommodation. Overall, the series describes the journey of the six young people through university towards 'adult life' – with each journey varying depending on the student's family background, personal interests and financial situation, for example. The series covers many student-related issues including moving out of the family home; partying, drinking and sexual relationships; the advantages and disadvantages of living in a shared house; relationships between students and university staff; working while studying; exam pressure; job seeking; and the value of degrees.
Germany	*13 Semester*	This film is a story about Moritz and his friends, following their journey through student life at Darmstadt Technical University (in Germany) in the early 2000s. Moritz and Dirk leave their small hometown in Brandenburg to study mathematics for business. The film covers a range of themes related to student life such as finding accommodation, meeting new people, engaging with learning, and personal development. The film emphasises that each student takes his or her own unique path through university, and that there is no one 'correct' route. Some might be faster and efficient, while it can take longer for others. Regardless of such differences, it concludes that a bright future is possible for everyone.

(continued)

Table A.3: Plots of the analysed films and TV series (continued)

Country	Name	Plot summary
	Wir Sind Die Neuen (We Are the New Ones)	This film is a story of generational conflict between three students (Barbara, Thorsten and Katharina) and three pensioners (Anne, Johannes and Eddi) who live in neighbouring flats in central Munich (in Germany). The pensioners, having shared a flat during their student days, decide to try communal living again after many years. They move into a nice apartment just below a student flat. They are very excited to meet the students and hope that they can build a supportive communal environment and help each other. However, what they find is not quite what they had hoped for: it appears that student life has changed dramatically since their own student days. The three students are extremely focused on their studies and wish to be left alone. The roles between the two generations are turned upside down: the pensioners are portrayed as the ones living a relaxed life, having parties and looking for new experiences whereas the students are depicted as uptight, stressed, extremely organised and purely goal-driven. The students' lifestyle eventually drives them to a crisis point, and they are forced to turn to their neighbours for help. In the end, they all realise they can learn from each other, and they establish a small community rather than being 'just' neighbours.
Ireland	*Normal People*	*Normal People* is a drama series about two young people – Marianne and Connell – from Sligo, a small coastal town in rural Ireland. Marianne comes from an affluent family while Connell is raised by a working-class single mother. They are both high-achieving students and enjoy studying. In the high school in Sligo, Marianne is not popular with the other students, and she is often bullied and treated as an outcast. In contrast, Connell is popular: he has many friends, and plays football in the school team. Their roles are then reversed at university. At Trinity College Dublin, Marianne makes friends easily and is portrayed as fitting in easily to university life. Connell feels uneasy in the university environment and finds it hard to connect to other students. Throughout the series, Connell and Marianne's different experiences of university life – because of their social class and gender – are contrasted. Following their journey through university, the series provides insight to various themes related to student life such as choice of degree programmes and universities; moving out of family homes and settling into university life; experiences of teaching and learning; partying, drinking and sex; mental health problems; and working while studying. Alongside the student life-related topics, *Normal People* is a beautiful story of love and friendship between Connell and Marianne.
Spain	*Fuga de Cerebros (Brain Drain)*	*Fuga de Cerebros (Brain Drain)* is a romantic comedy and traditional 'teen film' containing typical themes for the genre: coming of age; attempting to fit in; bullying; peer pressure; and first love. The protagonists are also typical of the genre: the bright, beautiful and famous 'girl next door' Natalia, and the misfit and bullied Emilio, who has been in love with Natalia since they were children. Now, at

Table A.3: Plots of the analysed films and TV series (continued)

Country	Name	Plot summary
		the age of 18, he is 'ready' to declare his love. However, Natalia has won a scholarship to study Medicine at the University of Oxford in the UK. Emilio's outcast friends decide that they will all go to Oxford (from Spain) for Emilio to 'win her over'. The young men come up with various plans as to how Emilio can impress Natalia – most with disastrous consequences. In the end, Natalia and Emilio are shown to be 'meant for each other', regardless of their differences in terms of personalities, aspirations and family background.
	Merlí: Sapere Aude (Merlí: Dare to Know)	*Merlí: Sapere Aude (Merlí: Dare to Know)* is a TV series that follows the life of first year philosophy students at the University of Barcelona (in Spain). It follows a previous series, *Merlí*, which centred on a high school philosophy teacher (Merlí) and his students. The main character of the series, Pol Rubio, comes from a family with no experience of higher education, but was encouraged by Merlí to study philosophy at university. During their first semester at the University of Barcelona, Pol and his four philosophy student friends experience the joys, difficulties and possibilities of the student life. The series is a strong statement of the importance of philosophy and education, curiosity and love of learning. Alongside these themes, the drama also comprises topics related to social class, family relationships and social justice.

Table A.4: Profiles of staff at Danish higher education institutions, with labels used in text

Label	Gender	Role	Discipline/area	Years of experience			
				0–4	5–9	10–14	15+
HEI1_1	M	Leadership/professional services[2]	Law				×
HEI1_2	M	Teaching	Law			×	
HEI1_3	F	Teaching	Physics		×		
HEI1_4	F	Leadership/professional services	Admissions			×	
HEI2_1	F	Leadership/professional services	Admissions		×		
HEI2_2	F	Teaching	Nursing	×			
HEI2_3	F	Leadership/professional services	Social Work		×		
HEI2_4	F	Teaching	Teacher Education	×			
HEI3_1	M	Teaching	Psychology			×	
HEI3_2	F	Teaching	Communication		×		
HEI3_3	F	Leadership/professional services	Career and Guidance			×	
HEI3_4	M	Leadership/professional services	Geography			×	

Table A.5: Profiles of staff at English higher education institutions, with labels used in text

Label	Gender	Role	Discipline/area	Years of experience			
				0–4	5–9	10–14	15+
HEI1_1	F	Teaching	Media and Communications	×			
HEI1_2	F	Leadership/professional services	Education Development	×			
HEI1_3	M	Leadership/professional services	Student Recruitment		×		
HEI1_4	M	Teaching	Accountancy and Finance			×	
HEI2_1	M	Leadership/professional services	Education Strategy				×
HEI2_2	M	Teaching	Accounting			×	
HEI2_3	M	Leadership/professional services	Schools Development/Student Recruitment	×			
HEI2_4	F	Teaching	Geography		×		
HEI3_1	F	Leadership/professional services	Applied Linguistics, Teaching and Learning				×
HEI3_2	M	Teaching	Chemistry Education				×
HEI3_3	F	Teaching	English Literature		×		
HEI3_4	F	Leadership/professional services	Global Recruitment and Outreach			×	

Table A.6: Profiles of staff at German higher education institutions, with labels used in text

Label	Gender	Role	Discipline/area	Years of experience			
				0–4	5–9	10–14	15+
HEI1_1	F	Teaching	Culture Studies				×
HEI1_2	M	Teaching	Social Work		×		
HEI1_3	F	Teaching	Social Work			×	
HEI1_4	F	Teaching	Social Work			×	
HEI2_1	F	Teaching	Biology			×	
HEI2_2	F	Leadership/professional services	Education	×			
HEI2_3	F	Teaching	Education	×			
HEI2_4	M	Teaching	Psychology				×
HEI3_1	M	Teaching	Didactics of Political Education				×
HEI3_2	F	Teaching	Social Work	×			
HEI3_3	M	Leadership/professional services	Higher Education		×		
HEI3_4	M	Leadership/professional services	Study and Teaching Affairs			×	

Table A.7: Profiles of staff at Irish higher education institutions, with labels used in text

Label	Gender	Role	Discipline/Area	Years of experience			
				0–4	5–9	10–14	15+
HEI1_1	M	Teaching	Sport, Leisure and Childhood Studies				×
HEI1_2	M	Teaching	Biological Sciences		×		
HEI1_3	M	Leadership/ professional services	Academic Administration and Student Affairs		×		
HEI1_4	M	Leadership/ professional services	Communications and Marketing		×		
HEI2_1	F	Leadership/ professional services	Student affairs				×
HEI2_2	F	Teaching	TESOL and Linguistics		×		
HEI2_3	F	Leadership/ professional services	Admissions			×	
HEI2_4	M	Leadership/ professional services	Biological Sciences				×
HEI3_1	M	Teaching	Immunology	×			
HEI3_2	M	Leadership/ professional services	Marketing	×			
HEI3_3	M	Teaching	History			×	
HEI3_4	F	Teaching	Developmental Biology				×

Table A.8: Profiles of staff at Polish higher education institutions, with labels used in text

Label	Gender	Role	Discipline/area	Years of experience			
				0–4	5–9	10–14	15+
HEI1_1	F	Leadership/ professional services	Philosophy	×			
HEI1_2	F	Teaching	Celtic Studies		×		
HEI1_3	M	Teaching	Philosophy	×			
HEI1_4	F	Leadership/ professional services	Chemistry				×
HEI2_1	M	Leadership/ professional services	Balkan Studies, Comparative Literature			×	
HEI2_2	M	Teaching	Physics				×
HEI2_3	F	Teaching	Political Science and International Relations	×			
HEI2_4	F	Leadership/ professional services	International Relations Office	×			
HEI3_1	M	Leadership/ professional services	Mechatronics		×		
HEI3_2	F	Leadership/ professional services	Teaching Methods	×			
HEI3_3	M	Teaching	Computer Science			×	
HEI3_4	M	Teaching	Computer Science		×		

Table A.9: Profiles of staff at Spanish higher education institutions, with labels used in text

Label	Gender	Role	Discipline/area	Years of experience			
				0–4	5–9	10–14	15+
HEI1_1	M	Teaching	Political Science				×
HEI1_2	F	Teaching	Sociology	×			
HEI1_3	M	Teaching	Social Psychology				×
HEI1_4	M	Teaching	Sociology				×
HEI2_1	M	Teaching	Engineering	×			
HEI2_2	F	Teaching	Psychology and Education		×		
HEI2_3	F	Teaching	Educational Psychology				×
HEI2_4	F	Leadership/professional services	Social Education				×
HEI3_1	F	Teaching	Sociology		×		
HEI3_2	M	Leadership/professional services	Student support		×		
HEI3_3	M	Teaching	Mathematics				×
HEI3_4	F	Leadership/professional services	Applied Sociology				×

Table A.10: Characteristics of participants in student focus groups

	Denmark	England	Germany	Ireland	Poland	Spain	Total	Proportion
	N=42	N=52	N=49	N=51	N=45	N=56	N=295	100
Gender								
Male	15	11	14	10	15	26	91	30.8
Female	27	40	34	41	30	28	200	67.8
Others	0	1	1	0	0	1	3	1.0
Did not say	0	0	0	0	0	1	1	0.3
Ethnicity								
Minority	6	8	1	8	0	3	26	8.8
Non-minority ethnic	35	42	48	40	27	46	238	80.7
Did not say	1	2	0	3	18	7	31	10.5
Age group								
<22 years	9	46	18	27	24	40	164	55.6
22–24 years	25	4	15	18	20	14	96	32.5
25–29 years	5	1	13	1	1	1	22	7.5
30 years and older	2	1	3	4	0	1	11	3.7
Did not say	1	0	0	1	0	0	2	0.7
Subject								
Arts and humanities	6	6	2	5	4	7	30	10.2
Social sciences	13	34	45	30	27	42	191	64.7
STEM	14	7	2	15	11	7	56	19.0
Inter-disciplinary	9	5	0	1	3	0	18	6.1
Mode of study								
Full-time	38	52	49	49	45	51	284	96.3
Part-time	2	0	0	2	0	5	9	3.1
Other	2	0	0	0	0	0	2	0.7
Term time job								
Yes	24	12	29	29	14	25	133	45.1
No	16	37	20	22	30	30	155	52.5

(continued)

Table A.10: Characteristics of participants in student focus groups (continued)

	Denmark	England	Germany	Ireland	Poland	Spain	Total	Proportion
Did not say	2	3	0	0	1	1	7	2.4
Children								
Yes	3	0	3	2	0	0	8	2.7
No	37	52	46	49	45	53	282	95.6
Did not say	2	0	0	0	0	3	5	1.7
Family education								
First in family	12	19	28	20	15	21	115	39.0
Parent with HE	26	29	20	30	30	35	170	57.6
Did not say	4	4	1	1	0	0	10	3.4
Social class								
Middle class	33	45	37	33	35	44	227	76.9
Working class	7	6	10	11	7	9	50	16.9
Unclear	2	1	2	7	3	3	18	6.1
Year of study								
1	12	32	14	9	10	11	88	29.8
2	12	6	12	9	10	17	66	22.4
3	14	13	15	9	20	12	83	28.1
4	3	0	4	23	5	12	47	15.9
5 and more	0	0	3	1	0	4	8	2.7
Did not say	1	1	1	0	0	0	3	1.0

Notes

Chapter 1

1. Source: Eurydice (2017).
2. In Poland, there were no documents available from any employers' organisation, so only 12 Polish policy documents were analysed, rather than the 16 from each of the other countries.
3. The information provided in the table is from relevant national sources, and related to the period from 2011 to 2016. For Spain and Germany, the information is based on paid circulation whereas for other countries it is overall circulation.
4. The main differences between the two types of newspapers are related to the content. Tabloids devote a lot of attention to the personal and private lives of people and to topics such as sports, scandal, and popular entertainment, whereas broadsheets focus more on the public side of life and topics related to politics, economics and society (Sparks, 2000).
5. We also conducted an analysis of university websites. This is not drawn upon in this book, but details are available in Lažetić (2019).
6. We chose to exclude both postgraduates and international students from the sample, on the grounds that they may well have different perspectives, which would make it harder to make comparisons across HEIs and countries.

Chapter 3

1. 'No-platforming' is the practice of preventing someone – either through policy or through protest – from spreading their ideas via a particular event or other means of communication. The term has often been applied to when invitations to speak at an event have been rescinded.
2. A 'trigger warning' is a statement at the start of a piece of writing, video or class alerting the reader, viewer or participant to the fact that it contains potentially distressing material.
3. Here, they were referring to the legacy of the UK prime minister, Margaret Thatcher, who was in power from 1979–1990.

Chapter 4

1. English theologian, John Henry Newman (1858), argued that university education should be about pursuing intellectual interests, not for any instrumental purpose, but as an end in itself (see Chapter 1).

Chapter 6

1. Interestingly, despite indications that student debt can have a substantial impact on subsequent life-course trajectories, including on mental health (De Gayardon et al, 2018), very few of our participants made any reference to this, even in England where students typically complete their HE with a high level of debt.
1. As the full texts of the Polish speeches were not publicly available, news reports from the Ministry of Science and Higher Education have been used which contain lengthy quotations from ministerial speeches.
2. Those categorised under 'Teaching' often conducted research as well; our sampling strategy was to choose people who had a reasonable amount of contact with students through their own teaching, unless they were in a leadership/professional services role.

References

Abbas, A., Ashwin, P. and McLean, M. (2016) 'The influence of curricula content on English sociology students' transformations: the case of feminist knowledge', *Teaching in Higher Education*, 21(4): 442–456.

Abrahams, J. and Brooks, R. (2019) 'Higher education students as political actors: evidence from England and Ireland', *Journal of Youth Studies*, 22(1): 108–123.

Abrahams, J. and Ingram, N. (2013) 'The chameleon habitus: exploring local students' negotiations of multiple fields', *Sociological Research Online*, 18(4): 213–226.

Ahier, J., Beck, J. and Moore, R. (2003) *Graduate Citizens? Issues of Citizenship and Higher Education*, London: RoutledgeFalmer.

Ahmed, S. (2014) *Willful Subjects*, Durham, NC: Duke University Press.

Ahmed, S. (2015) 'Against students', *Feministkilljoys* [blog] 25 June. Available online at: https://feministkilljoys.com/2015/06/25/against-students/ (Accessed 29 November 2020).

Allen, K., Quinn, J., Hollingworth, S. and Rose, A. (2013) 'Becoming employable students and "ideal" creative workers: exclusion and inequality in higher education work placements', *British Journal of Sociology of Education*, 34(3): 431–452.

Altbach, P. (1997) *Student Politics in America: A Historical Analysis*, New York: Routledge.

Amaral, A. (2008) 'Transforming higher education', in A. Amaral, I. Bleiklie and C. Musselin (eds) *From Governance to Identity*, Berlin: Springer, pp 81–94.

Amoore, L. (2005) *The Global Resistance Reader*, Hove: Psychology Press.

Anderson, R.D. (2004) *European Universities from the Enlightenment to 1914*, Oxford: Oxford University Press.

Andersson, J., Sadgrove, J. and Valentine, G. (2012) 'Consuming campus: geographies of encounter at a British university', *Social and Cultural Geography*, 13(5): 501–515.

Antonowicz, D., Pinheiro, R. and Smuzewska, M. (2014) 'The changing role of students' representation in Poland: an historical appraisal', *Studies in Higher Education*, 39(3): 470–484.

Antonowicz, D., Kulczycki, E. and Budzanowksa, A. (2020) 'Breaking the deadlock of mistrust? A participative model of the structural reforms in higher education in Poland', *Higher Education Quarterly*, 74(4): 391–409.

Antonucci, L. (2016) *Students' Lives in Crisis. Deepening Inequality in Times of Austerity*, Bristol: Policy Press.

Armstrong, E. and Hamilton, L. (2013) *Paying for the Party: How College Maintains Inequality*, Cambridge, MA: Harvard University Press.

Arnett, J.J. (2004) *Emerging Adulthood: The Winding Road from the Late Teens through the Twenties*, New York: Oxford University Press.

Ashwin, P., Abbas, A. and McLean, M. (2015) 'Representations of a high-quality system of undergraduate education in English higher education policy documents', *Studies in Higher Education*, 40(4): 610–623.

Ashwin, P., Abbas, A. and McLean, M. (2016) 'Conceptualising transformative undergraduate experiences: a phenomenographic exploration of students' personal projects', *British Educational Research Journal*, 42(6): 962–977.

Ask, K. and Abidin, C. (2018) 'My life is a mess: self-deprecating relatability and collective identities in the memification of student issues', *Information, Communication and Society*, 21(6): 834–850.

Auerbach, R.P., Alonso, J., Axinn, W.G., Cuijpers, P., Ebert, D.D., Green, J.G., et al (2016) 'Mental disorders among college students in the World Health Organization World Mental Health Surveys', *Psychological Medicine*, 46(14): 2955–2970.

Bacchi, C. (2000) 'Policy as discourse: What does it mean? Where does it get us?', *Discourse: Studies in the Cultural Politics of Education*, 21(1): 45–57.

Baker, D.P. (2011) 'Forward and backward, horizontal and vertical: transformation of occupational credentialing in the schooled society', *Research in Social Stratification and Mobility*, 29 (1): 5–29.

Baker, D. (2014) *The Schooled Society: The Educational Transformation of Global Culture*, Stanford, CA: Stanford University Press.

Ball, S.J. (2007) *Education Plc: Understanding Private Sector Participation in Public Sector Education*, London: Routledge.

Ball, S.J., Davies, J., David, M. and Reay, D. (2002a) ' "Classification" and "Judgement": social class and the "cognitive structures" of choice of Higher Education', *British Journal of Sociology of Education*, 23(1): 51–72.

Ball, S., Reay, D. and David, M. (2002b) ' "Ethnic choosing": minority ethnic students, social class and higher education choice', *Race, Ethnicity and Education*, 5(4): 333–357.

Bathmaker, A.-M. (2021) 'Constructing a graduate career future: working with Bourdieu to understand transitions from university to employment for students from working-class backgrounds in England', *European Journal of Education*, 56(1): 78–92.

Bathmaker, A-M., Ingram, N. and Waller, R. (2013) 'Higher education, social class and the mobilisation of capitals: recognising and playing the game', *British Journal of Sociology of Education*, 34(5–6): 723–743.

Becker, G.S. (1975) 'Investment in human capital: effects on earnings', in *Human Capital: A Theoretical and Empirical Analysis, with Special Reference to Education* (2nd edn), Cambridge, MA: NBER, pp 13–44.

Becker, G.S. (1993) *Human Capital: A Theoretical and Empirical Analysis, with Special Reference to Education* (3rd edn), Chicago: The University of Chicago Press.

Bennett, D., Knight, E., Divan, A. and Bell, K. (2019) 'Marketing graduate employability: the language of employability in higher education', *Education for Employability*, 2: 105–116.

Bennett, K., Cochrane, A., Mohan, G. and Neal, S. (2017) 'Negotiating the educational spaces of urban multiculture: skills, competencies and college life', *Urban Studies*, 54(10): 2305–2321.

Berg, T., Bowen, T., Smith, C. and Smith, S. (2017) 'Visualising the future: surfacing student perspectives on post-graduation prospects using rich pictures', *Higher Education Research & Development*, 36(7): 1339–1354.

Bessant, J. (2020) *Making Up People: Youth, Truth and Politics*, London: Routledge.

Bhabha, H. (1983) 'The other question: the stereotype and colonial discourse', *Screen*, 24(6): 18–36.

Biesta, G. (2002) '*Bildung* and modernity: the future of *Bildung* in a world of difference', *Studies in Philosophy and Education*, 21(4): 343–351.

Biesta, G. (2009) 'What kind of citizenship for European higher education? Beyond the competent active citizen', *European Educational Research Journal*, 8(2): 146–158.

Bills, D.B. (2003) 'Credentials, signals, and screens: explaining the relationship between schooling and job assignment', *Review of Educational Research*, American Educational Research Association, 73(4): 441–469.

Bleikie, I. and Michelsen, S. (2013) 'Comparing higher education policies in Europe', *Higher Education*, 65: 113–133.

Blichfeldt, B.S. and Gram, M. (2013) 'Lost in transition? Student food consumption', *Higher Education*, 65(3): 277–289.

Bloom, A. (1987) *The Closing of the American Mind: How Higher Education Has Failed Democracy and Impoverished the Souls of Today's Students*, New York: Simon and Schuster.

Boden, R. and Nedeva, M. (2010) 'Employing discourse: universities and graduate "employability"', *Journal of Education Policy*, 25(1): 37–54.

Böhme, G. (2010) *Kritik der Leistungsgesellschaft*, Bielefeld and Basel: Edition Sirius and Aisthesis Verlag.

Boliver, V. (2013) 'How fair is access to more prestigious UK universities?' *British Journal of Sociology*, 64(2): 344–364.

Bonal, X. and Tarabini, A. (2013) 'The role of PISA in shaping hegemonic educational discourses, policies and practices: the case of Spain', *Research in Comparative and International Education*, 8(3): 335–341.

Bonnard, C. (2020) 'What employability for higher education students?', *Journal of Education and Work*, 33(5–6): 425–445.

Bourdieu, P., Passeron, J.-C. and Nice, R. (1977) *Education, Society and Culture*, London: Sage.

Bradbeer, J., Healey, M. and Kneale, P. (2004) 'Undergraduate geographers' understandings of geography, learning and teaching: a phenomenographic study', *Journal of Geography in Higher Education*, 28(1): 17–34.

Bregnbaek, S. (2016) *Fragile Elite: The Dilemmas of China's Top University Students*, Stanford, CA: Stanford University Press.

Bristow, J., Cant, S. and Chatterjee, A. (2020) *Generational Encounters with Higher Education: The Academic–Student Relationship and the University Experience*, Bristol: Bristol University Press.

Brooks, R. (2007) 'Friends, peers and higher education', *British Journal of Sociology of Education*, 28(6): 693–707.

Brooks, R. (2018a) 'Higher education mobilities: a cross-national European comparison', *Geoforum*, 93: 87–96.

Brooks, R. (2018b) 'The construction of higher education students in English policy documents', *British Journal of Sociology of Education*, 39(6): 745–761.

Brooks, R. (2018c) 'Understanding the higher education student in Europe: a comparative analysis', *Compare: A Journal of Comparative and International Education*, 48(4): 500–517.

Brooks, R. (2020) 'Diversity and the European higher education student: policy influencers' narratives of difference', *Studies in Higher Education*, 45(7): 1507–1518.

Brooks, R. (2021) 'The construction of higher education students within national policy: a cross-European comparison', *Compare: A Journal of Comparative and International Education,* 51(2): 161–180.

Brooks, R. and Abrahams, J. (2018) 'Higher education students as consumers? Evidence from England', in A. Tarabini and N. Ingram (eds) *Educational Choices, Aspirations and Transitions in Europe*, London: Routledge, pp 185–202.

Brooks, R. and Abrahams, J. (2021) 'European higher education students: contested constructions', *Sociological Research Online*, 26(4): 810–832.

Brooks, R. and Holford, J. (2009) 'Citizenship, learning and education: themes and issues', *Citizenship Studies*, 13(2): 85–103.

Brooks, R., Abrahams, J., Lažetić, P., Gupta, A. and Jayadeva, S. (2020a). 'Access to and experiences of higher education across Europe: the impact of social characteristics', in A. Curaj, L. Deca and R. Pricopie (eds) *European Higher Education Area: Challenges for a New Decade*, Cham: Springer, pp 197–209.

Brooks, R., Gupta, A., Jayadeva, S., Abrahams, J. and Lažetić, P. (2020b) 'Students as political actors? Similarities and differences across six European countries', *British Educational Research Journal*, 46(6): 1193–1209.

Brooks, R., Abrahams, J., Gupta, A., Jayadeva, S. and Lažetić, P. (2021a) 'Higher education timescapes: temporal understandings of students and learning', *Sociology*, 55(5): 995–1014.

Brooks, R., Gupta, A. and Jayadeva, S. (2021b). 'Higher education students' aspirations for their post-university lives: evidence from six European nations', *Children's Geographies*, pp 1–14 (advance online access).

Brown, P. (2013) 'Education, opportunity and the prospects for social mobility', *British Journal of Sociology of Education*, 34(5–6): 678–700.

Brown, P. and Hesketh, A. (2004) *The Mismanagement of Talent: Employability and Jobs in the Knowledge Economy*, Oxford: Oxford University Press.

Brown, P. and Souto-Otero, M. (2020) 'The end of the credential society? An analysis of the relationship between education and the labour market using big data', *Journal of Education Policy*, 35(1): 1–24.

Brown, P., Lauder, H. and Cheung, S.Y. (2020) *The Death of Human Capital? Its Failed Promise and How to Renew It in an Age of Disruption*, Oxford: Oxford University Press.

Brown, P., Power, S., Tholen, G. and Allouch, A. (2016) 'Credentials, talent and cultural capital: a comparative study of educational elites in England and France', *British Journal of Sociology of Education*, 37(2): 191–211.

Budd, R. (2017) 'Undergraduate orientations towards higher education in Germany and England: problematizing the notion of "student as customer"', *Higher Education*, 73: 23–37.

Bunce, L., Baird, A. and Jones, S. (2017) 'The student-as-consumer approach in higher education and its effects on academic performance', *Studies in Higher Education*, 42(11): 1958–1978.

Burke, J.P., Crozier, G. and Misiasze, L. (2017) *Changing Pedagogical Spaces in Higher Education Diversity, Inequalities and Misrecognition*, London: Routledge.

Calver, K. and Michael-Fox, B. (2021) 'Constructing the university student in British documentary television', in R. Brooks and S. O'Shea (eds) *Reimagining the Higher Education Student: Constructing and Contesting Identities*, London: Routledge, pp 152–169.

Cardoso, S., Carvalho, T. and Santiago, R. (2011) 'From students to consumers: reflections on the marketisation of Portuguese higher education', *European Journal of Education*, 46(2): 271–284.

Chevalier, T. (2016) 'Varieties of youth welfare citizenship: towards a two-dimension typology', *Journal of European Social Policy*, 26(1): 3–19.

Chevalier, T. (2018) 'Social citizenship of young people in Europe: a comparative institutional analysis', *Journal of Comparative Policy Analysis: Research and Practice*, 20(3): 304–323.

Christie, H. (2009) 'Emotional journeys: young people and transitions to university', *British Journal of Sociology of Education*, 30(2): 123–136.

Clancy, P. (2015) *Irish Higher Education: A Comparative Perspective*, Dublin: Institute of Public Administration.

Clark, B.R. and Trow, M. (1966) 'The organisational context', in T.M. Newcomb and E.K. Wilson (eds) *College Peer Groups: Problems and Prospects for Research*, Chicago: Aldine, pp 17–70.

Clarke, J. (2005) 'New Labour's citizens: activated, empowered, responsibilised, abandoned?', *Critical Social Policy*, 25(4): 447–463.

Clarke, J., Newman, J., Smith, N., Vidler, E. and Westmarland, L. (2007) *Creating Citizen-Consumers*, London: Sage.

CMA [Competition and Markets Authority] (2020) *About Us*. Available online at: www.gov.uk/government/organisations/competition-and-markets-authority/about (Accessed 18 June 2020).

Coffey, A. (2004) *Reconceptualising Social Policy: Sociological Perspectives on Contemporary Social Policy*, Maidenhead: Open University Press.

Collins, R. (1979) *The Credential Society: An Historical Sociology of Education and Stratification*, New York: Academic Press.

Côté, J.E. (2000) *Arrested Adulthood: The Changing Nature of Maturity and Identity*, New York: New York University Press.

Cunningham, S. and Lavalette, M. (2004) '"Active citizens" or "irresponsible truants"? School student strikes against the war', *Critical Social Policy*, 24(2): 255–269.

Cvetkovski, S., Jorm, A. and Mackinnon, A. (2019) 'An analysis of the mental health trajectories of university students compared to their community peers using a national longitudinal survey', *Studies in Higher Education*, 44(1): 185–200.

Daniels, J. and Brooker, J. (2014) 'Student identity development in higher education: implications for graduate attributes and work-readiness', *Educational Research*, 56(1): 65–76.

Danvers, E. (2018) 'Who is the critical thinker in higher education? A feminist re-thinking', *Teaching in Higher Education*, 23(5): 548–562.

De Gayardon, A., Callender, C., DesJardins, S. and Deane, K. (2018) *Graduate indebtedness: its perceived effects on behaviour and life choices – a literature review (CGHE Working Paper 38)*. Available online at: www.researchcghe.org/publications/working-paper/graduate-indebtedness-its-perceived-effects-on-behaviour-and-life-choices-a-literature-review/ (Accessed 28 December 2020).

de la Torre, E. and Perez-Esparrells, C. (2019) 'Reforms in the Spanish higher education system', in B. Broucker, K. De Wit, J. Verhoeven and L. Leišytė (eds) *Higher Education System Reform. An International Comparison after Twenty Years of Bologna*, Leiden: Brill Publishing, pp 119–135.

Della Porta, D., Cini, L. and Guzman-Concha, C. (2020) *Contesting Higher Education: Student Movements Against Neo-Liberal Universities*, Bristol: Bristol University Press.

Devinney, T., Auger, P. and DeSailly, R. (2012) *What Matters to Australians: Our Social, Political and Economic Values*, Report from the Anatomy of Civil Societies Research Project.

Dobbins, M. (2011) *Higher Education Policies in Central and Eastern Europe: Convergence Towards a Common Model?*, Basingstoke: Palgrave.

Dobbins, M. and Leišyté, L. (2014) 'Analysing the transformation of higher education governance in Bulgaria and Lithuania', *Public Management Review*, 16(7): 987–1010.

Doblyté, S. (2020) 'Shame in a post-socialist society: a qualitative study of healthcare seeking and utilisation in common mental disorders', *Sociology of Health and Illness* (advance online access).

Donald, W.E., Ashleigh, M.J. and Baruch, Y. (2018) 'Students' perceptions of education and employability: facilitating career transition from higher education into the labor market', *Career Development International*, 23(5): 513–540.

Donnelly, M. and Gamsu, S. (2018) 'Regional structures of feeling? A spatially and socially differentiated analysis of UK student im/mobility', *British Journal of Sociology of Education*, 39(7): 961–981.

Duffy, A., Keown-Stoneman, C., Goodday, S., Horrocks, J., Lowe, M., King, N., et al (2020) 'Predictors of mental health and academic outcomes in first-year university students: identifying prevention and early-intervention targets', *BJPsych Open*, 6(3): E46. Doi:10.1192/bjo.2020.24

Dwyer, P. and Wyn, J. (2001) *Youth, Education and Risk*, New York: RoutledgeFalmer.

Ecclestone, K. and Hayes, D. (2009) *The Dangerous Rise of Therapeutic Education*, London: Routledge.

Ecclestone, K., Biesta, G. and Hughes, M. (2009) 'Transitions in the lifecourse: the role of identity, agency and structure', in K. Ecclestone, G. Biesta and M. Hughes (eds) *Transitions and Learning through the Lifecourse*, Oxon: Routledge, pp 25–39.

Edwards, R. and Usher, R. (1994) 'Disciplining the subject: the power of competence', *Studies in the Education of Adults*, 26(1): 1–14.

Elias, M. (2010) 'Impact of the Bologna process on Spanish students' expectations', *International Journal of Iberian Studies*, 23(1): 53–62.

Ertl, H. (2013) *The impact of the post-Bologna reforms on German higher education and the transition of graduates into the labour market* (Skope Research Paper), Skope: University of Oxford.

Eskin, M., Sun, J., Abuidhail, J., Yoshimasu, K., et al (2016) 'Suicidal behavior and psychological distress in university students: a 12-nation study', *Archives of Suicide Research*, 20(3): 369–388.

Eurostat (2019a) *Eurostat* [European Statistics Portal]. Available online at: https://ec.europa.eu/eurostat/371 (Accessed 24 August 2021)

Eurostat (2019b) *EU employment rate for recent graduates*. Available online at: https://ec.europa.eu/eurostat/web/products-eurostat-news/-/DDN-20190704-1 (Accessed 28 December 2020).

Eurostudent (n.d.) *Eurostudent VI database* Available online at: http://database.eurostudent.eu (Accessed 26 November 2019).

Eurostudent (2005) *Eurostudent report 2005: social and economic conditions of student life in Europe 2005.* Available online at: www.eurostudent.eu/download_files/documents/report2005.pdf (Accessed 1 October 2016).

Eurostudent (2011) *Social and economic conditions of student life in Europe.* Available online at: www.eurostudent.eu/download_files/documents/Synopsis_of_Indicators_EIV.pdf (Accessed 1 October 2016).

Eurostudent (2018) *Eurostudent VI: overview and selected findings. Social and economic conditions of student life in Europe.* Available online at: www.eurostudent.eu/download_files/documents/EUROSTUDENT_VI_short_report.pdf (Accessed 14 January 2022).

Eurydice (2017) *National Student Fee and Support Systems in European Higher Education – 2017/18*, Eurydice.

Evans, K. (1995) 'Competence and citizenship: towards a complementary model for times of critical social change', *British Journal of Education and Work*, 8(2): 14–27.

Farber, P. and Holm, G. (2005) Selling the dream of higher education: marketing images of university life, in S. Edgerton, G. Holm, T. Daspit and P. Farber (eds) *Imagining the Academy: Higher Education and Popular Culture*, London: RoutledgeFalmer, pp 117–130.

Finn, K., Ingram, N. and Allen, K. (2021) 'Student millennials/millennial students: how the lens of generation constructs understandings of the contemporary HE student', in R. Brooks and S. O'Shea (eds) *Reimagining the Higher Education Student*, London: Routledge, pp 188–205.

Fleming, T., Loxley, A. and Finnegan, F. (2017) *Access and Participation in Irish Higher Education*, London: Palgrave.

Fotiadou, M. (2020) 'Denaturalising the discourse of competition in the graduate job market and the notion of employability: a corpus-based study of UK university websites', *Critical Discourse Studies*, 17(3): 260–291.

France, A. (2007) *Understanding Youth in Late Modernity*, Maidenhead: Open University Press.

Frey, C. (2008) 'κλῆσισ/Beruf: Luther, Weber, Agamben', *New German Critique*, 35(3): 35–56.

Furedi, F. (2017) *What's Happened to the University? A Sociological Exploration of its Infantilisation*, London: Routledge.

Furlong, A. and Cartmel, F. (2007) *Young People and Social Change* (2nd edn), Maidenhead: Open University Press.

Fyfe, I. and Wyn, J. (2007) 'Young activists making the news: the role of the media in youth political and civic engagement', in L.J. Saha, M. Print and K. Edwards (eds) *Youth and Political Participation*, Rotterdam: Sense Publishers, pp 113–132.

Gabriel, Y. (1993) 'Organizational nostalgia – reflections on "the golden age"', in S. Fineman (ed) *Emotion in Organizations*, London: Sage, pp 118–141.

Gagnon, J. (2018) 'Unreasonable rage, disobedient dissent: the social construction of student activists and the limits of student engagement', *Learning and Teaching*, 11(1): 82–108.

Gale, T. and Parker, S. (2014) 'Navigating change: a typology of student transition in higher education', *Studies in Higher Education*, 39(5): 734–753.

Gangl, M. (2001) 'European patterns of labour market entry: a dichotomy of occupationalized vs. non-occupationalized systems?', *European Societies*, 3(4): 471–494.

Gedye, S. and Beaumont, E. (2018) '"The ability to get a job": student understandings and definitions of employability', *Education + Training*, 60(5): 406–420.

Gierus, J., Mosiolek, A., Koweszko, T. and Szulc, A. (2017) 'Institutional discrimination against psychiatric patients in Poland', *The Lancet*, 4: 743.

Grant, B. (2017) 'On delivering the consumer-citizen: new pedagogies and their affective economies', in S. Wright and C. Shore (eds) *Death of the Public University? Uncertain Futures for Higher Education in the Knowledge Economy*, New York: Berghahn Books, pp 138–155.

Grant, J., Hewlett, K.A., Nir, T. and Duffy, B. (2019) *Freedom of expression in UK universities*. Available online at: https://doi.org/10.18742/pub01-010 (Accessed 5 August 2021)

Gravett, K. (2019) 'Troubling transitions and celebrating becomings: from pathway to rhizome', *Studies in Higher Education*, doi:10.1080/03075079.2019.1691162 (advance online access).

Gravett, K., Kinchin, I.M. and Winstone, N.E. (2020) 'Frailty in transition? Troubling the norms, boundaries and limitations of transition theory and practice', *Higher Education Research & Development*, 39(6): 1169–1185.

Green, A. (2006) 'Education, globalization and the nation-state', in H. Lauder, P. Brown, J. Dillabough and A. Halsey (eds) *Education, Globalization and Social Change*, Oxford: Oxford University Press, pp 192–197.

Greenfield, L. (2013) *Mind, Modernity and Madness: The Impact of Culture on Human Experience*, London: Harvard University Press.

Gregersen, A., Holmegaard, H. and Ulriksen, L. (2021) 'Transitioning into higher education: rituals and implied expectations', *Journal of Further and Higher Education* (advance online access).

Grigsby, M. (2014) *College Life through the Eyes of Students*, Albany, NY: SUNY Press.

Haj, C.M., Geanta, I.M. and Orr, D. (2018) 'A typology of admission systems across Europe and their impact on the equity of access, progression and completion in higher education', in A. Curaj, L. Deca and R. Pricopie (eds) *European Higher Education Area: The Impact of Past and Future Policies*, Cham: Springer, pp 171–187. Available online at: https://link.springer.com/chapter/10.1007/978-3-319-77407-7_12 (Accessed).

Hammond, C. and Keating, A. (2018) 'Global citizens or global workers? Comparing university programmes for global citizenship education in Japan and the UK', *Compare*, 48(6): 915–934.

Hansen, K.-H. (2008) 'Rewriting *Bildung* for postmodernity: books on educational philosophy, classroom practice, and reflective teaching', *Curriculum Inquiry*, 38(1): 93–115.

Harris, A., Cuervo, H. and Wyn, J. (2021) *Thinking about Belonging in Youth Studies*, London: Palgrave.

Harrison, N. (2019) 'Students-as-insurers: rethinking 'risk' for disadvantaged young people considering higher education in England', *Journal of Youth Studies*, 22(6): 752–771.

Hazelkorn, E. (2015) *Rankings and the Reshaping of Higher Education* (2nd edn), London: Palgrave.

Hill, D.W. (2020) 'Communication as a moral vocation: safe space and freedom of speech', *The Sociological Review*, 68(1): 3–16.

Hirsch, J. and Khan, S. (2020) *Sexual Citizens: A Landmark Study of Sex, Power and Assault on Campus*, New York: W.W. Norton and Company.

Hodkinson, P., Hodkinson, H. and Sparkes, A.C. (2013) *Triumphs and Tears: Young People, Markets, and the Transition from School to Work*, London: Routledge.

Holdsworth, S., Turner, M. and Scott-Young, C. (2018) 'Not drowning, waving. Resilience and university: a student perspective', *Studies in Higher Education*, 43(11): 1837–1853.

Holton, M. and Finn, K. (2018) 'Being-in-motion: THE everyday (gendered and classed) embodied mobilities for UK university students who commute', *Mobilities*, 13(3): 426–440.

Hopmann, S. (2007) 'Restrained teaching: the common core of Didaktik', *European Educational Research Journal*, 6(2): 109–124.

Horlacher, R. (2015) *The Educated Subject and the German Concept of Bildung: A Comparative Cultural History*, London: Routledge.

Hoskins, B. (2006) *A Framework for the Creation of Indicators on Active Citizenship and on Education and Training for Active Citizenship*, European Commission, ISPRA.

Hubbard, P. (2013) 'Carnage! Coming to a town near you? Nightlife, uncivilised behaviour and the carnivalesque body', *Leisure Studies*, 32(3): 265–282.

Hudson, B. (2007) 'Comparing different traditions of teaching and learning: what can we learn about teaching and learning?', *European Educational Research Journal*, 6(2): 135–146.

Hurst, A.L. (2010) 'Schoolcraft vs. becoming somebody: competing visions of higher education among working-class college students', *Qualitative Studies*, 1(2): 75–90.

Hurst, A.L. (2013) 'Student types as reflection of class habitus: an application of Bourdieu's scholastic fallacy', *Theory and Research in Education*, 11(1): 43–61.

Hüther, O. and Krücken, G. (2014) 'The rise and fall of student fees in a federal higher education system: the case of Germany', in H. Ertl and C. Dupuy (eds) *Students, Markets and Social Justice*, Oxford: Symposium Books, pp 85–110.

Ingram, N. (2011) 'Within school and beyond the gate: the difficulties of being educationally successful and working class', *Sociology*, 45(2): 287–302.

Irwin, S. (2020) 'Young people in the middle: pathways, prospects, policies and a new agenda for youth research', *Journal of Youth Studies*, DOI: 10.1080/13676261.2020.1792864 (advance online access).

Isopahkala-Bouret, U., Lappalainen, S. and Lahelma, E. (2014) 'Educating worker-citizens: visions and divisions in curriculum texts', *Journal of Education and Work*, 27(1): 92–109.

Jackson, C. and Nyström, A.-S. (2015) '"Smart students get perfect scores in tests without studying much": why is an effortless achiever identity attractive, and for whom is it possible?', *Research Papers in Education*, 30(4): 393–410.

Jayadeva, S., Brooks, R. and Lazetic, P. (2021) 'Paradise lost or created? The perceived impact of policy on higher education students', *Journal of Education Policy* (advance online access).

Jayadeva, S., Brooks, R. and Abrahams, J. (2022) 'The (stereo)typical student: how European higher education students feel they are viewed by relevant others', *British Journal of Sociology of Education*, 43(1): 1–21.

Jones, G. (2009) *Youth*, Cambridge: Polity Press.

Keating, A. (2014) *Education for Citizenship in Europe: European Policies, National Adaptations and Young People's Attitudes*, Berlin: Springer.

Keeling, R. (2006) 'The Bologna Process and the Lisbon Research Agenda: the European Commission's expanding role in higher education discourse', *European Journal of Education*, 41(2): 203–223.

Kehm, B.M. (2013) 'To be or not to be? The impacts of the Excellence Initiative on the German system of higher education', in J. Shin and B. Kehm (eds) *Institutionalization of World-Class University in Global Competition: The Changing Academy – The Changing Academic Profession in International Comparative Perspective*, Dordrecht: Springer, pp 81–97.

Klemenčič, M. (2014) 'Student power in a global perspective and contemporary trends in student organising', *Studies in Higher Education*, 39(3): 396–411.

Klemenčič, M. and Park, B. (2018) 'Student politics: between representation and activism', in B. Cantwell, H. Coates and R. King (eds) *Handbook on the Politics of Higher Education*, Cheltenham: Edward Elgar, pp 468–486.

Kosmützky, A. (2015) 'In defence of international comparative studies: on the analytical and explanatory power of the nation state in international comparative higher education research', *European Journal of Higher Education*, 5(4): 354–370.

Kwiek, M. (2016) 'From privatisation (of the expansion era) to de-privatisation (of the contraction era): a national counter-trend in a global context', in S. Slaughter and B. Taylor (eds) *Higher Education, Stratification, and Workforce Development*, Dordrecht: Springer, pp 311–329.

Kwiek, M. (2018) 'Building a new society and economy: high participation higher education in Poland', in B. Cantwell, S. Marginson and A. Smolentseva (eds) *High Participation Systems of Higher Education*, Oxford: Oxford Scholarship Online, pp 334–357.

Lainio, A. and Brooks, R. (2021) 'Constructing students as family members: contestations in media and policy representations across Europe', in R. Brooks and S. O'Shea (eds) *Reimagining the Higher Education Student*, London: Routledge, pp 170–187.

Landrum, D. (2002) 'Citizenship, education and the political discourse of New Labour', *Contemporary Politics*, 8(3): 219–232.

Larcombe, W., Finch, S., Sore, R., Murray, C., Kentish, S., Mulder, R.A., et al (2016) 'Prevalence and socio-demographic correlates of psychological distress among students at an Australian university', *Studies in Higher Education*, 41(6): 1074–1091.

Lažetić, P. (2019) 'Students and university websites: consumers of corporate brands or novices in the academic community?' *Higher Education*, 77(6): 995–1013.

Leaker, A. (2020) *Against Free Speech*, London: Rowman & Littlefield.

Leathwood, C. (2006) 'Gender, equity and the discourse of the independent learner in higher education', *Higher Education*, 52: 611–633.

Leathwood, C. and O'Connell, P. (2003) ' "It's a struggle": the construction of the "new student" in higher education', *Journal of Education Policy*, 18(6): 597–615.

Lesko, N. (2012) *Act Your Age! A Cultural Construction of Adolescence*, New York: RoutledgeFalmer.

Littler, J. (2013) *Against Meritocracy: Culture, Power and Myths of Mobility*, London: Routledge.

Llamas, J.M.C. (2006) 'Technologies of disciplinary power in action: the norm of the "good student"', *Higher Education* 52(4): 665–686. doi:10.1007/s10734-004-1449-1.

Loader, B., Vromen, A., Xenos, M., Steel, H. and Burgum, S. (2015) 'Campus politics, student societies and social media', *The Sociological Review*, 63(4): 820–839.

Lomer, S. (2017) *Recruiting International Students in Higher Education: Representations and Rationales in British Policy*, London: Palgrave.

Loukakis, A. and Portos, M. (2020) 'Another brick in the wall? Young people, protest and non-protest claims making in nine European countries', *American Behavioral Scientist*, 6(5): 669–685.

Loveday, V. (2016) 'Embodying deficiency through "affective practice": shame, relationality, and the lived experience of social class and gender in higher education', *Sociology*, 50(6): 1140–1155.

Lukianoff, G. and Haidt, J. (2018) *The Coddling of the American Mind: How Good Intentions and Bad Ideas are Setting up a Generation for Failure*, London: Penguin Press.

Lynch, K., Grummell, B. and Devine, D. (2012) *New Managerialism in Education*, London: Palgrave.

Macfarlane, B. (2020) 'Myths about students in higher education: separating fact from folklore', *Oxford Review of Education* (advance online access).

McManus, L. and Rook, L. (2021) 'Mixed views in the academy: academic and student perspectives about the utility of developing work-ready skills through WIL', *Studies in Higher Education*, 46(2): 270–284.

Madsen, M. (2019) *Entangled Simplicities. A Metricography on 'Relevance' and 'Graduate Employability' Configurations in Danish University Education*. PhD thesis, Aarhus University. Available online at: https://pure.au.dk/portal/files/199271655/Entangled_Simplicities_final.pdf (Accessed 12 March 2021).

Madsen, M. (2021) 'The configurative agency of metrics in education: a research agenda involving a different engagement with data', *Journal of Education Policy*, 36(1): 64–83.

Maguire, M., Braun, A. and Ball, S. (2018) 'Discomforts, opposition and resistance in schools: the perspectives of union representatives', *British Journal of Sociology of Education*, 39(7): 1060–1073.

Marginson, S. (2019) 'Limitations of human capital theory', *Studies in Higher Education*, 44(2): 287–301.

Marqués, A.C. and Navarro-Pérez, J.J. (2019) 'The care crisis in Spain: an analysis of the family care situation in mental health from a professional psychosocial perspective', *Social Work in Mental Health*, 17(6): 743–760.

Marsh, D., O'Toole, T. and Jones, S. (2007) *Young People and Politics in the UK: Apathy or Alienation?*, Basingstoke: Palgrave.

Martínez-Campillo, A. and Fernández-Santos, Y. (2020) 'The impact of the economic crisis on the (in)efficiency of public higher education institutions in Southern Europe: the case of Spanish universities', *Socio-Economic Planning Sciences*, 71(1).

Massey, D. (2005) *For Space*, London: Sage.

Matthews, K.E., Dwyer, A., Hine, L. and Turner, J. (2018) 'Conceptions of students as partners', *Higher Education*, 76: 957–971.

McGettigan, A. (2013) *The Great University Gamble: Money, Markets and the Future of Higher Education*, London: Pluto Press.

Mendick, H., Allen, K., Harvey, L. and Ahmad, A. (2018) *Celebrity, Aspiration and Contemporary Youth: Education and Inequality in an Era of Austerity*, London: Bloomsbury.

Molesworth, M., Nixon, E. and Scullion, E. (2009) 'Having, being and higher education: the marketization of the university and the transformation of the student into consumer', *Teaching in Higher Education*, 14(3): 277–287.

Moore, T. and Morton, J. (2017) 'The myth of job readiness? Written communication, employability, and the "skills gap" in higher education', *Studies in Higher Education*, 42(3): 501–609.

Moreno, L. (2013) 'Spain's catch up with the EU core: the implausible quest of a "flying pig"?', *South European Society and Politics*, 18(2): 217–236.

Morley, L. (2003) 'Restructuring students as consumers', in M. Slowey and D. Watson (eds) *Higher Education and the Lifecourse*, London: SRHE and Open University Press, pp 79–92.

Moutsios, S. (2013) 'The de-Europeanization of the university under the Bologna Process', *Thesis Eleven*, 119(1): 22–46.

Muddiman, E. (2020) 'Degree subject and orientations to civic responsibility: a comparative study of Business and Sociology students', *Critical Studies in Education*, 61(5): 577–593.

Müller, W. and Gangl, M. (eds) (2003) *Transitions from Education to Work in Europe: The Integration of Youth into EU Labour Markets*, Oxford: Oxford University Press.

Naidoo, R. and Williams, J. (2015) 'The neoliberal regime in English higher education: charters, consumers and the erosion of the public good', *Critical Studies in Education*, 56(2): 208–223.

Naidoo, R., Shankar, A. and Veer, E. (2011) 'The consumerist turn in higher education: policy aspirations and outcomes', *Journal of Marketing Management*, 27(11–12): 1142–1162.

Neves, J. and Hillman, N. (2018) *The HEPI/Advance HE 2018 Academic Experience Survey*, Oxford: Higher Education Policy Institute.

Newman, J.H. (1996) [1858] *The Idea of a University*, New Haven, CT: Yale University Press.

Nielsen, G. (2011) 'Peopling policy: on conflicting subjectivities of fee-paying students', in C. Shore, S. Wright and D. Però (eds) *Policy Worlds: Anthropology and the Analysis of Contemporary Power*, New York: Berghahn Books, pp 68–85.

Nielsen, G.B. (2015) *Figuration Work: Student Participation, Democracy and University Reform in a Global Knowledge Economy*, New York: Berghahn Books.

Nielsen, G. and Sarauw, L.L. (2017) 'Tuning up and tuning in: the European Bologna Process and students' time of study', in S. Wright and C. Shore (eds) *Death of the Public University? Uncertain Futures for Higher Education in the Knowledge Economy*, Oxford: Berghahn, pp 156–172.

Nissen, S. (2019) *Student Debt and Political Participation*, London: Palgrave.

Nissen, S. and Hayward, B. (2017) 'Students' associations: the New Zealand experience', in R. Brooks (ed) *Student Politics and Protest: International Perspectives*, London: Routledge, pp 129–142.

Nixon, E., Scullion, R. and Molesworth, M. (2010) 'How choice in higher education can create conservative learners', in M. Molesworth, R. Scullion and E. Nixon (eds) *The Marketisation of Higher Education and the Student as Consumer*, London: Routledge, pp 196–208.

Nixon, E., Scullion, R. and Hearn, R. (2018) 'Her majesty the student: marketised higher education and the narcissistic (dis)satisfactions of the student-consumer', *Studies in Higher Education*, 43(6): 927–943.

Nyland, C. and Tran, L. (2020) 'The consumer rights of international students in the Australian vocational education and training sector', *Journal of Vocational Education and Training*, 72(1): 71–87.

Nyström, A.-S., Jackson, C. and Salminen Karlsson, M. (2019) 'What counts as success? Constructions of achievement in prestigious higher education programmes', *Research Papers in Education*, 34(4): 465–482.

OECD (2018) *Health at a Glance: Europe 2018*, Paris: OECD Publications.

OECD (2020) *Education at a Glance 2020*, Paris: OECD Publications.

Olcese, C., Saunders, S. and Tzavidis, N. (2014) 'In the streets with a degree: how political generations, educational attainment and student status affect engagement in protest politics', *International Sociology*, 29(6): 525–545.

O'Shea, S. (2014) 'Transitions and turning points: exploring how first-in-family female students story their transition to university and student identity formation', *International Journal of Qualitative Studies in Education*, 27(2): 135–158.

O'Shea, S. (2015) 'Avoiding the manufacture of "sameness": first-in-family students, cultural capital and the higher education environment', *Higher Education*, 72: 59–78.

O'Shea, S. and Delahunty, J. (2018) 'Getting through the day and still having a smile on my face! How do students define success in the university learning environment?' *Higher Education Research and Development*, 37(5): 1062–1075.

Ozga, J. and Lingard, B. (2007) 'Globalisation, education policy and politics', in B. Lingard and J. Ozga (eds) *The RoutledgeFalmer Reader in Education Policy and Politics*, London: Routledge, pp 65–82.

Pappa, S., Elomaa, M. and Perala-Littunen, S. (2020) 'Sources of stress and scholarly identity: the case of international doctoral students of education in Finland', *Higher Education*, 80(1): 173–192.

Philips, D. and Schweisfurth, M. (2014) *Comparative and International Education*, London: Continuum.

Phillips, L. (2008) 'Anti-Bologna movement spreads in Spain', *EU Observer*, 15 December 2008. Available online at: https://euobserver.com/educat ion/27303 (Accessed 6 April 2021).

Phipps, A. and Young, I. (2015) 'Neoliberalisation and "lad cultures" in higher education', *Sociology*, 49(2): 305–322.

Pickard, S. (2019) *Politics, Protest and Young People: Political Participation and Dissent in 21st Century Britain*, London: Palgrave.

Pilkington, H. and Pollack, G. (2015) '"Politics are bollocks": youth, politics and activism in contemporary Europe', *The Sociological Review*, 63(S2): 1–35.

Pole, C., Pilcher, J. and Williams, J. (2005) 'Young people in transition: becoming citizens? An introduction', in C. Pole, J. Pilcher and J. Williams (eds) *Young People in Transition: Becoming Citizens?*, London: Palgrave, pp 1–11.

Powell, J.J., Graf, L., Bernhard, N., Coutrot, L. and Kieffer, A. (2012) 'The shifting relationship between vocational and higher education in France and Germany: towards convergence?', *European Journal of Education*, 47(3): 405–423.

Pusey, A. and Sealey-Huggins, L. (2013) 'Neoliberalism and depoliticisation in the academy: understanding the "new student rebellions"', *Graduate Journal of Social Science*, 10(3): 80–99.

Raaper, R. (2018) 'Students' unions and consumerist policy discourses in English higher education', *Critical Studies in Education*, 61(2): 245–261.

Reay, D. (2017) *Miseducation: Inequality, Education and the Working Classes*, Bristol: Policy Press.

Reay, D., Crozier, G. and Clayton, J. (2009) '"Strangers in Paradise"? Working-class students in elite universities', *Sociology*, 43(6): 1103–1121.

Reay, D., Crozier, G. and Clayton, J. (2010) '"Fitting in" or "standing out": working-class students in UK higher education', *British Educational Research Journal*, 36(1): 107–124.

Reher, D. (1998) 'Family ties in Western Europe: persistent contrasts', *Population and Development Review*, 24(2): 203–234.

Reimer, D. and Thomsen, J.P. (2019) 'Vertical and horizontal stratification in higher education', in R. Becker (ed) *Research Handbook on the Sociology of Education*, Cheltenham: Edward Elgar Publishing Limited, pp 308–328.

Rivera, L.A. (2015) *Pedigree: How Elite Students Get Elite Jobs*, Princeton, NJ: Princeton University Press.

Roberts, S. and Li, Z. (2017) 'Capital limits: social class, motivations for term-time job searching and the consequences of joblessness among UK university students', *Journal of Youth Studies*, 20(6): 732–749.

Robertson, K. and Tustin, K. (2018) 'Students who limit their drinking, as recommended by national guidelines, are stigmatized, ostracized, or the subject of peer pressure: limiting consumption is all but prohibited in a culture of intoxication', *Substance Abuse: Research and Treatment*. Available online at: https://pubmed.ncbi.nlm.nih.gov/30093798/ (Accessed 5 August 2021).

Rochford, F. (2014) 'Bringing them into the tent: student association and the neutered academy', *Studies in Higher Education*, 39(3): 485–499.

Rømer, T.A. (2021) 'Gert Biesta: education between Bildung and post-structuralism', *Educational Philosophy and Theory*, 53(1): 34–45.

Sam, C. and van der Sijde, P. (2014) 'Understanding the concept of the entrepreneurial university from the perspective of higher education models', *Higher Education*, 68: 891–908.

Sarauw, L.L. and Madsen, S.R. (2020) 'Higher education in the paradigm of speed: student perspectives on the risks of fast-track degree completion', *Learning and Teaching*, 13(1): 1–23.

Schultz, T.W. (1961) 'Investment in human capital', *The American Economic Review*, American Economic Association, 51(1): 1–17.

Shaw, J. (2001) ' "Winning territory": changing place to change pace', in J. May and N. Thrift (eds) *Timespace: Geographies of Temporality*, London: Routledge, pp 120–132.

Shin, J.-C., Kim, H.-H. and Choi, H.-C. (2014) 'The evolution of student activism and its influence on tuition fees in South Korean universities', *Studies in Higher Education*, 39(3): 443–454.

Sidhu, R. (2006) *Universities and Globalization: To Market, To Market*, Mahwah, NJ: Lawrence Erlbaum Associates Ltd.

Slaughter, S. and Cantwell, B. (2012) 'Transatlantic moves to the market: the United States and the European Union', *Higher Education*, 63: 583–606.

Sloam, J. and Henn, M. (2019) *Youthquake 2017: The Rise of Young Cosmopolitans in Britain*, Berlin: Springer Nature.

Sparks, C. (2000) 'Introduction: the panic over tabloid news', in Sparks, C. and Tulloch, J. (eds) *Tabloid Tales: Global Debates Over Media Standards*, Oxford: Roman and Littlefield Publishers, pp 1–40.

Spence, M. (1973) 'Job market signaling', *The Quarterly Journal of Economics*, 87(3): 355–374.

Spiegler, T. and Bednarek, A. (2013) 'First-generation students: what we ask, what we know and what it means: an international review of the state of research', *International Studies in Sociology of Education*, 23(4): 318–337.

Stankiewicz, Ł. (2020) 'Discourse, resistance and organization: critical discourse analysis of the "revolt of the humanities" in Poland', *Discourse: Studies in the Cultural Politics of Education*, 1–13 (advance online access).

Stein, G.L., Gonzalez, G.M., Cupito, A., Kiang, L. and Supple, A. (2015) 'The protective role of familism in the lives of Latino adolescents', *Journal of Family Issues*, 36(10): 1255–1273.

Stiwne, E. and Alves, M. (2010) 'Higher education and employability of graduates: will Bologna make a difference?' *European Educational Research Journal*, 9(1): 32–44.

Storrie, K., Ahern, K. and Tuckett, A. (2010) 'A systematic review: students with mental health problems – a growing problem', *International Journal of Nursing Practice*, 16(1): 1–6.

Sukarieh, M. and Tannock, S. (2015) *Youth Rising? The Politics of Youth in the Global Economy*, London: Routledge.

Sykes, G. (2021) 'Dispelling the myth of the "traditional" university undergraduate student in the UK', in R. Brooks and S. O'Shea (eds) *Reimagining the Higher Education Student*, London: Routledge, pp 80–97.

Szukalska, H. (2020) Stigmatisation and medication: Poland's outdated approach to mental health, *Notes from Poland*, 1 May 2020. Available online at: https://notesfrompoland.com/2020/05/01/stigmatisation-and-medication-polands-outdated-approach-to-mental-health/ (Accessed 28 December 2020).

Tabor, E., Patalay, P. and Bann, D. (2021) 'Mental health in higher education students and non-students: evidence from a nationally representative panel study', *Social Psychiatry and Psychiatric Epidemiology*, 56: 879–882.

Tavares, O. and Cardoso, S. (2013) 'Enrolment choices in Portuguese higher education: do students behave as rational consumers?', *Higher Education*, 66: 297–309.

Teichler, U. (2009) *Higher Education and the World of Work: Conceptual Frameworks, Comparative Perspectives and Empirical Findings*, Rotterdam: Sense Publishers.

Teichler, U. and Kehm, B.M. (1995) 'Towards a new understanding of the relationships between higher education and employment', *European Journal of Education*, 30(2): 115–132.

Thornham, S. and Purvis, T. (2005) *Television Drama: Theories and Identities*, London: Palgrave Macmillan.

Tidman, Z. (2021) 'Gavin Williamson to announce "free speech champion" with power to sanction universities', *Independent* [online] 14 February. Available online at: www.independent.co.uk/news/education/education-news/free-speech-champion-universities-b1802203.html (Accessed 9 April 2021).

Tight, M. (2013) 'Students: customers, clients or pawns?' *Higher Education Policy*, 26: 291–307.

Tobolowsky, B.F. and Reynolds, P.J. (2017) 'Concluding thoughts on media representations of higher education: anti-intellectualism and other themes', in B.F. Tobolowsky and P.J. Reynolds (eds) *Anti-Intellectual Representations of American Colleges and Universities: Fictional Higher Education*, New York: Palgrave Macmillan, pp 179–198.

Tomlinson, M. (2007) 'Graduate employability and student attitudes and orientations to the labour market', *Journal of Education and Work*, 20(4): 285–304.

Tomlinson, M. (2008) '"The degree is not enough": students' perceptions of the role of higher education credentials for graduate work and employability', *British Journal of Sociology of Education*, 29(1): 49–61.

Tomlinson, M. (2010) 'Investing in the self: structure, agency and identity in graduates' employability', *Education, Knowledge & Economy*, 4(2): 73–88.

Tomlinson, M. (2013) *Education, Work and Identity: Themes and Perspectives*, London; New York: Bloomsbury Academic.

Tomlinson, M. (2017) 'Student perceptions of themselves as "consumers" of higher education', *British Journal of Sociology of Education* 38(4): 450–467.

Tran, L.T. and Vu, T.T.P. (2016) '"I'm not like that, why treat me the same way?" The impact of stereotyping international students on their learning, employability and connectedness with the workplace', *The Australian Educational Researcher*, 43(2): 203–220.

Tyler, I. (2013) *Revolting Subjects: Social Abjection and Resistance in Neoliberal Britain*, London: Zed Books.

Ulriksen, L. (2009) 'The implied student', *Studies in Higher Education*, 34(5): 517–532.

Ulriksen, L. and Nejrup, C. (2021) 'Balancing times: university students' practices and policy perspectives of time', *Sociological Research Online* (advance online access).

Usher, R. and Edwards, R. (1994) *Postmodernism and Education: Different Voices, Different Worlds*, London: Routledge.

Van Oorschot, W. (2006) 'Making the difference in social Europe: deservingness perceptions among citizens of European welfare state', *Journal of European Social Policy*, 16(1): 23–42.

Vromen, A. (2003) '"People try to put us down …": participatory citizenship of "Generation X"', *Australian Journal of Political Science*, 38(1): 79–99.

Vromen, A., Loader, B., Xenos, M. and Bailo, F. (2016) 'Everyday making through Facebook engagement: young citizens' political interactions in Australia, the United Kingdom and the United States', *Political Studies*, 64(3): 513–533.

Walsemann, K., Gee, G. and Gentile, D. (2015) 'Sick of our loans: student borrowing and the mental health of young adults in the United States', *Social Science and Medicine*, 124: 85.

Waters, J. (2009) 'In pursuit of scarcity: transnational students, "employability" and the MBA', *Environment and Planning A*, 41(8): 1865–1883.

Waugh, C. (2019) 'In defence of safe spaces: subaltern counter-publics and vulnerable politics in the neoliberal university', in M. Breeze, Y. Taylor and C. Costa (eds) *Time and Space in the Neoliberal University*, Cham: Springer Palgrave Macmillan, pp 143–168.

Weeden, K.A. (2002) 'Why do some occupations pay more than others? Social closure and earnings inequality in the United States', *American Journal of Sociology*, 108(1): 55–101.

Weedon, E. and Riddell, S. (2015) 'Higher education in Europe: widening participation', in M. Shah, A. Bennett and E. Southgate (eds) *Widening Higher Education Participation*, Oxford: Elsevier, pp 49–61.

Weiss, F., Klein, M. and Grauenhorst, T. (2014) 'The effects of work experience during higher education on labour market entry: learning by doing or an entry ticket?', *Work, Employment and Society*, 28(5): 788–807.

Whyte, W.H. (2019) *Somewhere to Live: Why British Students Study Away from Home, and why it Matters*, London: Higher Education Policy Institute. Available online at: www.hepi.ac.uk/wp-content/uploads/2019/11/HEPI_Somewhere-to-live_Report-121-FINAL.pdf (Accessed 5 August 2021).

Wilkinson, L.C. and Wilkinson, M.D. (2020) 'Value for money and the commodification of higher education: front-line narratives', *Teaching in Higher Education* (advance online access).

Wilkinson, R. and Pickett, K. (2010) *The Spirit Level: Why Equality is Better for Everyone*, London: Penguin.

Williams, J. (2011) 'Constructing consumption', in M. Molesworth, R. Scullion and E. Nixon (eds) *The Marketisation of Higher Education and the Student as Consumer*, London: Routledge, pp 170–182.

Williams, J. (2013) *Consuming Higher Education: Why Learning Can't Be Bought*, London: Bloomsbury.

Wimmer, A. and Glick Schiller, N. (2002) 'Methodological nationalism and beyond: nation-state building, migration and the social sciences', *Global Networks*, 2(4): 301–334.

Winkler, P., Krupchanka, D., Roberts, T., Kondratova, L., Machů, V., Höschl, C., et al (2017) 'A blind spot on the global mental health map: a scoping review of 25 years' development of mental health care for people with severe mental illnesses in central and eastern Europe', *Lancet Psychiatry*, 4(8): 634–642.

Wong, B. and Chiu, Y.L.T. (2019) 'Exploring the concept of "ideal" university student', *Studies in Higher Education* (advance online access).

Wong, B. and Chiu, Y.L.T. (2020) 'University lecturers' construction of the "ideal" undergraduate student', *Journal of Further and Higher Education* (advance online access).

Woodall, T., Hiller, A. and Resnick, S. (2014) 'Making sense of higher education: students as consumers and the value of the university experience', *Studies in Higher Education*, 39(1): 48–67.

Woodman, D. and Wyn, J. (2015) *Youth and Generation: Rethinking Change and Inequality in the Lives of Young People*, London: Sage.

Wright, K. (2008) 'Theorizing therapeutic culture', *Journal of Sociology*, 44(4): 321–336. DOI:10.1177/1440783308097124.

Wright, S. and Shore, C. (eds) (2017) *Death of the Public University? Uncertain Futures for Higher Education in the Knowledge Economy*, New York: Berghahn Books.

Ylijoki, O.-H. (2005) 'Academic nostalgia: a narrative approach to academic work', *Human Relations*, 58(3): 555–576.

Yosso, T.J. (2005) 'Whose culture has capital? A critical race theory discussion of community cultural wealth', *Race Ethnicity and Education*, 8(1): 69–91.

YouGov (2016) *One in four students suffer from mental health problems.* Available online at: https://yougov.co.uk/topics/lifestyle/articles-reports/2016/08/09/quarter-britains-students-are-afflicted-mental-hea (Accessed 22 May 2021).

Zamponi, L. and González, J.F. (2017) 'Dissenting youth: how student and youth struggles helped shape anti-austerity mobilisations in Southern Europe', *Social Movement Studies*, 16(1): 64–81.

Index

References to figures appear in *italic* type;
those in **bold** type refer to tables. References to
endnotes show the page number and the note
number, followed by the chapter number, e.g. 187n4(ch1).

Hansen, K.-H. 109
hard workers 78–82, 120–124
Harris, A. 47
Harrison, N. 27
Hayes, D. 115, 141
Hazelkorn, E. 17, 20, 87, 89
HE-related data by country **15**
hedonistic students 151–154
Henn, M. 55
Hesketh, A. 119
hierarchies between disciplines of
    study 82–86, 166
hierarchies between HEIs 86–88, 166
hierarchy of learners 82–91
higher education
  HE-related data by country **15**
  human capital discourse 93
  Humboldtian model 15, 19, 20, 39, 70,
    109, 123, 159
  public responsibility model 6
  residential model 6, 34, 160
  social investment model 5–6
  see also university education
higher education institutions (HEIs) **178**
  hierarchies between 86–88, 166
  staff profiles **181–184**
higher education policy 93–95
higher education students *see* students
Hill, D.W. 141
Hillman, N. 114
Hirsch, J. 114
Hodkinson, P. 99
Holford, J. 46
Holm, G. 11
Hopmann, S. 109
Horlacher, R. 109
Hoskins, B. 46, 47
Hudson, B. 109
human capital discourse 5, 92–100,
    112
humanities 82, 83, 84, 85
Humboldtian model 15, 19, 20, 39, 70,
    109, 123, 159
Hurst, A.L. 77

I

ideal students 133–144, 139, 141, 146,
    148, 150, 161
identity politics 143
identity work 25
implied students 133, 134
incompetent, students as lazy and 80,
    134–139, 155
  student perspectives 148–150
independent learners 134, 136, 139
individualised citizenship 37
Ingram, N. 13
institutional habitus 89
institutional perspectives 11–12

instrumental learners 69–73, 75, 78
Ireland
  country characteristics **8**
  dependence on family 146–148
  habitus disconnect 125
  HE-related data **15**
  hierarchies between disciplines of
    study 84–85
  hierarchies between HEIs 88
  human capital discourse 94, 97
  labour market transition 29
  national policy contexts 19–20
  newspapers **10**
  social class 88–89
  staff profiles **183**
  stress 128, 129–30
  students as citizens 50, 51, 53, 54, 55,
    56, 58
  students as hard workers 79
  students as lazy and
    incompetent 137–138
  students as learners 72, 73, 76
  students as political actors 66
  students' mental wellbeing 116
  students' political activism 139–141
  transition to adulthood 32–35
  TV series and films **11**
  vocational perspective 108
Irish Independent **10**, 62, 140
Irish Times **10**, 61, 116, 135, 140
Irwin, S. 27
Isopahkala-Bouret, U. 52

J

Jones, G. 133

K

Keating, A. 46, 47, 55
Keeling, R. 92
Kehm, B.M. 19, 102
Khan, S. 114
Klememčič, M. 65, 67
Kosmützky, A. 7
Kwiek, M. 4, 20, 21, 157, 158

L

labour market 107
labour market participation 52
  see also future workers, students as
labour market transition 28–31
  see also employability
Lainio, A. 131, 147
language 13–14
Larcombe, W. 114
Lavalette, M. 47
Lažetić, P. 92
lazy and incompetent, students as 80,
    134–139, 155
  student perspectives 148–150

Wilkinson, R. 129
Williams, J. 5, 6, 9, 17, 48, 70, 114
Wimmer, A. 7, 163
Winkler, P. 118
Wir sind die Neuen **11**, 81, 120–121, **180**
Wong, B. 133, 139
Woodman, D. 146
worker-citizens 52, 54, 58
　see also future workers, students as
Wright, K. 141
Wyn, J. 133, 146

Y

Ylijoki, O.-H. 145
Yosso, T.J. 139
Young, I. 129
youth studies 133
youth unemployment 21
youthhood 40, 43

Z

Zamponi, L. 60, 143